Oliver Sensen
Kant on Human Dignity

Kantstudien

Ergänzungshefte

im Auftrage der Kant-Gesellschaft
herausgegeben von
Manfred Baum, Bernd Dörflinger,
Heiner F. Klemme und Thomas M. Seebohm

166

De Gruyter

Oliver Sensen

Kant on Human Dignity

De Gruyter

ISBN 978-3-11-048154-9

e-ISBN 978-3-11-026716-7

ISSN 0340-6059

Library of Congress Cataloging-in-Publication Data

Sensen, Oliver.
    Kant on human dignity / Oliver Sensen.
        p. cm. − (Kantstudien. Ergänzungshefte, ISSN 0340-6059 ; Bd. 166)
    Includes bibliographical references (p.   ) and index.
    ISBN 978-3-11-026621-4 (hardcover : alk. paper)
    1. Kant, Immanuel, 1724−1804.   2. Dignity.   3. Respect for persons.
I. Title.
    B2799.M25S46   2011
    179.7092−dc23

                                                                    2011030744

Bibliographic information published by the Deutsche Nationalbibliothek

The Deutsche Nationalbibliothek lists this publication in the Deutsche
Nationalbibliografie; detailed bibliographic data are available in the Internet
at http://dnb.d-nb.de.

Printing: Hubert & Co. GmbH & Co. KG, Göttingen
∞ Printed on acid-free paper

Printed in Germany

www.degruyter.com

To
Kathryn and Lily

Contents

VIII   Contents

Acknowledgments

The present book is an enlarged and much-revised treatment of subjects I first took up in my dissertation. I want to begin by thanking my supervisors at Cambridge University, Onora O'Neill and Simon Blackburn, who presented the initial guidance and challenges that shaped this work. Friedo Ricken, Jimmy Altham and Franz-Josef Wetz at an early stage enlarged my understanding of the historical background of human dignity. Christine Korsgaard helped me to spend a year at Harvard, and the DAAD, AHRB, and the Studienstiftung des Deutschen Volkes provided financial support while I was writing my dissertation. As an assistant professor I was fortunate to receive a fellowship from Tulane's Center for Ethics and Public Affairs.

Since completing my dissertation I have had the privilege of presenting my interpretation in eight different countries on three continents, and I would like to thank the audiences of my talks for their helpful challenges. I am grateful to have had the chance to discuss aspects of my interpretation with many friends and scholars, including Henry Allison, Stefano Bacin, Ralf Bader, Gary Banham, Marcia Baron, Robert Berman, Adam Cureton, Stephen Darwall, Lara Denis, Stephen Engstrom, Katrin Flikschuh, Jerry Gaus, Georg Geismann, Joshua Glasgow, Ina Goy, Paul Guyer, Otfried Höffe, Patrick Kain, Samuel Kahn, Samuel Kerstein, Amanda Perreau-Saussine, Doug Portmore, Andy Reath, Dieter Schönecker, Sally Sedgwick, Susan Shell, Houston Smit, Jens Timmermann, Mark Timmons, Andreas Trampota, and Richard Velkley.

I would like to single out Thomas Hill for particular thanks; he took a philosophic interest in my work and offered me invaluable friendly support, without the slightest obligation to do so. For reading the full manuscript and offering valuable comments I would like to thank Anne Margaret Baxley as well as the three reviewers for the de Gruyter *Kant-Studien* series. Thanks also go to my employer, Tulane University, and to my genial colleagues in the Philosophy Department there. I would like to thank my parents for being my first educators, and my daughter Lily for being a delightful distraction. But above all I am grateful to my wife, Kathryn, who read and commented on every draft at every stage of this project;

her brilliant mind and continued challenges have helped to make this book much better.

Finally, I would like to acknowledge permission to include some material from my published articles in this book. Sections of Chapter 1 are from my "Kant on Inner Value," *European Journal of Philosophy* 19, pp. 262–280. The key idea for Chapter 3 was first developed in my "Dignity and the Formula of Humanity," in *Kant's* Groundwork. *A Critical Guide*, ed. Jens Timmermann (Cambridge: Cambridge University Press, 2010), pp. 102–118. Chapter 4 includes sections from my "Human Dignity in Historical Perspective," *European Journal of Political Theory* 10, pp. 71–91; and I incorporated parts of my "Kant's Conception of Human Dignity," *Kant-Studien* 100, pp. 309–331 in my Chapters 4 and 5.

Abbreviations

In referring to Kant's texts I use the following abbreviations:

Anth   *Anthropologie in pragmatischer Hinsicht. Anthropology from a Pragmatic Point of View*

BDG   *Der einzig mögliche Beweisgrund zu einer Demonstration des Daseins Gottes. The Only Possible Argument in Support of a Demonstration of the Existence of God*

Collins   *Moralphilosophie Collins. Lectures on Ethics Collins*

GMS   *Grundlegung zur Metaphysik der Sitten. Groundwork of the Metaphysics of Morals*

GSE   *Beobachtungen über das Gefühl des Schönen und Erhabenen. Observations on the Feeling of the Beautiful and Sublime*

IaG   *Idee zu einer allgmeinen Geschichte in weltbürgerlicher Absicht. Idea for a Universal History with a Cosmopolitain Aim*

Log   *Logik. Lectures on Logic*

KpV   *Kritik der praktischen Vernunft. Critique of Practical Reason*

KrV   *Kritik der reinen Vernunft. Critique of Pure Reason*

KU   *Kritik der Urteilskraft. Critique of the Powers of Judgment*

Mrong   *Moral Mrongovius II. Lectures on Ethics Mrongovius II*

NF   *Kants Naturrecht Feyerabend. Lectures on Natural Law Feyerabend*

NG   *Versuch, den Begriff der negativen Größen in die Weltweisheit einzuführen. Attempt to Introduce the Concept of Negative Magnitudes into Philosophy*

Päd   *Pädagogik. Lectures on Pedagogy*

PG   *Physische Geographie. Lectures on Physical Geography*

Refl   *Reflexion. Reflection Note*

RezUlrich   *Kraus' Recension von Ulrich's Eleutheriologie. Kraus's Review of Ulrich's Eleutheriology*

RGV   *Die Religion innerhalb der Grenzen der bloßen Vernunft. Religion within the Boundaries of Mere Reason*

RL   *Metaphysische Anfangsgründe der Rechtslehre. Doctrine of Right*

SF   *Der Streit der Fakultäten. The Conflict of the Faculties*

TL   *Metaphysische Anfangsgründe der Tugendlehre. Doctrine of Virtue*

TP   *Über den Gemeinspruch: Das mag in der Theorie richtig sein, taugt aber nicht für die Praxis. On the Common Saying: That May Be True in Theory, But It Is of No Use in Practice*

Vigil   *Die Metaphysik der Sitten Vigilantius. Lectures on Ethics Vigilantius*

WA   *Beantwortung der Frage: Was ist Aufklärung? An Answer to the Question: What is Enlightenment?*

ZeF   *Zum ewigen Frieden. Toward Perpetual Peace*

All references are to *Kants gesammelte Schriften*, Deutsche Akademie der Wissenschaften (formerly: Königlich Preußische Akademie der Wissenschaften), Berlin: Walter de Gruyter (1902 ff). Only references to *KrV* refer to the "A" and "B" pages of the first and second editions, all other references list volume, page number and sometimes the line number of the Prussian Academy edition of Kant's works, e.g.: *GMS* 4:420.17. All translations are taken – unless otherwise stated – from *The Cambridge Edition of the Works of Immanuel Kant*, Cambridge: Cambridge University Press.

Introduction

Over the last 65 years the concept of human dignity has gained prominence in politics, philosophy, and ordinary thought. Human dignity is
now the cornerstone of the constitution of many states and political man-
ifestos, and United Nations documents present dignity as the justification
for human rights. Rights "derive from the inherent dignity of the human
person", as the *International Covenants on Human Rights* (1966) put it.

In this context human dignity is often assumed to be an inherent
value all human beings posses; as such, it is thought to be a value that
grounds the requirement to respect other human beings. In accordance
with this the German dictionary *Duden* defines dignity (*Würde*) as a
"value inherent in human beings that commands respect."[1] On this common view, it is because another person has dignity that one should respect
him or her. For a philosophical account and justification of this idea,
scholars often turn to Immanuel Kant.[2]

This book began as just such a project. What prompted my research
initially was the desire to understand human dignity more clearly and to
analyze Kant's justification for it. But the more closely I studied Kant's
texts and the secondary literature, the less convinced I became that the
contemporary view of human dignity was shared by Kant. Many puzzles
emerge when one reads Kant under the assumptions of many contemporary scholars that he grounds the requirement to respect others on a value
they possess. For instance, Kant says that all human beings should be respected, but that only a morally good will has absolute value; yet not all
human beings have a morally good will. Or if value is supposed to be the
foundation of moral requirements, why does Kant argue that no value
can ground moral requirements? Similarly, why does he say that
human beings have dignity because they should be respected (cf. *TL*
6:462, 435), not that they should be respected because they have dignity?

---

1 *"Achtung gebietender Wert, der dem Menschen innewohnt"* (*Duden* 1997, 821; my
   translation).
2 Cf., e.g., Gewirth 1982; Seifert 1997; Wood 2008; Dürig's object formula in
   German law; and the discussion in Chapter 4.

Finally, why does Kant neither refer to value nor dignity where he says he justifies moral requirements, or where he summarizes his position?

Thinking through these puzzles, I was led to the conclusion that Kant asks us to radically shift perspectives, and turn our thinking around from what we ordinarily assume about the relationship between value and the requirement to respect others – a shift similar to his Copernican Revolution in metaphysics. It seems natural to assume that if one should respect others, it must be because there is something valuable about them. Kant agrees that this assumption is natural, but paradoxical as it may seem, he turns the relationship around. It is not because others have a value that one should respect them, but it is because one should respect them that they have an importance and a dignity. The justification for the requirement to respect others is that it is a direct command of reason. In this respect Kant's moral philosophy is parallel to his theoretical philosophy: Kant conceives of human beings not as passive observers, either in knowing the world, or in discovering what ought to be done. Rather, in both cases, reason approaches the world with its own a priori principles, and the principle of respect for others is one such principle. Very recently there has been a growing recognition in the Kant literature that Kant's moral philosophy cannot be based on a value, but that a shift in perspectives is needed.[3] In accordance with this, I argue in this book that one can read Kant's positions on dignity and the requirement to respect others without a prior value as their foundation.

When one recognizes the character of this Copernican Revolution concerning dignity and respect, the striking result is that Kant's texts become coherent. If one does not look in Kant for a value that grounds moral requirements, then it is not surprising that neither value nor dignity plays any role in the texts where Kant says he justifies moral requirements, nor where he describes the essence of his moral philosophy. This way of reading Kant, then, can make sense of the passages in which Kant says that nothing can have a value other than that which the moral law determines for it; and one can likewise make sense of the passages in which, on the one hand, he says that only a morally good will can have an absolute value, but on the other, that even a morally vicious human being deserves respect. If all human beings deserve respect, but

---

3   Cf. Engstrom 2009; Reath 2012a; Herman 2010, Formosa 2012; Vogt (unpublished). For earlier skeptics see Onora O'Neill 1989, ch. 7; Hill 1992, ch. 2; Herman 1993, 239; Schneewind 1996; Dean 2000; and Johnson 2007.

if not all have a value (the absolute value of a morally good will), then value is not the ground of the requirement to respect others.

So I ask the reader to bear with me and try to enter into a different way of thinking about dignity. One can see my study as an attempt to see how far one can read Kant without invoking a foundational value, and it seems to me that one can do so all the way down. Kant's justification of the requirement to respect others is not what one would ordinarily expect – and he admits that – but following his train of thought can lead us to think more clearly about the possibilities for justifying that requirement. That is a task which the present work is intended to prepare rather than to complete.

Since what interests us most in the concept of human dignity is the question of whether there is a value all human beings possess, a value that grounds the requirement to respect others, I begin the book with that question. In Chapter 1 I examine Kant's conception of value to see whether he puts forth a value that grounds moral requirements. If value is supposed to be the foundation of moral requirements, what is this value? For instance, is it a metaphysical property human beings possess, something we do value, or something we should value? In Chapter 2 I discuss the most prominent attempts in the secondary literature to argue for a value that would ground respect for all human beings. Are these arguments really in Kant's texts? Are they valid? In Chapter 3 I lay out my interpretation of how Kant justifies the requirement to respect others. If, as I argue, Kant does not ground the requirement on a prior value, then how is it grounded? In the last two chapters I then look more closely at Kant's usage of 'dignity'. If Kant does not have a value that grounds moral requirements, how could he use 'dignity' as the name for such a value? In Chapter 4 I point out that, historically, there was a different way of understanding dignity, and that Kant's usage often reflects this older view. Finally, in Chapter 5 I take a close look at the famous passages in the *Groundwork* and *Doctrine of Virtue* where Kant does seem to define 'dignity' as an absolute inner value. Even if Kant often adheres to an older usage of 'dignity', does he not also use it to define 'absolute inner value'? The following overview of the argument of each chapter will provide a preview of my answers to these questions.

Overview of the Book

In Chapter 1 I interpret Kant's conception of value. If he did conceive of dignity as a value all human beings possess, a close look at his notion of value would seem to be essential for understanding his notion of dignity. Dignity is not supposed to be just any value, but a very special kind of value: a value that not only justifies the requirement to respect human beings, but also one that trumps other considerations, and one that a person cannot forfeit. But does Kant have such a conception of value? My conclusion is that he does not, and that his arguments rule out the possibility that any value could be the foundation of moral requirements. I had this conclusion in mind in comparing Kant's moral philosophy to a Copernican Revolution. But what is his argument?

Kant himself discusses the question of how value could ground moral requirements. His point is that if one tries to ground morality on any value (this would include a distinct metaphysical property a human being possesses inherently), heteronomy would result. For if one tries to ground morality on a value, one still has to explain how one could discern this value and why one could be motivated to follow it. For Kant external objects are given to human beings by sensibility. This relates to his arguments in the *Critique of Pure Reason* about how one can discern external entities. If the value is nothing one can sense through the five senses, then it must be a feeling, according to Kant. This means that the only indication one could have of a value external to one's own will is a feeling. Feelings, however, are fleeting, relative and contingent. As such they cannot ground a necessary and universal moral law, as Kant argues moral laws must be. One could object that Kant's argument does not rule out the possibility that there really is such a value in other human beings, but it raises the stakes. To dispute Kant's views one would have to develop an alternative epistemology to show how such a value could be discerned and ground moral requirements (e.g., a moral intuitionism). Within Kant's framework a grounding on an external value (i.e., a value outside one's own will and awareness) is not possible. Instead, he conceives of value as a prescription of reason. Value is something one is committed to valuing by the dictates of one's own reason. These dictates are not based upon a prior and independent value 'out there' in other human beings; rather Kant says that they follow from an a priori moral law – hence the Copernican Revolution in morality.

In Chapter 2 I discuss the most prominent arguments in the Kant literature that attempt to demonstrate a value of human beings that can ground the requirement to respect others – such as dignity is supposed to be. If value is not an external property, could it be internal to the will and ground moral requirements, as has been argued in the literature? In this respect the arguments offered by Christine Korsgaard, Allen Wood, Paul Guyer, Richard Dean, and Samuel Kerstein do not necessarily contradict the interpretation of value I have offered in Chapter 1. This is because most of these scholars – with notable exceptions – do not conceive of value as a distinct metaphysical property, but rather as something one is committed to valuing, or something a perfectly rational being would value. To this extent I agree with the arguments that have been offered. However, I also agree with commentators who conclude that these arguments fail to derive a moral conclusion (that one should respect others) from non-moral premises (e.g., from the ends human beings set themselves in everyday life). The arguments mostly fail to establish that one really is committed to valuing other human beings.

In Chapter 3 I spell out the alternative reason why one should respect others, according to Kant. In Kant's view, morality is based on laws. Value is secondary to and determined by laws. These laws cannot be given by any external authority (including a value external to one's will), as this would yield heteronomy. If the law were given by an external authority, one would still need a reason why one should obey this authority. If this reason were said to be an inclination one has, then morality would be based on this inclination, thereby undermining the external authority. Accordingly, Kant conceives of the law to respect others as an internal law, given by one's own reason. Again the parallel to his first *Critique* is at play. There Kant argues that human beings are not passive observers of the world, but shape their perception of the world by a priori principles. Similarly in determining how one should act, one approaches the problem with a priori principles, according to Kant. One of these principles is the Formula of Humanity: *"So act that you use humanity, whether in your own person or in the person of any other, always at the same time as an end, never merely as a means."* (GMS 4:429) Kant says that this principle is at bottom the same as the Categorical Imperative, which he argues is a priori. I argue that the passage in which Kant first formulates the Formula of Humanity (GMS 4:427–9) confirms the view that Kant conceives of the Categorical Imperative and the Formula of Humanity as one requirement, expressed in different ways.

In Chapter 4 I explain how the previous analyses fit with Kant's conception of dignity. Kant cannot conceive of human dignity as a value that grounds the requirement to respect others: He does not have such a conception of value, and he grounds the owed respect on a law of reason. In this chapter I point out that there is another conception of dignity, widespread in the history of philosophy, and that Kant frequently employs it. In this fundamentally Stoic conception, 'dignity' is not the name for a value property. Rather 'dignity' is used to express the idea that something is raised above something else. For instance, a Roman senator is raised above the rest of the citizens in virtue of his political power. Human beings are said to be raised above the rest of nature in virtue of possessing reason (or sometimes freedom). In this conception dignity is not in the first instance a moral or normative notion, but it expresses a relation, that one thing X is raised above another Y. What it is raised above and why depends on the context in which the concept is used. Kant frequently employs this conception when, for instance, he talks about the dignity of a teacher or the dignity of mathematics. But does he also use it in the famous passages in the *Groundwork* and *Doctrine of Virtue* where 'dignity' appears in conjunction with 'value'?

In Chapter 5 I provide a close reading of the famous passages in which Kant is often thought to define 'dignity' as an 'absolute inner value'. There is a way in which one can read these passages as a definition of dignity as value, without contradicting what I have said about value or worth in Chapter 1. If value is simply another expression for what is commanded by the moral law, and dignity is another expression for value, then dignity might likewise be what is commanded by the law. However, the passages in which 'dignity' appears in conjunction with 'value' are more complicated than that. In them Kant argues that morality is raised above all other forms of behavior. This is because only moral behavior is commanded unconditionally (by the moral law). Kant uses 'dignity' to express the idea that morality is raised above something else (in that only morality should be pursued unconditionally). Dignity is not a definition of value, but a way of saying that morality is elevated or special. In short, even here Kant uses a fundamentally Stoic conception of dignity.

* * *

My interpretation is novel in several ways. I explain more fully than has been done before exactly why Kant does not ground moral requirements on a value; I provide a new interpretation of the passages that lead up to the Formula of Humanity; including a novel reading of concepts like 'end in itself', 'respect', and 'humanity'; and I show that Kant adheres to a fundamentally Stoic conception of dignity. My interpretation makes Kant's texts coherent. It makes sense of the fact that Kant makes only a scarce and scattered use of 'dignity', and especially of the fact that he never relies on value or dignity whenever he says that he justifies moral requirements or whenever he summarizes his position. It also eliminates the apparent conflict between two very different justifications for morality that scholars detect in the *Groundwork:* the faculty of reason in the third section, and supposedly a value in the second section (where he explicitly says that he does not justify moral requirements, and where he refers to the third section for a justification). Thus a further strength of my interpretation is that it shows Kant's texts to be coherent.

In presenting these chapters to different audiences, I have received two main reactions. On the one hand, people grant that Kant is not a moral realist. He does not conceive of value as a distinct metaphysical property. On the other hand, people do not want to go back to the Categorical Imperative. Scholars have discussed extensively how one can derive concrete duties from the imperative, and the method has been found wanting. I believe that Kant did not intend the imperative to be a clear procedure for deriving specific duties, but in any case one does not have to reopen the debate. Rather my interpretation can satisfy both reactions. One can read Kant as anti-realist about value, since the requirement to respect others is *justified* with reference to the Categorical Imperative. However, since the Formula of Humanity is at bottom the same as the imperative, one can now use the formula to derive concrete duties.

The difference between my interpretation and the contemporary paradigm of dignity therefore does not lie in the application. Kant is adamant that one should respect all human beings. My interpretation merely offers a different *justification* for the requirement to respect others. My argument is also not a systematic claim. I am not trying to show that the contemporary paradigm of dignity is false or unfounded. My interpretation merely poses a dilemma for the contemporary conception: If one wants to justify the contemporary paradigm of dignity (as a value that grounds respect), one cannot just refer to Kant for a justification. One would have to look elsewhere. On the other hand, if one is interested to know how Kant viewed the matter, one finds support in his texts for a different conception of dignity. And there might be advantages to following Kant here. Kant reminds us that we do not directly perceive a value that would induce respect, but that the requirement to respect other human beings need not wait upon the discovery of any property so elusive.

Part I
Respect for Others

Three months before his death, Kant received a visit from his physician. Although he was nearly collapsing from weakness, Kant remained standing even after his doctor invited him to sit. Wasianski, a former student and now a trustee of Kant's, explained to the physician that Kant would only sit down after his visitor had been seated. When the physician reacted with disbelief, Kant took all his strength to say: "The sense of humaneness has not yet left me." (Wasianski 1804, 263 f.)

It is central to Kant's moral philosophy that one should always respect all other human beings. He famously credits Rousseau for his appreciation of the importance of respecting all human beings:

> I am an inquirer by inclination. I feel a consuming thirst for knowledge [...]. There was a time when I believed this constituted the honor of humanity, and I despised the people, who know nothing. Rousseau set me right about this. This binding prejudice disappeared. I learned to honor humanity, and I would find myself more useless than the common laborer if I did not believe this attitude of mine can give worth to all others in establishing the rights of humanity.[4]

Kant holds that *all* human beings should be respected. Even a vicious man [*Lasterhafte*] deserves respect as a human being (cf. *TL* 6:463). Kant articulates this requirement in his Formula of Humanity as an end in itself, which he calls the supreme limiting condition of one's freedom: *"So act that you use humanity, whether in your own person or in the person of any other, always at the same time as an end, never merely as a means."* (*GMS* 4:429)

However, the exact reason why one should respect others remains a matter of debate. The prevailing view in the Kant literature is that one should respect other human beings because of an absolute inner worth or value[5] all human beings possess. The absolute value is often called "dignity"[6], and this value is said to be the reason why one should respect others.[7] The value is often seen not just as the reason why one should re-

---

4 Remarks on *SE* 20:44; the translation is from Wood 1996, xvii.
5 In the following I shall use "worth" and "value" interchangeably as Kant only used one word: *"Werth"*.
6 Cf., for instance, Paton 1947, 189; Lo 1987, 165; Löhrer 1995, 34–44; Forschner 1998, 38; Wood 1999, 115; Schönecker/Wood 2003, 142. For a skeptical note on this prominent view see Meyer 1989, 520–534.
7 See Jones 1971, 130: "It is because of this kind of absolute value that one ought to treat persons as ends-in-themselves and never as mere means"; but also Wood 1998b, 189: "Kant's moral philosophy is grounded on the dignity of humanity as

spect others, but even as Kant's "most fundamental value"[8], and as a value that is the foundation even of the Categorical Imperative.[9] The debate focuses on the question whether human beings have this value or dignity in virtue of a pre-moral capacity they possess (such as freedom or the capacity to set ends)[10], or because of a morally good will.[11]

The prevailing view is intuitively plausible. If one asks whether one should respect others because they have a value, or if they have a value because they should be respected, the first option seems more natural. If one should respect others, it seems that it is something about them – a value they possess – that grounds this requirement.[12] However, Kant scholars seldom reflect upon the meta-ethical questions of what this value itself is supposed to be. What does one mean in saying that human beings have an absolute value? What is this value ontologically? How can one discern it, and why should one be motivated to pursue it? What exactly is the relationship between having a capacity (to set ends or be moral) and absolute value? If, for instance, one finds out during a Hobbesian war of all against all that the other has reason and freedom, does this not give more reason to be afraid of him (cf. *NF* 27:1320)? What exactly has Hobbes overlooked? And how does the claim that all human beings as such have value square with passages in which Kant says, for instance, that "nothing can have a worth other than that which the law determines for it" (*GMS* 4:435 f.), or that the absolute value of a human being can only be given to oneself in being morally good (cf. *KU* 5:443, cf. 208 f.; *GMS* 4:439, 449 f., 454; *KpV* 5:110 f., 147 f., 86)?

Kant himself reflects on the nature of value in connection with questions about the ground of the Categorical Imperative. Following his train of thought in the first chapter will bring out what Kant means by 'abso-

---

its sole fundamental value"; cf. Paton 1947, 171; Ross 1954, 52–4; Hutchings 1972, 287, 290; Lo 1987, 165; and Löhrer 1995, 124, 34–36.

8   Wood 1998b, 189; cf. his 2008, 94.
9   See Guyer 2000, 150–157. Here and throughout the rest of the book with "Categorical Imperative" I shall refer to the Universal Law Formula: *"act only in accordance with that maxim through which you can at the same time will that it become a universal law."* (*GMS* 4:421)
10 Cf. Guyer 2000, ch. 4; Korsgaard 1996a, ch. 4; Wood 1999, ch. 4.
11 Cf. Paton 1947, 168 f.; Ross 1954, 51 f.; Ricken 1989, 246; Dean 2006, chs. 1–5; and Kerstein 2006, 219. For an alternative grounding of morality (other than on a value) cf. Engstrom 2009; Reath 2012a; and Herman 2010.
12 Cf. Watkins/FitzPatrick 2002, 364.

lute inner value', what his most fundamental value is, and whether there could be a value underlying the Categorical Imperative, in either the requirement to universalize one's maxim, or in the requirement to respect others. In order to pursue these questions I shall first look at the metaethical question of what the ontological nature of absolute inner value is for Kant (Chapter 1). I shall then relate this to the standard views that have been given in the Kant literature (Chapter 2). Finally, I shall look at the justification for the requirement to respect others, as expressed in Kant's Formula of Humanity (Chapter 3). I claim that Kant in fact reverses the relationship between value and the requirement to respect others. For him it is not that one should respect others because they have a value or an importance, but that they have an importance because they should be respected. The requirement to respect others is justified with reference to a direct command of reason. In this Kant's moral philosophy is parallel to his theoretical philosophy. It is a priori principles that shape theoretical and practical knowledge.[13]

---

13 Cf. Schneewind 1998, 484; Engstrom 2009; Rauscher 2002.

Chapter 1: Kant's Conception of Value

Introduction

What is the value that is often said in the Kant literature to be the ground of the requirement to respect others? At this point the question is not in virtue of which feature human beings have value – for instance, the capacity to set ends, freedom, or morality. Rather, it is the meta-ethical question about the nature of this value. If human beings have the capacity to set ends, what does one mean in saying that this capacity has value? For instance, does one mean to say that there is an additional property adhering to the capacity to set ends, or that the capacity to set ends is valued, or that it should be valued? What is value in Kant's framework?

One possibility is that the value of human beings is a distinctive property all human beings possess. In addition to one's properties of body and soul (e. g., freedom and the property of being a self) that are part of a theoretical description of a human being, one would also possess the value property of being precious. In this chapter I shall first argue that Kant does not have such a conception of value (Section 1), and that his arguments rule out that such a value could be the foundation of moral requirements (Section 2). I shall then consider what else value could be, and whether these conceptions could ground the requirement to respect others (Section 3). Next I shall outline an alternative reading of how Kant uses phrases like 'absolute inner value' (Section 4), and confirm this interpretation in looking at more of Kant's writings (Section 5). My conclusion will be that Kant does not place a value as the foundation for the requirement to respect others. While some of his passages could be read as if Kant had a conception of a foundational value, a close look at these passages and his arguments points away from this conclusion.

Section 1: Kant on Value as a Property

Despite the emphasis on value in recent Kant scholarship, the literature seldom reflects on the nature of this value. Scholars who do so tend to compare the value of humanity to a non-natural property, a conception that is often ascribed to G.E. Moore.[14] On this account, value is a property a thing possesses inherently, i. e., a property that would belong to the thing even if it were the only thing that existed or if it existed in total isolation from everything else. Value would then be "part of the fabric of the world" (Mackie 1977, 15) in the widest sense: a distinct property, substance, or an instance of a Platonic form. To say that a human being has an absolute inner value, could refer to something inside a human being, an "inherent, intrinsic preciousness" (Seifert 1997, 96; cf. Korsgaard 1996a, 257, 250 f.). It could be that in comparing a good will to a jewel (cf. *GMS* 4:394), Kant implies that human beings have something precious inside of them. Because value might be a property inherent in human beings, this form of objective value does not have to exist 'out there' in the world, i. e., independently of human beings. Similarly, since value might be a property that supervenes on human minds, it might not exist independently of the mind.

A common way to describe this value would be to say that it is an intrinsic property and that Kant would be a moral realist in holding that it exists. I have deliberately avoided both classifications, because the terms are used in a variety of ways. For instance, even a property a thing would have if it existed in complete isolation might only be described with reference to something else (cf. Langton 2007, 179). The property would then be relational or extrinsic and not intrinsic. One example would be a dispositional property: One could describe the absolute value of human beings as a property that would instill awe in an observer, were he to encounter it. Similarly, the label of 'moral realist' is too unspecific (cf. Rauscher 2002, 480–4). Kant could be a realist about the Categorical Imperative, but not about the good. He could be a realist not in the sense that the imperative or value exists as a distinct property or entity, but in the sense that sentences about them have a truth value. Accordingly, one could refer to the claim that one should follow the Categorical Imperative independently of what one wants to as 'moral realism'. However, these

---

14 See esp. Langton 2007; Schönecker 1999, 387–389; and Watkins/FitzPatrick 2002. Langton adds Barbara Herman and Karl Ameriks, however, Herman explicitly denies that there is an independent value that justifies the Categorical Imperative, see her 1993, 239; and Ameriks does not talk about value, but whether the Categorical Imperative rests on an anti-realist metaphysics, see his 2003, ch. 11. In her earlier papers Korsgaard makes it sound as if she endorses this conception of objective value, cf., e. g., her 1996a, 257, 250 f., but I shall argue in the next chapter that this is not her view. There I shall also argue that it is not Guyer's view, but Wood's exact position is harder to establish, cf. Kain 2010.

usages of 'realism' do not settle anything about the question with which I am concerned here.

The question I want to address here is whether Kant upholds a value of human beings as a distinct (non-natural) property that a human being would possess even if one existed in complete isolation. A Kantian who wants to defend the claim that there is such a value property underlying Kant's moral philosophy might use an argument – similar to G.E. Moore's – that such a value is indemonstrable (cf. Guyer 2000, 170; Langton 2007, 184; Wood 1999, 125) and can be known by intuition. While it seems like a promising route to take in order to ground the re-quirement to respect others, there is a growing literature that suggests that Kant does not have such a conception of value.[15] In the following I shall seek to add to these doubts by arguing that Kant did not even entertain such a conception, but that his arguments would rule it out even if he had considered it.

First, there is reason to believe that Kant did not even entertain a con-ception of value as a separate property (or substance). What suggests this claim is that Kant does not list this conception when he aims to list "all possible" (*KpV* 5:39) conceptions of the good or value. This indicates that such a conception is not even a candidate for how one could under-stand the good or value (notions which I take to be equivalent for Kant[16]). Throughout his mature writings Kant always gives the same can-didates for what the good could be: Kant thinks that one could conceive of the good as the "basis of morality" (*Mrong* 29:620) as pleasure, a moral feeling, perfection, or a divine command (cf. *GMS* 4:441 f.; *KpV* 5:39 f., 64; *Mrong* 29:628; *Collins* 27:252–5). Kant sometimes adds education and civil constitution as candidates that could be the good on which to base morality (cf. *KpV* 5:40; *Mrong* 29:621; *Collins* 27:252–5). He claims that the extended list includes "all previous" attempts to ground morality on the good, as well as – more importantly – "all possible" at-tempts to ground morality (cf. *KpV* 5:40; *GMS* 4:432, 441).

Kant considers this list exhaustive because the good would have either empirical (subjective) or rational (objective) grounds. Within each cate-gory the grounds could be external or internal. Empirical grounds are ed-

---

15 Cf. Hill 1992, 48; Schneewind 1996, 285–8; Dean 2000, 34; Rauscher 2002, 484 f.; Reath 2003, 127–155; Johnson 2007, 133–148; and Engstrom 2009, 11–14; Herman 2010; Formosa 2012; and Vogt (unpublished).

16 Consider how seamlessly he switches between both expressions at the beginning of the *Groundwork* (cf. 4:393 f.).

ucation/civil constitution (external), or a feeling of pleasure (internal). The rational grounds can also be internal (perfection) or external (divine command) (cf. *KpV* 5:40; *Mrong* 29:620–9). Kant thinks that these possibilities form a "table in which all possible cases are actually exhausted, except the one formal principle" (*KpV* 5:40), Kant's moral law or Categorical Imperative. What is important to note is that Kant does not consider the good or value to be a metaphysical property or substance.[17] Instead he labels as the "metaphysical" options a divine command theory and the perfectionism he associates with Wolff and Baumgarten (cf. *Mrong* 29:622, 627, 628). This suggests that a 20th century Moorean conception of value as a non-natural property was not something Kant even considered.

On reflection, the conclusion that Kant did not have a conception of objective value should not be surprising if one recalls how the terms were used in Kant's time. In his own time the German term 'Werth' and its English equivalents were economic terms (cf. Hügli 2004, 556). They referred to the price an object can fetch on the market. Even the distinction between intrinsic and extrinsic value was used in that context. It did not refer to an ontological distinction, but marked the price an object can fetch before and after human labor was attached to it (cf. Lichtblau 2004, 587 f.). One therefore cannot take a Moorean conception of value to be the default position Kant would have naturally assumed. On the contrary, one would need to provide strong evidence that Kant held such a conception against the views of his time. But what would have been Kant's position if he had encountered a conception of value as a metaphysical property?

The second point to note is that arguments Kant gives in the *Critique of Practical Reason* equally apply to a Moorean conception of value (cf. Pieper 2002, 117 f.). The relevant arguments appear in the chapter "On the concept of an object of pure practical reason" (*KpV* 5:57–65). At first it may seem as if the chapter is merely concerned with the question which objects a morally good reason may and may not pursue: "By a concept of an object of practical reason I understand the representation of an object as an effect possible through freedom." (*KpV* 5:57) One could therefore think that the chapter is merely about which effects are allowed by pure reason (cf. Wood 1998a, 170). However, the chapter

---

17 Among the candidates he mentions, he does not include the Platonic form of the good. However, elsewhere he argues directly against Platonic forms as such, cf. *KrV* B370–375 and B8 f.

seems to be about more than that. Kant wants to make the point that the objects of pure practical reason follow from the principle of pure practical reason, the moral law or Categorical Imperative. In this respect the second *Critique* reverses the order of the first. While theoretical knowledge starts from the senses, proceeds to objects, and then principles, practical insight has to start from a principle, the moral law. Only from there can practical inquiry go to objects and then the senses (cf. *KpV* 5:16). The second chapter in the *Critique of Practical Reason* is then essentially about the "method of ultimate moral investigation" (*KpV* 5:64): Is the moral law to be derived from a prior conception of the good, or is the good to be determined by the moral law?

Kant's treatment of this question contains two arguments. The first claims that if one were to place a good prior to the law, there would not be anything immediately good (in contrast to good as a means). The second argues that if one were to place a good prior to the law, there would not be a moral law. In this section I shall look at the first argument. I shall try to explain why it also rules out a conception of value as a metaphysical property. In short: Kant rules out any possible conception of the good as being prior to and independent of the moral law because it would yield heteronomy (cf. *KpV* 5:64, *GMS* 4:441). The idea is not that there is a value 'autonomy' that would be violated. Kant's point is rather that even if there were a divine command or – I may add – a metaphysical value property, one still would have to give an account of how one can *discern* this value, and why one should be *motivated* to follow it. Kant's answer is that it would have to be a feeling of pleasure by which one discerns the value and by which one would be motivated to follow it. Pleasure, however, is contingent and subjective, and cannot ground a necessary and universal moral law (cf. *KpV* 5:64).

In detail: The argument takes the form of a *reductio ad absurdum*. Kant argues that if the concept of the good is to be the basis of the moral law, then there would be nothing immediately good, but the good would be "always only good *for something*" (*KpV* 5:59). The reason is that pleasure would be needed to discover the good and motivate the will:

> If the concept of the good is not to be derived from an antecedent practical law, but, instead, is to serve as its basis, it can be only the concept of something whose existence promises pleasure and thus determines the causality of the subject, that is, the faculty of desire, to produce it (*KpV* 5:58).

Why does Kant think that the concept of the good could only be something that promises pleasure? Kant had argued for this point earlier in the second *Critique* (cf. 5:22). There he argues that the way one can relate to any external object (this includes a value property other human beings possess) only by receptivity and sensibility, not the faculty of understanding or thought:

> Pleasure [...], insofar it is to be a determining ground of desire for this thing, is based on the *receptivity* of the subject, since it *depends* upon the existence of an object; hence it belongs to sense (feeling) and not to the understanding (*KpV* 5:22).

One has to read this claim while keeping in mind the first *Critique*. There he argues that human beings do not possess an intellectual intuition, but that the way an object is given to human beings is via sensibility (cf. *KrV* A50 f./B74 f.). I take it that Kant would make the following point: If the good is – by assumption – not a natural property that can be detected by one of the five senses (e. g., if value is conceived of as a non-natural property one cannot see, feel, hear, touch or smell), then the only remaining avenue for sensibility to receive the object is a feeling of pleasure. Similarly, in order to be motivated to pursue this value, one would need a feeling of pleasure. In Kant's view, human beings are either motivated by pleasure or by an a priori law (cf. *KpV* 5:63[18]). Why does he maintain this? Kant's main target is a Humean theory of motivation. Hume had argued that reason is merely the slave of the passions, and that only passions can motivate (cf. *Treatise of Human Nature* 2.3.3). If this were true, then Kant's a priori moral law would be powerless to effect actions by itself, and would be dependent upon some prior and independent desires for its efficacy. Against this Kant argues in the second *Critique* that one could also be motivated by a law of pure reason (cf. *KpV* 5:15). His concern is not that there might be a third alternative in addition to pleasure or an a priori law.

Given these premises, Kant argues that if the good or a value were prior to the law, then it could only motivate via pleasure. If one follows Kant in this, the result is that "the concept of that which is immediately good would be directed only to that with which the feeling of *gratification* is immediately connected" (*KpV* 5:58). Determining the good by pleasure is against the common way of speaking, Kant continues, which re-

---

18 Cf. also *GMS* 4:400: "the will stands between its a priori principle, which is formal, and its a priori incentive, which is material, as at a crossroads".

quires that the good can be appraised by reason, i.e., through concepts that can be universally communicated (cf. *KpV* 5:58). He therefore concludes that if the concept of the good were the basis of the moral law, then there would be nothing good absolutely.

It is important to note that this argument equally applies to a conception of value as a distinct metaphysical property. If one wants to base the requirement to respect others on a value property the other possesses, then one still has to account for how one can discern this value, and why one should be motivated to follow it. In Kant's epistemology, if one is to know a value 'out there', it would first have to be given in sensibility: If one cannot see, hear, feel, touch or smell the metaphysical value property, then it could only be given by a feeling of pleasure. So even if there were a value property 'out there' (which has not been shown), the only way human beings could know about it – according to Kant – is by means of a feeling of pleasure. In the next section I shall argue that Kant uses this reasoning to rule out that a value of others could ground the requirement to respect them. In this context it is just important to note that to human beings a metaphysical value property would not be known as such. The only access one would have to it is through a feeling of pleasure. So even if value existed as a distinct metaphysical property, human beings could never know it as such; the only thing we would have is a feeling of pleasure. The assumption that there is a value of human beings out there therefore reduces itself ad absurdum. If there were this value, it would drop out of the picture. We could not know of its existence. This means that Kant's arguments also rule out the knowledge and relevance of metaphysical value properties for moral philosophy (cf. again Pieper 2002, 117 f.).

One could object that Kant's argument is far from being watertight. For the argument that there would be nothing immediately good he relies on the common way of speaking, which might not be accurate. But more importantly a modern-day intuitionist or moral realist would not think that Kant's alternatives exhaust all the options.[19] Why could there not be an intellectual intuition for discerning a value of human beings, and why could one not be motivated by the same feeling of respect Kant puts forth for the moral law? My aim here is not to defend Kant systematically. Kant gives the answer to these questions in the first *Critique*. There he argues: "Our nature is so constituted that our *intuition* can never be other than sensible" (*KrV* A51/B75; cf. *KpV* 5:58). Kant takes

---

19 For more recent statements see Stratton-Lake 2002; and Shafer-Landau 2003.

attempts to gain insight beyond the senses to be fruitless, given the lack of progress that has been made in metaphysics (cf. *KrV* B20 f., Bvii); and in the 'Dialectic' he argues more extensively that reason gets into contradictions and commits fallacies if it tries to gain insight beyond the senses. My aim is not to defend these views, but they show how deep Kant's answer goes, and they raise the stakes for the opponent of Kant's views – he now has to show why Kant is wrong and defend an alternative epistemology. But what has become clear is that Kant does not have a conception of value as a distinct metaphysical property, and that he argues against such a conception. And this is the only point with which I am concerned here.[20]

But does Kant not endorse a metaphysical value property in other writings? There are two *Groundwork* passages in particular that scholars often cite in favor of a metaphysical reading of value. The clearest passage is at the beginning of the *Groundwork* where Kant compares the good will to a jewel. It is the clearest passage not only because he there uses the expression 'absolute value' (he also uses it, for instance, in *GMS* 4:428), but because he seems to elucidate the nature of value. He says that even if a good will were not able to effect anything, then still "like a jewel, it would shine by itself, as something that has its full worth in itself" (*GMS* 4:394). Is this not an endorsement of value as a metaphysical property (cf. Langton 2007, 158)?

In spite of the evocative image Kant uses here, this passage does not actually establish that Kant considered absolute value to be a metaphysical entity. The first thing to note about this analogy is that the emphasis is on 'shine', not on 'jewel'. Kant uses analogies to express the equality of relations: "*analogy*, which surely does not signify, as the word is usually taken, an imperfect similarity between two things, but rather a perfect similarity between two relations in wholly dissimilar things." (*Prol* 4:357; cf. *KrV* A179 f./B222). For instance, if one says that '4 is to 2 as 6 is to 3' one does not thereby express that 4 is like 6. Rather, in both cases the relation between the pair of numbers is the same: 'is twice as much'. Kant uses the jewel analogy to express that even if a good will does not effect anything, it still *shines* like a jewel, meaning it exacts respect from an observer: "before a humble common man in whom I perceive uprightness of character [...] *my spirit bows*, whether I want it or whether I do not" (*KpV* 5:76 f.).

---

20 In the next chapter I shall discuss attempts in the Kant literature to reason one's way to a value property of others.

Using a jewel as an analogy therefore does not commit Kant to an ontological claim about the nature of value. The same is true for a second passage that might be taken to express a metaphysical value claim:

> The essence of things is not changed by their external relations; and that which, without taking account of such relations, alone constitutes the worth of a human being is that in terms of which he also must be appraised by whoever does it, even by the supreme being (*GMS* 4:439; cf. Wood 2008, 112).

This passage likewise does not establish that Kant talks about a metaphysical value entity. What constitutes the worth of a human being is that he acts for the sake of the Categorical Imperative: "the proper worth of an absolutely good will [...] consists just in the principle of action being free from all influences of contingent grounds" (*GMS* 4:426).[21] Kant repeatedly says that the worth of a human being is only the one he can give himself in being morally good (cf. again *KU* 5:443, cf. 208 f.; *GMS* 4:439, 449 f., 454; *KpV* 5:110 f., 147 f.). As the jewel passage made clear, this value is independent of what a will effects. So, the essence of a good will does not change with its external relations, and a human being must simply be appraised by whether he follows the imperative for its own sake. Even a supreme being would not look at the consequences of what the will effects. However, the supreme being would not intuit a value property in a good will, he would merely look at whether the human being follows the Categorical Imperative for its own sake. This reading is confirmed by the sentence that immediately precedes the above quote. A human being is appraised with reference to the Categorical Imperative: "even this sole absolute lawgiver would [...] still have to be represented as appraising the worth of rational beings only by their disinterested conduct, prescribed to themselves merely from that idea" (*GMS* 4:439). The above passage about the essence of things merely reaffirms this point. While I still have to give an account of precisely how Kant uses 'absolute value' (cf. Section 4), there is no proof that this passage by itself puts forth a metaphysical value claim.

Finally, it could be argued that Kant thinks that human beings possess a metaphysical value property in virtue of being part of an intelligible world. After all, Kant does call the intelligible aspect of oneself the "prop-

---

21 Cf. *GMS* 4:437: *"That will is absolutely good* which cannot be evil, hence whose maxim, if made a universal law, can never conflict with itself."

er self" (*GMS* 4:457 f., 461).[22] However, this ontological superiority of the proper self does not by itself imply a moral value. For any object as it appears in the phenomenal world has an intelligible aspect. In the case of any table there is a 'proper table' (whatever it may be). But this does not mean that a table has a moral value. Likewise, Kant does not give an argument that a proper self has a moral value, and he directly argues that any knowledge of an intelligible self is impossible for human beings (cf. the 'Paralogisms', *KrV* A341/B399-A405/B431). How then could one know that the intelligible aspect of one's self has an objective value property? Rather, Kant talks about the "proper self" in the context of explaining why one should take an interest in the moral law: "the law interests because it is valid for us as human beings, since it arose from our will as intelligence and so from our proper self" (*GMS* 4:461). The law is valid because it has a genuine source that is not external; an external source could not ground a necessary and universal law (see Sections 1 and 2). Since the law is genuine, one should take an interest in it. There is no further argument that an intelligible world has value.

In conclusion, a proof that Kant conceives of the value of human beings as a distinct property all human beings possess is elusive. To the contrary, Kant does not even entertain such a conception, and his arguments rule out any knowledge of such a value as an independent starting point (in Kant's framework). Given these arguments, Kant's usage of phrases like 'inner value' is not enough to ascribe to him the conception of value as a distinct metaphysical property.[23]

Section 2: Kant's Argument Against Value as a Foundation

So far I have argued that Kant did not conceive of value as a distinct metaphysical property. But even if he had encountered an author who put forward such a conception, or even if Kant had conceived of it himself, he offers another argument that seems to rule out that such a value could ground any moral requirements, including the requirement to respect others. The second *Critique* passage under discussion does not explicitly

---

22 I thank Dieter Schönecker for raising that objection; on this point cf. his 1999, 387–389.

23 This seems to be what Langton and Korsgaard imply; cf. Langton 2007, 182–5; and Korsgaard 1996a, 257, 250 f. Korsgaard has since distanced herself from a metaphysical reading of this argument; see her 1998, 63 f.

mention that requirement to respect others, as expressed in the Formula of Humanity. But it is important to note that the argument will also be valid for the Formula of Humanity. The formula is also a command of reason and a categorical imperative. The formula commands that one treat others *never* merely as a means, but *always* at the same time as an end in itself. It is not only valid if one wants something else (e.g., to win the favor of the person affected), nor – according to Kant – can it be overridden if one is not inclined to follow it.

The argument is similar to the previous one, and can therefore be brief (cf. also Guyer 2000, 132 f.). Within his discussion of the good in the second *Critique* Kant addresses an objection a reviewer had made against the *Groundwork*.[24] The reviewer had said that Kant should have derived the Categorical Imperative from a prior conception of the good. This prompts Kant to explain his method for establishing the moral law (cf. *KpV* 5:8 note):

> This is the place to explain the paradox of method in a *Critique of Practical Reason*, namely, that the concept of good and evil must not be determined before the moral law (for which, as it would seem, this concept would have to be made the basis) but only (as was done here) after it and by means of it (*KpV* 5:62 f.).

Again, Kant is not concerned about the question which good one may pursue, but he poses the deeper question about the basis or justification of the moral law. The moral law is not based on a prior and independent value, for instance a value of human beings. This claim – that good or value cannot be prior to the moral law but must be determined by it – goes against a common way of thinking. Kant concedes that it is paradoxical, and elsewhere he grants that it is natural to *think* that there is a condition underlying the Categorical Imperative.[25]

However, he also argues that there cannot be a good or value underlying the imperative. His argument is another *reductio*. Again Kant begins by supposing that one could start with a conception of the good: "Suppose that we wanted to begin with the concept of the good in order to derive from it laws of the will" (*KpV* 5:63). His conclusion is that then there would be no a priori law of the will such as the Categorical Imperative: "the possibility of a priori practical laws would be at once excluded" (*KpV* 5:63). His reason is again that one could only determine what is good by the experience of a feeling of pleasure. If the criterion

---

24 Cf. *KpV* 5:8 note. The reviewer is often identified as Pistorius, see Kant 1996, 631.

25 Cf. *GMS* 4:463; I shall discuss this point in Chapter 3 below.

is dependent upon experience, it is a posteriori and not a priori, as he argues moral laws must be (cf. *GMS* 4:389).

To explain further: The criterion must be the experience of pleasure, "since this concept [of the good] had no practical a priori law for its standard" (*ibid.*). Kant does not consider a third option, given the candidates he considers for the concept of the good (cf. Section 1). If one does not begin with the moral law, then the good could be either pleasure or something external (e. g., God's will, but also a metaphysically distinct value property). If the good were external, it would have to be discovered by pleasure. (Again, pleasure would be all one has and knows of, cf. Section 1). So without a prior moral law, the criterion for the good would be pleasure; pleasure is relative and contingent, and therefore cannot yield an a priori moral law. Pleasure varies from person to person: "pleasure or displeasure [...] can never be assumed to be universally directed towards the same objects" (*KpV* 5:26). But even if all people were to desire the same thing (e. g., freedom or humanity), the shared desire still would not qualify as the basis of the moral law, since "this unanimity itself would still be only contingent" (*KpV* 5:26). Contingent inclinations cannot ground an a priori moral law. This is because the sure signs of the a priori are necessity and strict universality: "Necessity and strict universality are therefore secure indications of an *a priori* cognition, and also belong together inseparably." (*KrV* B4) But why does the moral law have to be a priori? Kant had argued for this at the beginning of the *Groundwork*:

> Everyone must grant that a law, if it is to hold morally [...] must carry with it absolute necessity; that, for example, the command "thou shalt not lie" does not hold only for human beings (*GMS* 4:389; cf. 412, 425).

Kant's *reductio* can be summarized as follows: If one does not begin with the moral law, then one would have to be moved by pleasure; pleasure is relative and contingent, and therefore cannot yield the moral law.

Like the first argument presented in the previous section, Kant's argument that the good is dependent upon the moral law is not watertight. The arguments share the crucial premise that an external good could only be known by a feeling of pleasure (and that pleasure is all one would have of this value). Again a modern-day intuitionist might take issue with Kant's first *Critique* and argue that human beings do have an intellectual intuition or a sixth sense for discovering a metaphysical value property. Nonetheless, the argument again makes clear that Kant does not think that *any* value could ground the Categorical Imperative as the moral law: "it is on the contrary the moral law that first determines and makes possible the concept of the good, insofar as it deserves this name absolutely" (*KpV* 5:64).

In this respect one could compare Kant's views on the relationship between value and the moral law to his 'Copernican Revolution' in his theoretical philosophy (cf. Engstrom 2009, 13 f., 183; Allison 2011, ch. 9[26]). The relevant feature is that Kant proposes a revolution in our way of thinking [*"Revolution der Denkungsart"*] (*KrV* B xviiif.). It is a natural way to think that human cognition must conform to the object. Similarly, it is a common way to think that moral laws must conform to something that has value or is precious. Kant reverses both relationships. In his theoretical philosophy Kant argues that the object must conform to a priori elements of human cognition. In his moral philosophy Kant argues that absolute value is dependent upon an a priori law of human reason (cf. also *GMS* 4:435 f.).[27]

However, there is a deeper way in which Kant's views on value relate to his 'Copernican Revolution' in theoretical philosophy. If one construes value as a distinct metaphysical property, it is an object 'out there' that first has to be discerned. In this respect knowing a value property would be no different from knowing any object as it is in itself:

> If we let outer objects count as things in themselves, then it is absolutely impossible to comprehend how we are to acquire cognition of their reality outside us, since we base this merely on the representation, which is in us. (*KrV* A378)

If one wants to start with a metaphysical value property, one is faced with the same problem. One could not know the value as it is in itself, merely one's own subjective reaction to it. In the case of value – Kant argues (see Sections 1 and 2 above) – this could only be a feeling of pleasure. To construe value as a distinct metaphysical property therefore seems to be ruled out by Kant's 'Copernican Revolution' in theoretical philosophy as well.

However, is there not also textual evidence for the opposite view? Does Kant not explicitly say that an absolute value is the ground of the Categorical Imperative, since without such a value, no supreme principle would be found anywhere? Consider the following passage: "if all worth were conditional and therefore contingent, then no supreme prac-

---

26 For earlier comparisons of Kant's ethics to his 'Copernican Revolution' cf. Silber 1959/60; Carnois 1987, 45; Sullivan 1989, 45; and Trampota 2003, 16, 116, 118–20.

27 Similarly Kant will argue that human beings have dignity because they should be respected, cf. *TL* 6:435, 462.

tical principle for reason could be found anywhere" (*GMS* 4:428). Does this not show that there must be a value underlying the Categorical Imperative? This passage is more complicated than it may seem. I shall give it a fuller treatment in Chapters 2 and 3. For now it is sufficient to note that the statement can be equally true if value is dependent upon the Categorical Imperative, as Kant has argued. If the imperative somehow brings about absolute worth, but if one could not find anything of absolute worth, then there would be no imperative. Take the following *modus tollens*:

> If there is a Categorical Imperative, then there is something of absolute worth.[28]
> There is nothing of absolute worth (all worth is conditioned).
> There is no Categorical Imperative.

Kant would deny the second premise. The sentence "if all worth were conditional and therefore contingent, then no supreme practical principle for reason could be found anywhere" can then be read as a way one can *find out* whether there is a Categorical Imperative, not as a statement about the ground of the imperative. It would give a *ratio cognoscendi* of the imperative, not the *ratio essendi* (cf. *KpV* 5:4 note). The passage therefore does not contradict Kant's arguments against the priority of value to the imperative.[29]

Section 3: Alternative Conceptions of Value

It is not yet clear that Kant would have to understand the value of human beings as a distinct metaphysical property in order for it to ground the requirement to respect others. Could not value be something else and fulfill this function? In this section I shall look at whether there is any other conception of value that Kant or Kantians consider and whether it could ground Kant's moral philosophy. What else could value be?

If value is not a property an object has in isolation (or something that can exist by itself like a substance or Platonic form), it could be a relation

---

28 Cf. *GMS* 4:436: "For, nothing can have a worth other than that which the law determines for it." Cf. *KpV* 5:62 f.

29 There is another objection. Does Kant not say that every action needs an end (cf. *TL* 6:385), and do not actions that follow the Categorical Imperative therefore need a special moral end as the ground of the imperative? I shall address this objection in Chapter 2 below.

between two objects. The prime case is the instrumental relation. For instance, food is valuable for living beings because it is instrumental in maintaining the life and health of those beings. However, there is no need to postulate a value property an object would have in isolation. In this respect to say that 'x is valuable' is to say that 'x is beneficial or useful for y' (cf. von Wright 1963, 42 f., 47 f.). The instrumental relation is not the only relation that might be relevant for the question of what value could be. Another example is the relation of fittingness. To say that a practice is good, e.g., a certain etiquette, might be to express that this behavior is fitting under the circumstances (cf. Scanlon 1998, 98).

There are further possibilities. If value is neither a separate property an object would also have in isolation, nor a relation between two objects, it could be that value is simply what people do in fact value. In a Kantian framework one can distinguish two forms of this. What one values could be based on inclinations, or it could be based on pure reason. If one construes value as what one in fact values based on inclinations, value would then not refer to a separate property, but merely describe the subjective desire or preference. It might be that in this respect one ultimately only values happiness or pleasure, and in making statements about what is good one might try to influence others based on one's desires, but value itself is nothing beyond that. Objects would be good merely in a derivate sense: To call an object good would be to say that one does prefer or value the object, and again one might try to influence others. In short, we would not desire something because it has value, but it would be valuable because we desire it.

Finally, value might not be a description of what a being values based on his desires, but it could be a *prescription* of what one should value (e.g., what it would be rational to value). Value then would not be a property an object has in isolation, nor a relation between objects, nor a description of what people actually value, but rather a shorthand for saying what should be valued. To say that human beings have value would be to say that they should be valued and respected. The prescription could have different sources. It could be external, e.g., a command from one's parents, society, or God, or the source could be internal, such as one's rationality or a feeling of conscience. In a Kantian framework the source cannot be external (see Sections 1 and 2 above). Rather it would be a command of pure reason – or something a being would value if it were wholly governed by reason (cf. *GMS* 4:412 f.; 449; 453–5). This prescription is what Kant presents as the Categorical Imperative.

This fourth alternative, prescriptivism, seems to be often overlooked. One attempt to clarify Kant's position on value is to try to locate it within the following dichotomy: In Kant's view, is something good because it is desired, or is it desired because it is good? (Cf. Langton 2007, 170–185; Wood 2008, 110.) But the possibilities considered in this Euthyphro-style question are not exhaustive, for if what is good is prescribed by the Categorical Imperative (and the imperative is not itself grounded in a value), then something is neither good because it is desired, nor is it desired because it is good. If, for instance, the Categorical Imperative prescribes that one not lie, then not lying is good not because it is desired, and it is prescribed regardless of whether it is desired. The Euthyphro-style dilemma is not exhaustive.

There are now four possibilities to consider regarding the ontological nature of value. Value could be a distinct metaphysical property, in the sense that it is a property an object possesses even if it were to exist in isolation. Second, value could be a relation between two objects, e. g., a relation of usefulness or fittingness. Third, value could be subjective, in the sense that it is what a subject does value (e. g., pleasure, happiness). Finally, value statements could be nothing more than a (rational) prescription that commands what one should value.[30] If Kant does not understand value to be a distinct metaphysical property – as I have argued in the previous sections – might he construe value in any of the other three senses in order to ground the requirement to respect others?

First, Kant does not seem to think that value could be a *relation* and ground the moral law. This comes out, for instance, in Kant's famous discussion of hypothetical imperatives in the *Groundwork* (cf. 4:413–419). The relations Kant considers, and that figure in the Kant literature,[31] are relations of utility or instrumentality. Statements about these relations express the means to any possible end or to the given end of happiness. As such they are rules of skill or counsels of prudence (cf. *GMS* 4:416). Ex-

---

30 Are there further possibilities? I do not see anything in Kant's text that suggests that he might hold a hybrid or composite view of value. One example of such a view would be that value is the composite of an object plus its subjective enjoyment (e. g. the enjoyment of a piece of art, or what G.E. Moore calls an 'organic whole', cf. his 1903; Korsgaard 1996a, 252). Another example could be if one construed value parallel to a secondary property (cf. McDowell 1985, 110–129). On the other hand, in a buck-passing account of reasons value might be construed as a Moorean non-natural property, cf. Scanlon 1998, 97. Value would then be a distinct metaphysical property.

31 Cf. Wood 1999, 61–65; but also Korsgaard 1996a, 250–3.

amples are rules for a physician to heal, or for a poisoner to kill. These counsels are all hypothetical; they only say which means would be good with a view to a given end, and they are clearly distinguished from the Categorical Imperative, which commands unconditionally (cf. *GMS* 4:414–419).

Even happiness, which can be presupposed a priori to be a necessary end for each human being, does not ground categorical commands. One reason is that happiness is not a determinate concept, according to Kant. It is therefore not clear what exactly will make one happy. So, instead of precepts one should definitely follow, statements about what promotes happiness dissolve into empirical counsels: "for example, of a regimen, frugality, courtesy, reserve and so on" (*GMS* 4:418). But even if there were a definite concept of happiness, statements about what would be good or what one should do would be "still always *hypothetical*; the action is not commanded absolutely but only as a means to another purpose" (*GMS* 4:416). In addition, this purpose (happiness) and any rules of how to bring it about would not be strictly universal; for they would be merely valid for human beings, but not for all rational beings as such – as Kant argues that morality must be (cf. *GMS* 4:389; 412; 425).

Second, value could not be *subjective* and ground morality, because it would violate Kant's basic premise that morality is necessary and universal: "moral laws are to hold for every rational being as such" (*GMS* 4:412; cf. 389, 425). For Kant, what people value based on inclinations cannot ground the universal moral law, since pleasure and desires vary from person to person (cf. again *KpV* 5:26). But even if all people were to desire the same thing, this unanimity would be contingent (*ibid.*). Contingent inclinations cannot ground a necessary moral law (cf. Section 2 above).

Finally, statements about value could be a *prescription* of what one should value. I shall argue in the next section that this is how Kant understands value. If the faculty of reason deems a maxim or an action as necessary, Kant can say that this maxim or action 'has value', without ascribing a metaphysical property to the action. 'Has value' is merely another way of saying 'should value' or 'would value if he were fully rational'. This is why Kant says that the good has to be determined by the moral law (cf. *KpV* 5:62 f., *GMS* 4:435 f.). One could also express the prescription about what one should value in saying that human beings are committed to valuing it, or that they would value it if they were fully in accord with reason. However, value as a prescription would not *ground* the moral law. One still needs to explain why and how something is prescribed. If the prescription is not grounded in something external

(e. g., a divine command or a value), then it might be justified in reference to a principle, for instance, Kant's Categorical Imperative.

The question here is whether this account of value could ground the Categorical Imperative. A prescription could not ground Kant's Categorical Imperative if it were merely contingent on something else one wants: e. g., 'rent a luxury car if you like comfort on your travels', or 'tithe 10 % of your income if you want to please your church'. These rules are only valid upon a condition, and do not furnish an unconditional and categorical imperative. However, even if the prescription were *necessary* and not conditioned, in that it commands what one has to value simply, it could not ground or justify Kant's imperative. The simple reason is that such a prescription would have exactly the same characteristics as the Categorical Imperative. For Kant, a prescription that commands necessarily, i. e., one that is not conditioned on ends that one may set for oneself based on desires, can only prescribe the form of the law, i. e., to universalize one's maxim (cf. *GMS* 4:420 f., *KpV* 5:29 f.). That prescription would be the Categorical Imperative, and not a separate value. So in construing a prescription of what one should value, one would not thereby introduce a value that is prior to and independent of the moral law.[32]

To conclude, Kant does not ground moral requirements on a prior or independent value. (I shall discuss how Kant grounds the Categorical Imperative instead in Chapter 3 below.) It is important to note that this holds for *any* conception of value. It does not depend upon how exactly one construes it. The reason is that to ground morality on value would yield heteronomy. If one construes value as something external (e. g., a divine command or a distinct metaphysical property), the way it could be discerned is a feeling of pleasure, according to Kant's epistemology. Whether value is something external or is what one actually desires, the only thing one would have would be a feeling of pleasure for Kant. Pleasure is relative and contingent, and cannot yield a necessary and universal moral law. One can construe value as the prescription to do some-

---

32 Many arguments in the literature that seem to put a value as the foundation of Kant's moral philosophy implicitly rely on the Categorical Imperative. For instance, if one argues that one should value humanity, since the value of humanity cannot be subordinated without contradiction (cf. Korsgaard 1996a, 123), it is really the prohibition of a contradiction that does the work. This prohibition is established by the Categorical Imperative (cf. *GMS* 4:424). Andrews Reath argues along similar lines that to hold the value of human beings as equal involves the Categorical Imperative, cf. his 2003, 142.

thing (or a description of what a person fully in accord with reason would do). However, in that case one still has to give an account of why one should do it. Since one cannot base this 'should' on a prior value (which would be reduced to a feeling of pleasure), it can only be a prior moral law, according to Kant's framework.

So, while Kant would grant that placing a value as foundation is a natural way of thinking, he argues that it cannot be the basis of morality. He thinks that this is the mistake of all previous moral systems, and all possible moral system that have a value as their cornerstone (cf. again *KpV* 5:39). My aim has not been to give a systematic defense of this view. However, there is clear evidence that Kant did not base his morality on a value. In the next section I shall spell out the evidence that Kant considered statements about value to be nothing more than a prescription of reason.

Section 4: Kant's Conception of Absolute Inner Value

Kant talks about value at prominent places, most notably at the beginning of the First Section of the *Groundwork* where he argues that only a morally good will could be called good without limitation (cf. *GMS* 4:393 f.), and in the Second Section where he distinguishes between price and inner value (cf. *GMS* 4:434 f.). So far I have argued merely negatively in ruling out several conceptions for what Kant could mean by phrases like 'absolute inner value', and I have argued that Kant does not base moral requirements on any value. But what does he mean by 'value', and how does he justify moral requirements? I shall treat the latter question in Chapters 2 and 3. In this section I shall spell out how I take him to use 'absolute inner value'.

What is absolute inner value for Kant? It cannot be a distinct metaphysical property. As I have argued, Kant does not have such a conception of value (see Section 1 above). But it also cannot be a description of what one values subjectively, or of a relation that holds between two entities (e.g., a relation of utility). Kant says that what one values subjectively based on inclinations has "relative" value (*GMS* 4:428), and he contrasts that with absolute or inner value. I shall argue that for Kant the expression 'absolute inner value' is nothing more than a *prescription* of what one should value independently of inclinations. It is not a description of a property or entity that exists 'out there'. It is merely a shorthand expression for a prescription, or a description of what a perfectly rational being would value.[33] To say that something has inner value is to say that it should be valued unconditionally. The reason why one should value something this way is that it is commanded by the Categorical Imperative. Value is nothing more than the prescription, and the prescription is justified with reference to the imperative (cf. Schneewind 1998, 512).

This is how Kant explains it in his texts. Value in general is what reason judges (independently of inclinations) to be necessary: "the will is a capacity to choose *only that* which reason independently of inclinations cognizes as practically necessary, that is, as good" (*GMS* 4:412). This means: To say that something 'is good' or 'has value' is merely a different way of expressing that reason deems it necessary or prescribes it (cf. Hill 1992, 124; Wood 2008, 91). What is thereby judged to be good or valuable is expressed in an imperative: "All imperatives [...] say that to do or to omit something would be good" (*GMS* 4:413[34]). 'Good' in the absolute sense in which it is contrasted with what relates to one's well-being [*Wohl*] is only predicated of actions, and the will that carries them out:

> Thus good or evil is, strictly speaking, referred to actions [...], and if anything is to be good or evil absolutely (and in every respect and without any further condition), [...] it would be only the way of acting, the maxim of the will, and consequently the acting person himself as a good or evil human being, that could be so called, but not a thing. (*KpV* 5:60)

For Kant, 'good' or 'value' is dependent upon reason's judgment. If reason judges an action to be necessary (i. e., good) as a means to something else one wants, then it issues hypothetical imperatives: 'Do x if you want y' (cf. *GMS* 413 f.). The value of x is then conditioned and relative to one's wanting y (cf. *GMS* 4:428). If reason deems an action to be necessary irrespective of how one is inclined, e. g., if reason deems it necessary not to lie, its command is categorical, and the value is not relative to and not conditioned upon inclinations, but in itself good (i. e., commanded simply):

> Now, if the action would be good merely as a means *to something else* the imperative is *hypothetical*; if the action is represented as *in itself* good, hence as necessary in a will in itself conforming to reason, as its principle, *then it is categorical.* (*GMS* 4:414)

---

33 Cf. Ross 1954, 50 f.; Hill 2003, 19; Hill 1992, 48; Dean 2000, 34; Schneewind 1996, 285–8; Engstrom 2009, 11–14.

34 Cf. *GMS* 4:414: "The imperative thus says which action possible by me would be good".

In accordance with the opening statement of the *Groundwork* Kant maintains that only a good will could be judged to be good without limitation
or absolutely. Non-rational things can have a relative value, but not an
absolute value.

This means that when Kant talks about absolute or inner value he is
likewise talking about a *judgment* of reason, not about a property of an
existing thing. The grammatical form of 'x has absolute inner value' therefore does not commit Kant to an ontological claim that x has a distinct
value property. How then does Kant use *'absolute'* or *'inner* value?' I shall
argue that Kant uses phrases like 'x has absolute inner value' to express
that reason deems x to be necessary simply and that reason's judgment
is not conditioned (e.g., by the consequences of x or one's inclinations
to x). Something is deemed necessary in this way if it follows in accordance with the Categorical Imperative, e.g., that one should not lie. To
elucidate: First, 'absolute inner value' refers to how one has to *judge*, or
to what reason deems necessary. This becomes clear in the famous opening passage of the First Section of the *Groundwork*. Kant says that it is
"impossible to *think*" of anything that "could be *considered* good without
limitation except a good will" (*GMS* 4:393; emphasis mine). He goes on
to say that an *"impartial rational spectator* can take no delight" in seeing
happiness without a good will. Even secondary virtues lack much of what
"would be required to *declare* them good without limitation," and he
notes that the coolness of the scoundrel makes him "more abominable
in our eyes" (*GMS* 4:393 f.; emphasis mine). For Kant, 'absolute inner
value' is accordingly not equivalent to 'a value a thing *has* in itself,' literally speaking,[35] but is tied to one's judgment of it.

Second, to say that something has an absolute inner value expresses
that reason judges an action to be necessary *regarded for itself* (i.e., independently of inclinations, its usefulness, functions and circumstances
etc.). 'Inner' and 'absolute' become interchangeable: "The word **absolute**
is now more often used merely to indicate that something is valid of a
thing considered **in itself** and thus **internally** [*innerlich*]" (*KrV* A324/
B381; cf. *KpV* 5:60 above). 'Inner' and 'absolute' therefore refer to the
same kind of judgment, one that is made in abstracting from all relations.
If one judges looking at the object in isolation, then one's judgment is
also unconditioned. It is not conditioned by any relation that may
hold (e.g., a utility relation). This is the tenor of Kant's remarks at the

---

35 Again, this seems to be how Korsgaard (in her earlier papers) and Langton read it,
    cf. Korsgaard 1996a, 257, 250 f.; Langton 2007, 182–185.

beginning of the *Groundwork*. He asks whether one judges talents of mind, qualities of temperament, gifts of fortune, happiness, and secondary virtues to be good in every respect, or only under the condition of a good will (cf. *GMS* 4:393 f.). In the end it is only a good will that is unconditionally good:

> A good will is not good because of what it effects or accomplishes, [...] but only because of its volition, that is, [...] regarded for itself, [it] is to be valued incomparably higher than all that could merely be brought about by it in favor of some inclination (*GMS* 4:394).

A judgment about absolute inner value is accordingly a judgment of what is to be valued irrespective of any condition (inclinations, consequences etc.). This judgment is made in accordance with the Categorical Imperative, and therefore follows from it. Value is not the ground of it.

Clarifications

To avoid misunderstandings, my view is not that the value of human beings is merely relational (*pace* Foreman 2010). Of course, human beings might also have a relational value – for instance, they might be useful for all sorts of purposes (cf. *TL* 6:434) – but this is not my concern here. First, my interpretation leaves untouched Kant's key claim that *all* human beings should be respected. I have merely argued that Kant cannot refer to a value to *justify* this claim. Second, on my reading value is not something anyone or anything has, literally speaking. It is not a distinct metaphysical property of a human being or thing. Rather the function of using the term 'value' in a proposition is to prescribe or recommend something. What one adds in saying that something is good or has value is that this something is prescribed by reason (either as a means to something else or *simpliciter*). Reason might prescribe or recommend something in virtue of distinct metaphysical properties an object has, but value is not itself such a property. It is merely another way of expressing the prescription or recommendation.

Third, to adopt this view does not commit one to constructivism (*pace* Wood 2008, 110). It is a false dichotomy to say that there are only two positions, constructivism and realism. There are at least three positions. One could be a realist about value (i. e., there are distinct metaphysical value properties 'out there'), one could be a realist about the moral law (i. e., the moral law is valid irrespective of what one wants), or one could be a constructivist (i.e., the moral law is not an in-built principle of reason, but it is merely constructed by human beings in a volitional act). To deny that Kant is a value realist does not mean that one has to read Kant as a constructivist. He could be a realist about the moral law (cf. Ameriks 2003, ch. 11). Indeed I shall argue in Chapter 3 below that Kant is a realist about the moral law in the sense that the moral law is an in-built principle of reason. So even a hermit is under the moral law. One way to express this is to say that the moral law is constitutive of one's reason (cf. Reath 2006, 4, 176–180). However, I have tried to avoid labels, simply because they are often read in different ways.

Fourth, so far I have merely talked about the justification of the requirement to respect others. I have not yet said anything about the application or the question of how one can derive concrete duties from the requirement to respect others. So I have not yet addressed the question of whether one might need a value to answer the question *who* should be respected. Could it not be that one might still have to refer to a value in order to explain, for instance, why one should respect other human beings, but not tables and chairs?[36] I shall address these questions in Chapter 3 below. However, it is important to note that the same difficulties hold in regard to application: What is this value supposed to be ontologically? How can one discern it, and why should one be motivated to respect it? The same arguments I have presented in Sections 1 and 2 above apply here as well. So in Chapter 3 I shall sketch Kant's alternative answer to these questions that does not refer to a value of human beings.

Finally, there is still one loophole I have not yet addressed. So far I have merely argued that Kant cannot ground the requirement to respect others on a value *external* to one's own will, e.g., a value that is 'out there' or that another person has. However, it could be that value is not something that is external to one's will, but something that is *internal* to one's will (cf. Wood 2008, 93). It could be that one can discover a value that is possessed by all human beings by virtue of looking into oneself. Value would then not be a property external to one's own will, and the above arguments might not apply. I shall address this loophole in Chapter 2. For now I have merely argued that moral requirements cannot be grounded on a value that one discerns in the other.

---

36 I thank Sally Sedgwick, Marcia Baron, Joshua Glasgow, and Jens Timmermann for pressing me on this point.

The Goodness of the Good Will

I have argued that to say that something has value is to say that it *should* be valued. What does it mean then to say that a good will has value? How could one say that a particular person has a good will?[37]

This objection does not seem to pose a problem for the interpretation of value I have offered. First, it does not seem to be Kant's concern to determine whether someone actually has a morally good will. He famously says that one cannot even in one's own case know whether one's will has full moral worth:

> in fact we can never, even by the most strenuous self-examination get entirely behind our covert incentives, since, when moral worth is at issue, what counts is not actions, which one sees, but those inner principles of actions that one does not see. (*GMS* 4:407)

In his moral philosophy Kant is not concerned with determining whether someone actually has a morally good will (cf. *GMS* 4:406–8). Rather Kant's conception is forward-looking. The question of his moral philosophy is: "What should I do?" (*KrV* A805/B833)

Second, even if one could determine whether a particular person has a good (or evil) will, this would not pose a special difficulty for the interpretation of value I have offered. For to say that 'Peter has a good will' would still be meaningful if it merely amounts to saying that 'Peter has a will that one should value'. The function of the sentence would be to recommend or *prescribe* what kind of will one should value. A good will is good if it follows the Categorical Imperative for its own sake: "the proper worth of an absolutely good will [...] consists just in the principle of action being free from all influences of contingent grounds" (*GMS* 4:426; cf. 437). This requirement is the requirement of the Categorical Imperative (cf. 4:420 f.). To add that a will that follows the imperative for its own sake 'is good', adds that it is prescribed to value such a will.

This interpretation also explains the following cryptic passage from Kant's discussion of the different formulas of the Categorical Imperative, that what determines the good must be unconditionally good:

> For, nothing can have a worth other than that which the law determines for it. But the lawgiving itself, which determines all worth, must for that very reason have a dignity, that is, an unconditional, incomparable worth; and

---

37 I thank Jens Timmermann for pressing me on this question.

the word *respect* alone provides a becoming expression for the estimate of it that a rational being must give. (*GMS* 4:435 f.)

This passage is not an argument for the view that the condition of the value of things must have an unconditional value.[38] I shall discuss such an argument in Chapter 2. Rather, the passage first confirms the view that I have been arguing for in this chapter, that value is merely another way of expressing the prescription of the moral law: "For, nothing can have a worth other than that which the law determines for it." There is no (absolute) value besides the prescription of the law. Value is a secondary notion that is dependent upon the moral law (cf. Schneewind 1996, 286). When Kant says that "the lawgiving, which determines all worth, must for that very reason have [...] an unconditional, incomparable worth," he does not introduce a different conception of value. Rather, here too 'value' is just another expression for a prescription. The law determines what should be done (and should be valued). The main request the law poses is that one's maxim can be willed as a universal law (cf. *GMS* 4:421). The passage under discussion appears in the context of the Formula of Autonomy, or "the *principle* of every human will as *a will giving universal law through all its maxims*" (*GMS* 4:432). In other words, what one should do is choose maxims that could be given as universal laws. This lawgiving of lower-level (or more concrete) laws is commanded by the moral law. The moral law requires that one participate in the process of lawgiving, i.e., in adopting universalizable maxims for its own sake. If one does so, then one has a morally good will and an unconditional value (i.e., one behaves exactly as one should). Therefore Kant can say that participating in the "lawgiving, which determines all worth, must [...] have [...] an unconditional, incomparable worth". The moral law determines all (unconditional) value (i.e., what one should value). What one should value is universal lawgiving. This lawgiving therefore has an unconditional worth as it is what is unconditionally commanded by the moral law.

---

38 As such it would give supreme value to two different things, cf. Mulholland 1990, 110 f. I thank Rocco Porcheddu for pressing me on this, cf. also his 2012.

Section 5: The Appearance of 'Value' in Kant's Works

In the previous section I have argued that value is a secondary notion for Kant. It is merely another way of expressing the command of reason that Kant formulates in the moral law. My claim that value is a secondary notion for Kant should not be surprising if one looks at how Kant uses 'value' throughout his writings. What is striking is that 'good' or 'value' is missing where one should most expect it if it were a foundational concept for Kant. It does not play any role where he says that he justifies morality, in the Third Section of the *Groundwork* or the First Chapter of the *Critique of Practical Reason*. It also does not appear where Kant gives a summary of his moral philosophy, e.g., in the 'Introduction' to the *Metaphysics of Morals* as a whole (cf. 6:221–8), in his essay "On the Common Saying: That May Be True in Theory, But It Is of No Use in Practice" or in his *Lectures on Ethics*.

In the following I shall briefly survey Kant's writings on moral philosophy during his mature period for any obvious usages of 'value' or 'good'. My aim is not to give a thorough analysis of these passages, but to make sure that I have not overlooked a discussion of value that contradicts my previous analysis. What scholars who dispute the interpretation of the previous sections would need is a clear passage in which Kant does not merely use phrases like 'has absolute inner value', but in which he also specifies it as something prior to and independent of the moral law (and ideally explains the ontological nature of this value). In addition, they would need a passage that explains why Kant would have changed his views on value from the second *Critique*, and his epistemology of the first *Critique* more generally. In the following, I shall give a brief survey of other passages in which Kant refers to 'good' or 'value'. The question is whether there is anything in these passages that contradicts the account of value I have given so far.

Groundwork of the Metaphysics of Morals

With the exception of the *Groundwork*, value does not play a prominent role in Kant's writings. Since the *Groundwork* is often read, it might distort the picture of the role value plays in Kant's thought. The fact that Kant starts out the *Groundwork* with a discussion of the good will does not mean that value is the basic concept of his moral philosophy. After all, the *Groundwork* begins with 'common rational cognition', which is a different approach than Kant's usual emphasis on a priori insights. The beginning of the *Groundwork* is therefore not a reliable indicator of Kant's key concepts of moral philosophy. The emphasis on common cognition might be an attempt to make his work popularly accessible, and it has been plausibly argued that Kant's emphasis on value at the beginning of the *Groundwork* is an attempt to contrast his ethics with ancient Greek ethics, and in particular Garve's edition of Cicero's *De Officiis*.[39] Kant makes this clearer in a parallel passage in the lecture notes taken by Vigilantius (cf. 27:482 ff.). Finally, as I have argued in Section 4 above, the beginning of the *Groundwork* does not introduce a value that could be the *foundation* of morality. The beginning of the *Groundwork* is therefore no objection to the interpretation offered so far.

In the *Groundwork* 'value' also appears in connection with the Formula of Humanity. This passage should be of greater interest since it would establish a value all human beings possess – in contrast to the beginning of the *Groundwork* where it is merely tied to a good will which only some might have (cf. *GMS* 4:406–8). While the claim that only a good will is absolutely good is contestable, the view that all human beings possess equal value would usually be considered to be a welcome foundation for moral philosophy. I shall look at this passage very closely in the next two chapters. For now it is only important to note that there Kant does not specify value in a new way (e. g., as a distinct metaphysical property), and that one does not have to read that passage as claiming that a value underlies the Categorical Imperative (cf. Section 2 above). The passage can be read as conforming with Kant's explicit statements about the nature of value, and I shall present such an interpretation in Chapter 3 below.

In contrast 'value' does not play any role in the argument of the Third Section of the *Groundwork*, where Kant aims to justify his conception of morality. This is most significant – for if value were to be the foundation of Kant's moral philosophy, this would be the place to say it. Instead 'value' is mentioned merely in passing.[40] It does not appear in connection with the justification of morality, but merely in relation to the claim that even "the most hardened scoundrel" (*GMS* 4:454) deep down wishes to be morally good. By this wish, Kant says, "he can expect no satisfaction of

---

39   On the relationship between the *Groundwork* and *De Officiis* cf. Reich 1939; Allison 2011, ch. 2; Timmermann 2007, xxviif.; Schönecker 1999, 61–7; Schneewind 1996; Duncan 1958, 173–8; and Wood 2006.
40   Cf. *GMS* 4:449.34 & 36; 450.13 & 15; 454.37.

his desires [...]; he can expect only a greater inner worth of his person."
(*GMS* 4:454) This passage does not introduce a justification of morality.
It merely claims that everyone, even a scoundrel, has the moral motivation of respect for the law and thereby a desire to form a good will. In
accordance with the beginning of the *Groundwork*, Kant talks here
about the value of a good will (cf. Section 4 above); he does not introduce
a new kind of value that could be the foundation of morality.

Naturrecht Feyerabend

A second writing in which 'value' features prominently is a set of hitherto
un-translated lecture notes from a time when the *Groundwork* was in
press. The set of notes taken by Feyerabend record a lecture on natural
law Kant gave during the fall semester of 1784. The lecture will be crucial
for understanding what Kant means by 'end in itself', and I therefore
shall come back to it in Chapter 3 below. One might also think that it
contains an endorsement of a substantive account of value. For instance,
Kant says that:

> The human being [...] is an end in himself, that is why he can only have an
> inner value, i.e., dignity, in whose place no equivalent can be set. [...] The
> inner value of the human being rests on his freedom, that he has his own
> will. (*NF* 27:1319.33–8)[41]

However, the fact that Kant uses the expression 'inner value' once again
does not settle anything as to what he means by it. By itself this expression does not introduce a new account of value that differs from the one
specified in Section 4 above. What one would need is that Kant explicitly
specifies a different conception of value. However, even the lecture itself
speaks against a more substantial usage of 'value'. As it proceeds, it becomes clear that here too Kant uses 'inner value' merely as a specific
form of judgment, not as the name for a metaphysical property.

   To elucidate: Kant's question in this context is about humanity's place
in nature. In the blind play of nature one thing follows another. Human
beings stand out in that they are not simply pushed around, they have
their own free will and can use things as their means: "The whole of nature is subject to the will of the human being" (*NF* 27:1319.2). Things
only have value if they are regarded as means to something else: "I cannot

---

41 All quotations from this lecture are my own translation.

think of any value of other things unless I consider them as means to other ends, e. g., the moon has value for us insofar as it illuminates the earth" (*NF* 27:1319.6–8). It is important to note that in this context Kant merely talks about how one has to judge. He does not ascribe value properties to things. In this context, to say that a thing has value is merely to say that it is useful for something else (cf. *GMS* 4:428).

Similarly, Kant argues that reason must regard human beings not merely as means (as things pushed around by forces of nature). He contrasts being a mere means with being an end. However, by itself this is only a word that signifies a negative contrast (human beings are not merely means in the causal chain). By itself it does not generate any normative requirements. In the state of nature one's knowledge that the other is free makes one the more afraid of the other, since his actions are harder to predict (cf. *NF* 27:1320). It needs a normative premise to generate any requirement out of the fact that human beings are free. Like 'end in itself', Kant characterizes *"Bonum a se* [good in itself]" merely negatively, in contrast to *"Bonum ab alio* [good from another]" (*NF* 27:1321). If something is not just a means to another, and thereby not just useful for the fulfillment of the end of another, this by itself does not ascribe a normative standing to 'end in itself'. Similarly, 'good in itself' first of all expresses that something is not merely good for another. By itself it does not say that 'good in itself' refers to a distinct metaphysical property. Instead, Kant again merely talks about how one has to *judge*. In nature one event follows the other in a chain of events. Reason has to think that there is no infinite regress, and that the chain comes to an end. Similarly, reason has to think that the chain of means does not go on forever, but comes to a halt in a *Bonum a se:*

> It is necessary in the system of ends that the existence of some one thing must be an end in itself, and not all things can be mere means, as an *Ens a se* is necessary in the chain of efficient causes. (*NF* 27:1321.12–14)

However, this way of thinking is only a "need of reason" (*NF* 27:1321.27). Human questioning does not come to an end until it finds an unconditioned condition. In the chain of means and ends the questioning comes to a halt in a being that is not a mere means to another. By itself this is not a value claim, despite Kant's terminus of *"Bonum a se"*. Rather it merely says that human beings are not mere means because they are free and can govern themselves. It needs further argument to show that one *should* not treat others as mere means. For this Kant reverts to the Categorical Imperative: "This limitation [to treat others never merely as a means] rests (*beruht*) on the conditions of the most possible universal agreement of the will of others." (*NF* 27:1319.30–32; cf. 1322) The requirement to treat others never merely as a means *rests* [*beruht*] on universality. The justification for the requirement to respect others is the qualification of one's maxim as a universal law. This is the same requirement as the Categorical Imperative (see Chapter 3 below). The Feyerabend lecture notes therefore do not contradict Kant's elucidation of the nature of value as spelled out in Section 4.

Critique of Practical Reason

The *Critique of Practical Reason* is a central work to consider regarding Kant's conception of value. Since he derives and justifies the fundamental law of practical reason in the first chapter of the book (cf. 5:19–50), one would expect an important reference to value at that point. Instead, value plays no role whatsoever in that enterprise.[42] When Kant uses 'value' in that chapter it is to talk about the "immediate worth that compliance with it [the moral law] gives a person in his own eyes" (*KpV* 5:38). Kant merely talks about the value of a good will in the sense found at the beginning of the *Groundwork*. In accordance with that, Kant argues that if someone cheats at play, "he must *despise* himself as soon as he compares himself with the moral law". His reaction would be: "I am a *worthless* man [*Unwürdiger*]" (*KpV* 5:37). I have already discussed at length the appearance of 'good' in the first chapter of the *Critique of Practical Reason*. Rather than introducing a value as the foundation of morality, Kant does not even entertain the conception of good as a distinct metaphysical property under "all possible" conceptions of the good (see Section 1 above). The second chapter then rules out that any conception of value could be the foundation of morality as this would yield heteronomy (see Section 2).

'Value' still appears prominently in the 'Dialectic' of the second *Critique* (cf. *KpV* 5:107–119). There Kant discusses the highest good as "the whole and complete [...] object of the faculty of desire of rational finite beings" (*KpV* 5:110). The highest good combines morality and happiness, with "happiness distributed in exact proportion to morality (as the worth of a person and his worthiness to be happy)" (*KpV* 5:110 f.). It becomes clear that the highest good is not a new substantive value

---

42 Cf. the scattered usage of "worth" in *KpV* 5:23.36; 35.38; 38.26.

that is introduced, but merely states the complete aim a human being strives for, and that the highest good is still dependent upon morality. The second *Critique* therefore makes it harder to ascribe a substantive notion of value to Kant. This is an important result, since this is one of the three *Critiques*, which are Kant's three major works.

Metaphysics of Morals

The *Metaphysics of Morals* is often conceived as presenting a fuller picture of Kant's ethics than his earlier works.[43] I shall discuss this work much more thoroughly in subsequent chapters. For now the question is merely whether the text contains a conception of value that goes beyond the prescriptive account I have sketched in Section 4 above. The first thing that is striking is that value plays no role whatsoever in the summary Kant gives of his moral philosophy in the 'Introduction' to the *Metaphysics of Morals* as a whole. For instance, 'value' is not among the "Prior Concepts [*Vorbegriffe*] of the *Metaphysics of Morals*" (cf. *MS* 6:221–8). Instead, Kant summarizes his moral philosophy in the familiar terms of 'freedom', 'Categorical Imperative', and 'duty' (cf. Baum 2012).

But in the Introduction to the *Doctrine of Virtue* there seems at first glance to be a change. There he says that ethics provides a matter, "an **end** of pure reason which it represents as an end that is objectively necessary, that is, an end that, as far as human beings are concerned, it is a duty to have" (*TL* 6:380). However, it is important to note that Kant's introduction of this end is no departure from his earlier emphasis on the Categorical Imperative. This is because the ends that it is a duty to have are explicitly said to *follow* from the moral law, they are not the ground of it. Kant makes this clear in the Section 'Discussion of the Concept of an End that is also a Duty' (cf. *TL* 6:382):

> One can think of the relation of end to duty in two ways: one can begin with the end and seek out the *maxim* of actions in conformity with duty or, on the other hand, one can begin with the maxim of actions in conformity with duty and seek out the end that is also a duty. – The *doctrine of right* takes the first way. [...] But *ethics* takes the opposite way. [...] Hence in ethics the *concept of duty* will lead to ends and will have to establish *maxims* with respect to ends we *ought* to set ourselves, grounding them in accordance with moral principles. (*TL* 6:382)

---

43 Cf. Wood 1999, 321; and Oberer 2006, 259 f.

Kant says that the ends that it is a duty to have *follow* from the concept of duty and are grounded "in accordance with moral principles". This is reminiscent of the beginnings of the *Groundwork* and second *Critique.* Kant does not introduce a new substantial value; rather these moral ends are introduced to counter the influence of ends presented by inclinations (cf. *TL* 6:380). The agreement with his earlier works should not be surprising if one looks at what these moral ends are. Kant specifies them as *"one's own perfection"* and *"the happiness of others"* (*TL* 6:385). These correspond to the examples three and four in the *Groundwork* (cf. *GMS* 4:422 f.). This is not a new justification. The condition for moral bindingness is still the qualification as a universal law:

> The reason that it is a duty to be beneficent is this: since our self-love cannot be separated from our need to be loved (helped in case of need) by others as well, we therefore make ourselves an end for others; and the only way this maxim can be binding is through its qualification as a universal law (*TL* 6:393).

Even with the introduction of moral ends in the *Doctrine of Virtue*, it is still the Categorical Imperative that is at the heart of moral requirements: "Hence, if there is an end that is also a duty, the only condition that maxims of actions, as means to ends, must contain is that of qualifying for a possible giving of universal law." (*TL* 6:389; cf. 451)[44]

However, there are also at least two passages in the discussion of more concrete duties in which Kant talks about value. It is important to show that they do not introduce a new and more substantial account of value. The first passage appears in Kant's discussion of the duty of servility or false humility. Kant says: "But a human being [...] possesses a *dignity* (an absolute inner worth) by which he exacts *respect* for himself from all other rational beings in the world." (*TL* 6:434 f.) I shall discuss this passage twice below, once in the context of why one should respect others, and once in the context of Kant's usage of 'dignity' (cf. Chapters 3 and 5 below). In the following I shall just briefly argue for the following two points: First, Kant does not specify the value in a way that would introduce a new substantial account, e.g., he does not say that "inner value" refers to a metaphysically distinct property. Second, if one looks at the context of the passage, it becomes clear that Kant talks about the *moral* value of a good will, not a value that grounds moral requirements. "Absolute inner worth" refers to a "morally practical reason"

---

44 I shall consider in Chapter 3 whether there is a different justification for the Formula of Humanity.

(*TL* 6:434). There is no break with the conception of absolute value that can be found at the beginning of the *Groundwork*.

To elucidate: The passage starts out in explicitly denying that the mere existence of human beings gives them an important value. As such human beings, with their capacity to set ends, merely have an ordinary value:

> In the system of nature, a human being [...] is a being of slight importance and shares with the rest of the animals [...] an ordinary value [...]. Although a human being has, in his understanding, something more than they and can set himself ends, even this gives him only an *extrinsic* value for his usefulness (*TL* 6:434; cf. *KpV* 5:61; *NF* 27:1321 f.; cf. *Vigil* 27:545).

Kant contrasts the human being as a natural being with the human being as subject to morality: "But a human being regarded as a *person*, that is, as the subject of a morally practical reason, is exalted above any price" (*TL* 6:434). It is the moral aspect of oneself that is respected and that accounts for one's worth:

> from our capacity for internal lawgiving and from the (natural) human being's feeling himself compelled to revere the (moral) human being within his own person, at the same time there comes *exaltation* of the highest self-esteem, the feeling of his inner worth (*valor*), in terms of which he is above any price (*TL* 6:436).

The worth Kant is talking about is tied to one's moral capacity. Kant is not saying that everyone is morally good, or that only morally good people should be respected (cf. *TL* 6:462 f.). Rather, the context is the duty against false humility. A human being should not be servile towards others, for he is capable of achieving the worth that really counts, moral worth. A human being feels respect for the moral human being within, i. e., for the command of the moral law. He thereby feels that in following the law for its own sake he can acquire the inner worth of a morally good will. In being able to achieve that worth, "[h]e can measure himself with every other being of this kind and value himself on a footing of equality with them." (*TL* 6:435) Therefore he should not fall into a servile spirit.

I shall give a fuller discussion of this passage below (in Chapters 3 and 5). For now it is merely important to note that Kant does not specify a new form of value. Rather he talks about the value of morality familiar from the *Groundwork*. I shall argue that this is also true of the second passage in the *Doctrine of Virtue* where value figures prominently. In his discussion of duties towards others from respect, Kant says that "the *respect* that I have for others or that another can require from me [...] is therefore recognition [...] of a worth that has no price" (*TL* 6:462). I shall give a thorough discussion of this passage in Chapter 3 below. For now it is only important to note that Kant does not specify the value in any way that would contradict his earlier account specified in Section 4. Instead the passage can be read as specifying *what* should be respected – the moral capacity in others – not as introducing a new value. Kant explains it in the following way: "just as he [the agent] cannot give himself away for any price (this would conflict with his duty of self-esteem), so neither can he act contrary to the equally necessary self-esteem of others" (*TL* 6:462). As an argument for why one should respect others, this claim would not make much sense. Kant merely specifies what should be respected. As one should respect the moral aspect of oneself, so others have to respect *their own* moral capacity which gives them true self-esteem. If one should respect others, one should respect their striving for true self-esteem. I shall give a much fuller discussion in Chapter 3 below. For now it was only important to note that the passage does not contradict the interpretation of value I have offered.

Lectures on Ethics

It is striking that Kant's very comprehensive *Lectures on Ethics* also do not contain a substantial account of value. There are different sets of notes, taken by different people, from the lectures Kant gave over decades. The earlier sets show a greater similarity in their structure to the textbooks Kant used by Baumgarten, *Introduction to Practical First Philosophy*, and especially his *Philosophical Ethics* (cf. Schneewind 1997). One therefore could try to explain the absence of a treatment of the conception of value by the lack of such a treatment in the textbooks. However, throughout the notes Kant departs from the textbooks wherever he thinks they are going wrong. So, one would expect Kant to point out the importance of value if he thought that the textbooks miss that point. But this is not the case. In the following I shall focus on the set of notes taken by Vigilantius because they show a greater degree of independence from the textbooks. The notes where taken in the fall semester of 1793, well after the publication of the second *Critique* (1788) and not too far from the *Metaphysics of Morals* (1797).

In the Vigilantius notes the concept of value does not play any significant role. Again the emphasis is on freedom, the a priori moral law and duty. Value or good is secondary to these concepts, and connected to them. There is only one passage where he addresses the good directly:

> Thus an action is: a. Good in the positive sense when it agrees with certain *leges obligantes*, and in the negative sense when it does not conflict with the law of duty, and is thus neither bad nor positively good. (*Vig* 27:512)

This passage does not offer a new substantial account of value that could ground moral requirements. Again 'good' is predicated of actions, and not of human beings as such. More importantly, the passage reiterates that 'good' is another way of expressing the prescription of the moral law. This passage, together with the absence of any direct discussion of value throughout the different lecture notes (let alone a positive account of value as a distinct metaphysical property), confirms the interpretation of value I have offered in Section 4 above. Value is a secondary notion for Kant.

This is further supported by passages like these: "the existence of man is not by itself a *factum* that produces any obligation." (*Vigil* 27:545) This passage echoes a statement Kant had made in the *Groundwork:* "Here, then, we see philosophy put in fact in a precarious position, which is to be firm even though there is nothing in heaven or on earth from which it depends or on which it is based." (*GMS* 4:425) Kant does not think that there are any moral facts out there on which one can base morality. Rather the source of morality is the "principles that reason dictates, and that must have their source entirely and completely a priori" (*GMS* 4:425 f.). The *Lectures on Ethics* make it harder to ascribe to Kant a value as the foundation of his morality.

Reflection Notes

The picture is also confirmed if one goes through Kant's *Reflection Notes* in regard to 'value'. In a way they are even more explicit, since they clearly express that the value of human beings is dependent upon a morally good will. This does not mean that one should only respect human beings with a morally good will – even if one could know who has one and who has not. Rather it shows that for Kant value is not the reason why one should respect others. To talk about the value of human beings is Kant's way of saying what one should strive for, namely morality. Take, for instance, the following passage: "For that reason nothing except persons have an absolute value, and this consists in the goodness of their free choice." (*Refl*

6598 19:103) This echoes the passages cited earlier from the *Groundwork* and second *Critique*. For Kant nothing has absolute value except a good will. This is also confirmed in other reflection notes: "The value of the person rests on the freedom that agrees with itself in accordance with original (*ursprünglichen*) rules." (*Refl* 6861 19:183) The value of human beings depends upon having a will in accordance with the moral law (cf. also *Refl* 19:278 and 281).

Critique of the Powers of Judgment

Kant is equally explicit about the lack of a substantive conception of value in the *Critique of the Powers of Judgment*:

> [I]t is the value that he alone can give to himself, and which consists in what he does, in how and in accordance with which principles he acts, not as a link in nature but in the freedom of his faculty of desire; i.e., a good will is that alone by means of which his existence can have an absolute value. (*KU* 5:443.07–13; cf. 208 f.)

Kant emphasizes that is *only* through the proper use of one's freedom that one can acquire an absolute value:

> Only through that which he does without regard to enjoyment, in full freedom and independently of that which nature could passively provide for him, does he give his being as the existence of a person an absolute value (*KU* 5:208 f.).

Kant's position from the *Groundwork* that only a morally good will can have an absolute value did not change over time.

Critique of Pure Reason

While the *Critique of Pure Reason* does not contain an explicit discussion of the nature of value, its arguments make it harder to ascribe to Kant a position according to which 'absolute inner value' refers to a distinct metaphysical value property. This is for several reasons: First, Kant famously says that one can only know the relation of things, never what they are in themselves: "everything in our cognition [...] contains nothing but mere relations, [...] and not that which is internal to the object in itself" (*KrV* B 66; cf. A265/B321). If we cannot cognize what is internal to an object, this would seem to rule out cognition of a value property internal to an object.

The underlying story is familiar to Kantians. Kant argues that one can only have knowledge of objects that relate to possible sense-experience. One therefore cannot have knowledge of objects that would go beyond the senses, e.g., a Moorean non-natural value property, and we cannot introduce a non-sensible intuition that could detect these properties: "we cannot cook up [...] a single object with any new and not empirically given property [...]. Thus we are not allowed to think up any sort of new original forces, e.g., an understanding that is capable of intuition of its object without sense" (*KrV* A770/B798; similarly A254/B309). Since Kant explicitly states that one cannot assume any properties of objects that are non-sensible, one cannot construe the value of human beings in his account as a non-sensible value property: "merely intelligible properties of things of the sensible world cannot be assumed" (A772/B800), and "hyperphysical ones can never be permitted at all" (A773/B801).

One could object that these passages only refer to external objects, but that this leaves open the possibility that one could know the value of human beings from one's own case. However, here too Kant explicitly argues that one can only know oneself as one appears, leaving no room for cognition of a property one might have independently of one's internal sense: "I therefore have **no cognition** of myself **as I am**, but only as I **appear** to myself" (*KrV* B158). One is justified in assuming the existence of a self as the subject of one's thought, but "apart from this logical significance of the I, we have no acquaintance with the subject in itself" (*KrV* A350). If one does not know oneself beyond the introspection of inner sense, how could Kant hold that one possesses a distinct metaphysical value property?

My aim here is not to evaluate Kant's views about knowledge, but merely to bring out the fact that key tenets of the *Critique of Pure Reason* make it harder to ascribe to Kant the view that 'absolute inner value' could be a distinct metaphysical property – in contrast to being something one does or should value.

In conclusion, the conception of value Kant spells out in the *Groundwork* and *Critique of Practical Reason* is confirmed by other writings throughout his mature period. Scholars who interpret Kant as having a value as the foundation of his moral philosophy would need to support their view with passages in which Kant not merely uses the phrase 'has absolute inner value', but where he specifies this value as prior to and independent of the moral law. In addition, one would need a good explanation of why Kant should have forgotten his views about epistemology whenever he wrote on ethics. The aim of this section was to indicate that such an interpretation of Kant is not readily at hand if one goes through the moral writings of his mature period.

Conclusion

The common view in the literature, according to which Kant bases the requirement to respect others on an absolute inner value they possess, cannot be literally true. Kant does not seem to have a conception of absolute value that is prior to or independent of the moral law (cf. Section 1 above). Even if Kant had conceived of such a value, his arguments rule out that it could be the foundation of his moral philosophy. If value is supposed to be an independently existing fact, one still would need an account of how one can discern it. Kant argues that the only thing one would have would be a feeling of pleasure. However, pleasure is relative and contingent, and cannot ground a necessary moral law (cf. Section 2).

Instead, Kant grounds absolute value on the moral law. This law is given a priori by pure reason. Good is what reason deems necessary. If reason deems something necessary without condition, it is absolutely good or – as Kant can also say without making a metaphysical commitment – it has inner value. Absolute inner value follows from the moral law, it is not the basis of it (cf. Section 4). This view is not merely confined to the beginning of the *Groundwork*. There is no obvious passage in other writings where Kant contradicts these views. On the contrary, what Kant says elsewhere confirms the *Groundwork* picture (cf. Section 5).

To sum up: So far I have argued that value could not be the ultimate justification for moral requirements, including the requirement to respect others. This of course does not mean that one should not respect others. Kant is very clear that this is a necessary and universal moral requirement. The result of my argument is merely that value is not the reason why one should respect them, according to Kant. If all human beings should be respected, but not all have absolute value, then absolute value is not the reason why one should respect them. To argue against my interpretation, it is not enough to point to passages where Kant uses phrases like 'has absolute inner value'. One still has to look at how he uses those terms. In the absence of a direct specification to the contrary, I conclude that Kant uses 'has absolute inner value' to express that 'an action (or its will) is judged to be necessary in accordance with the moral law irrespective of inclinations'. This reading is also supported by Kant's epistemology. To argue against my interpretation, one would also have to explain why and where Kant changed his epistemology from the first *Critique* so as to allow an intellectual intuition or the knowledge of a non-sensible property.

At this point my results are negative. I have not yet spelled out why one should respect others, according to Kant. Before I lay out my reading of the Formula of Humanity in Chapter 3, I shall first look at the arguments presented in the Kant literature (in Chapter 2). One could argue that the preceding analysis leaves one important loophole. So far I have merely argued that value cannot be something *external* to the will (such as a distinct metaphysical property in others) and ground moral requirements. But could it not be that value is *internal* to the will, and can be discovered as such? For instance, value could be something one is committed to valuing, or something one necessarily wills, or something that is connected to a morally good will. There is not necessarily a disagreement between these views and the interpretation I offer in Section 4 above. For on these readings value is not necessarily a distinct metaphysical property. There is only a disagreement if one understands this value as being prior to or independent of the moral law, or if one grounds the requirement to respect others on the value of a good will, not on the moral law. In Chapter 2 I shall discuss these possibilities as they have been presented in the literature, before laying out my interpretation of the requirement to respect others in Chapter 3.

Chapter 2: The Value of Humanity

Introduction

In Chapter 1 I presented my interpretation of Kant's conception of value. In Kant scholarship the reason why one should respect others is often thought to be that all human beings as such possess a value. I have argued that Kant does not have such a conception of value, and that his arguments rule out the possibility that value is the justification for the moral requirements Kant puts forward. For Kant, absolute value is not prior to the moral law, but depends on it.

However, my previous discussion left open one important possibility. So far I have argued that value cannot be a property external to one's will (e. g., a value one would have to discover in other human beings), and ground moral requirements. But this leaves open the possibility that value is something *internal* to one's own will. Kant's arguments rule out that value is a foreign property which one still has to discover and be motivated to follow. If value is something internal to one's own will, on the other hand, it seems that heteronomy would not necessarily ensue. Maybe one can know the value of human beings immediately from one's own will, and then somehow infer that all other human beings have such a value too. In this chapter I shall look at prominent arguments that have been put forward in this vein by Christine Korsgaard, Allen Wood, Paul Guyer, Richard Dean, and Samuel Kerstein. As it turns out, the views of value employed in these arguments do not necessarily disagree with what I have said in Chapter 1. Nonetheless, there is reason to be skeptical about whether the prominent arguments in the literature can ground the requirement to respect others. In the next chapter I shall briefly refer to other prominent scholars, including Thomas Hill, Stephen Engstrom, Andrews Reath and Barbara Herman, whose views are closer to my own interpretation.

The arguments from the literature I shall discuss in this chapter can roughly be divided into two sets, mirroring a tension within Kant's text itself (cf. Kerstein 2002, 68). On the one hand, Kant seems to be saying that all human beings as such are ends in themselves and should be respected (cf. *GMS* 4:428; *TL* 6:463). On the other hand, he says that morality is the condition for something's being an end in itself (cf.

GMS 4:435), and that only a morally good will has an absolute value (cf. e.g. *GMS* 4:393). The prominent arguments I shall discuss emphasize one or the other of the two sets of passages. The first set offers arguments for the view that all human beings deserve respect wholly independently of whether they have a morally good will or not. The second claims that human beings deserve respect in virtue of (possibly) having a good will.

One might think that the prominent arguments in the literature are at odds with the interpretation of value I have offered in the previous chapter. But this is not necessarily the case, for the literature arguments do not necessarily conceive of the nature of value in a way that is at odds with the interpretation I have offered in Chapter 1. They often conceive of value as what one is committed to valuing (see Sections 2 and 3 below), or what everyone necessarily values (see Section 4 below). This is in agreement with the interpretation of value I have offered in Chapter 1 above. In the first case value would be a prescription, while in the second case it would be a description of what a perfectly rational being would value. Value would not (necessarily) be a distinct metaphysical property. There is only a discrepancy if one construes this value as independent of the Categorical Imperative. In that case, it seems to me that one cannot plausibly generate the requirement to respect others. However, if the arguments make an implicit reference to the Categorical Imperative, e.g., in explicating what one is committed to valuing 'on pain of contradiction' (cf. *GMS* 4:437), then there is not necessarily any disagreement with my view. For the prohibition of a contradiction is a feature of the Categorical Imperative (cf. *GMS* 4:424), and value would be dependent upon the imperative, as I have argued above.

Similarly, the view that one should value a morally good will does not necessarily contradict the interpretation of value I have offered in the previous chapter. For scholars who offer this interpretation often do not conceive of value as a distinct metaphysical property, but as a prescription or as something that an impartial rational spectator would value (cf. Section 5). There is only a conflict with my interpretation if one makes the good will of others the reason why one should respect them. So while there is not necessarily a disagreement about what value is, its nature so to speak, there is a potential disagreement about the reason why one should respect others, and about the question of whom one should respect. On my reading one should respect all human beings, not just the ones with morally good wills.

In the following I shall start my discussion with the prominent arguments made by Christine Korsgaard (Sections 1 and 2), Allen Wood (Section 3), Paul Guyer (4), as well as Richard Dean and Samuel Kerstein (5). There is a vast secondary literature on these arguments. The reaction to these arguments has been overwhelmingly negative. I ultimately share the skepticism of the critics about the success of these arguments in grounding the requirement to respect others. However, I do think that each contains valuable insights that should not be dismissed. In the next chapter I shall then give my own reading of the requirement to respect others as spelled out in Kant's Formula of Humanity.

Section 1: Korsgaard's Regress Argument

Perhaps the most influential interpretation of the Formula of Humanity was offered by Christine Korsgaard. Her essays collected in *Creating the Kingdom of Ends* sparked a huge interest in the literature. They promised a new and exciting way to read Kant, and thereby brought Kant's ethics back into systematic discussions about ethics more generally. Korsgaard was not the first and not the only one who put forward her interpretation,[45] but her version has inspired a whole generation of Kant scholars, and laid the tracks for the reading of Kant's Formula of Humanity. For instance, even scholars who do not agree with her particular interpretation nonetheless follow her in reading Kant's argument for the Formula of Humanity as proceeding in two parts: first, that in order for there to be a Categorical Imperative there has to be a necessary or unconditioned end, and second that this end is humanity as an end in itself.[46] Korsgaard later disavowed her original reconstruction of Kant's argument for a modified version (which I shall discuss in Section 2), but the original version is still widely discussed today.[47]

---

45 Cf. her 1996a, ch. 4 (initially published 1986) to, e.g., R.P. Wolff 1973, 71–77; Gewirth 1982, 29 f.; Löhrer 1995, 269–298; and Wood 1999, 130.
46 See 1996a, 109 f.; cf. Wood 1999, 112–4; Kerstein 2002, 47–54; Dean 2006, ch. 6.
47 See, for instance, Timmermann 2006; Darwall 2006, 229–234; Langton 2007; Wood 2008, 90–93; and Christiano 2008.

Summary of the Argument

According to Korsgaard's original reconstruction, Kant's argument for the view that all human beings have an absolute value (and should therefore be respected) has two parts. The first part argues that if there is a Categorical Imperative, then there must be an objective end that has absolute value. The second part argues that this end is humanity as an end in itself. The first part can be summarized along the following lines: Kant says that every action needs an end (cf. *TL* 6:385). Accordingly, it is claimed, morally worthy actions, in which the agent follows the Categorical Imperative for its own sake, also need an end: "if there is a categorical imperative there are necessary actions, and every action contains an end" (Korsgaard 1996a, 110). This end cannot be an end that the agent sets for himself based upon his inclinations, because such ends are relative and contingent; contingent ends cannot ground the necessary actions prescribed by the imperative. Therefore the end of moral actions must be a necessary end.[48] In a further step it is argued that this end in itself is humanity.

Korsgaard describes the second part of the argument as a regress upon the condition of the goodness of non-rational things (cf. her 1996a, 119–124). The argument begins with the view that 1) non-rational things only have value if they are valued by human beings. Take, for instance, a horse carriage. It only has value if it is valued by human beings (for traveling moderate distances, weddings, sight-seeing etc.). If human beings did not value them (because of inventing faster and more comfortable means like a car or plane), these objects would lose their value. 2) Reason, which strives to have its insights complete, has to seek the unconditioned condition of the value of things. 3) The regress comes to an end only in human beings' setting an end for which the thing in question is a means. 4) Human beings can confer the value of means on things only if they themselves have an unconditional value: "we find that the unconditioned condition of the goodness of things is rational nature [...]. To play this role, however, rational nature must itself be something of unconditional value." (Korsgaard 1996a, 123) 5.) Since humanity is an unconditional end (in an agent-neutral sense), one must respect it wherever one finds it. The steps of the second part can be summarized as follows:

1) Non-rational things are not unconditionally valuable, but their value depends upon something else.

---

48 Cf. Korsgaard 1996a, 109 f.; and Paton 1947, 167 f.

2) Reason seeks the unconditioned.
3) The unconditioned condition of the value of non-rational things is human (and other rational) beings' setting themselves ends.
4) Human beings can confer the value of means on things only if they themselves have an unconditional value.
5) One has to value humanity in virtue of its unconditional value wherever one finds it.

This argument is appealing because it promises a strong moral conclusion from minimal premises. From an uncontroversial non-moral starting-point – that human beings set themselves ends – one derives a substantial moral claim, that all human beings have an absolute value. However, is the argument really Kant's, and is valid?

Textual basis

Korsgaard gleans the argument from the passage that leads up to the Formula of Humanity in the *Groundwork* (4:425–429). It is a very cryptic passage, and Korsgaard can acknowledge that the argument is not literally spelled out in the text.[49] But how much does the text support the Regress Argument? I shall look at both parts separately.

The first part of the argument deserves attention since it is so popular in the literature.[50] To remind ourselves: The first part contains the view that since every action needs an end, moral actions need a special moral end underlying actions done for the sake of the Categorical Imperative. If it is successful, it can show that there must be something that is an end one should respect – at least on the Kantian premises. If the first part is not successful, there still might be a way in which the second part could stand on its own, as I shall explain shortly. Is the first part of the argument in the text?

One might think that the first part of the argument is contained in the *Groundwork* passage in the following way: After Kant's examples for the Formula of Universal Law of Nature, he asks whether his moral principle is a necessary law for all rational beings (cf. *GMS* 4:426). He postulates: "If there is such a law, then it must already be con-

---

49 Cf. e.g. Korsgaard 1996a, 260; and 123: "I read him as making the following argument."
50 See again Paton 1947, 167 f.; Korsgaard 1996a, 109 f.; Wood 1999, 112–4; Kerstein 2002, 47–54; Dean 2006, ch. 6.

nected (completely a priori) with the concept of the will of a rational being as such" (*GMS* 4:426). Kant subsequently considers the will of human beings, and emphasizes the role ends play in the determination of the will: "what serves the will as the objective ground of its self-determination is an end" (*GMS* 4:427). Subjective ends, which are ends adopted based on inclination, cannot ground a categorical imperative: "all these relative ends are only the ground of hypothetical imperatives." (*GMS* 4:428) For the laws that prescribe how to reach one's subjective ends are not unconditionally valid, but only valid if one shares the end. In contrast, Kant says that an *"end in itself* could be [...] the ground of a possible categorical imperative," and he affirms that "every rational being *exists* as an end in itself", at least every "human being necessarily represents his own existence in this way" (*GMS* 4:428 f.). So, does the passage not confirm that actions in accord with the Categorical Imperative need a special moral end underlying them?

In the *Groundwork* passage (4:425–9) Kant does not explicitly say that every action needs an end, and that therefore a morally good action needs a special moral end that underlies the Categorical Imperative. Kant does say that every action needs an end in the *Doctrine of Virtue* (*TL* 6:385). However, as I have argued above (cf. Chapter 1, Section 5), the moral ends Kant talks about there are not humanity, but *"one's own perfection* and *the happiness of others"* (*TL* 6:385). More importantly, the ends are said to *follow* from the Categorical Imperative, and are not said to be the ground of it: "the *concept of duty* will lead to ends and will have to establish *maxims* with respect to ends we *ought* to set ourselves, grounding them in accordance with moral principles". (*TL* 6:382) So the *Doctrine of Virtue* passage does not support the view that actions in accordance with the Categorical Imperative need a moral end *underlying* that imperative.

On closer inspection the view that actions done for the sake of the imperative need an underlying moral end is very surprising. It seems at odds with the rest of Kant's works (cf. Reath 2012b). When he addresses the question of the *justification* of the imperative in the *Groundwork* and second *Critique*, he refers to freedom as the ground of the imperative. Further, a special moral end does not seem necessary to *motivate* the agent.[51] When Kant addresses the question of the proper moral *motivation* in the same works, he says that the law aided by respect is enough (cf. *GMS* 4:400; *KpV* 5:71 ff.). A moral end is also not needed for *determin-*

---

51 Cf. again Reath 2012b, *pace* Guyer 2000, 145; Kerstein 2002, 48.

ing the rightness of actions. This comes out in the examples Kant gives in the *Groundwork* to illustrate the Formula of Law of Nature. The examples always have the same structure: Someone has an end based on an inclination, and is about to adopt a maxim to act accordingly. However, "he still has conscience enough to ask himself: is it not forbidden or contrary to duty" (*GMS* 4:422). Imagine someone adopted a maxim that would violate a *negative* duty (e. g., of lying or gluttony). If he refrains from acting on the maxim because it would be contrary to the Categorical Imperative, then his morally good action (of not lying, indulging in gluttony) would have its end or matter from the original inclination. This is similar if the original inclination was to tell the truth, and the agent acts on a maxim because it is in accordance with the Categorical Imperative. Kant does not introduce a further moral end as a necessary condition for acting morally.

The situation is similar but more complicated in cases where the agent would violate a *positive* duty (e. g., to help others or further one's talents). If an agent lacks an end to help others, or if he adopts an end *not* to help others based on an inclination, and if he finds that the corresponding maxim violates the Categorical Imperative, the end or matter of the action still comes from the initial inclination (and similarly if his end was to help others, and it passes the test). Again there does not seem to be need for a moral end in order to act for the sake of the Categorical Imperative. However, the case is more complicated for positive duties, since Kant does introduce moral ends in the *Doctrine of Virtue*. The *Doctrine of Right*, Kant says, only concerns itself with the universalizability of maxims, but not with the motive of actions. "But ethics goes beyond this and provides a *matter* [...], an **end** of pure reason which [...] it is a duty to have." (*TL* 6:380) The justification Kant gives for this is that such an end is needed to counter ends given by inclinations. Inclinations might tempt human beings to act contrary to the moral law. So, in order to be able to act morally, reason must provide its own end:

> For since the sensible inclinations of human beings tempt them to ends [...] that can be contrary to duty, lawgiving reason can in turn check their influence only by a moral end set up against the ends of inclination, an end that must therefore be given a priori (*TL* 6:380 f.).

This can be read as a requirement for the mechanism as to how one can act morally. In order to act morally, one needs a moral end that counterbalances the influence of sensible ends. My aim here is not to evaluate the plausibility of this claim. However, it is important to note that this claim does not help the first part of the Regress Argument. First, the moral ends Kant talks about are one's own perfection and the happiness of others (cf. again *TL* 6:385), not humanity, as the Regress Argument will claim. Second, the ends Kant gives are merely ends for *positive* duties, corresponding to the examples 3 and 4 in the *Groundwork* (cf. *GMS* 4:422 f.; *TL* 6:419), not ends for every moral action. Third, these ends *follow* from the imperative (cf. again *TL* 6:382), they are not the ground of it, as will be important for the *Groundwork* passage: "The ground of this principle [the Categorical Imperative[52]] is: *rational nature exists as an end in itself*" (*GMS* 4:428 f.). The *Doctrine of Virtue* therefore does not help the first part of the Regress Argument. Kant's view is not that, since every action needs an end, moral actions need a special moral end. However, this problem with the *first* part of the Regress Argument does not seem to affect the more important second part to which I shall now turn.

The *second* part of the argument does not seem undermined even if the popular first step is not really Kant's. If an inquiring mind reflects upon the value of things, and reaches the conclusion that things can only have value if human beings are of unconditional value, then the second part of the Regress Argument can stand on its own. The passage in Kant's text to which it is supposed to refer is *Groundwork* 428. Kant had said that relative ends cannot ground a categorical imperative, but that an end in itself could. He then asserts that "the human being [...] *exists* as an end in itself" (*GMS* 4:428). He rules out objects of inclinations, inclinations themselves and non-rational things as objective ends, repeating the argument that objects based on inclination are conditioned upon the inclinations, and therefore merely upon a subjective end, not an objective end (cf. *GMS* 4:428).

Again the passage is very cryptic, and Kant does not spell out why exactly the inclinations themselves or non-rational things can only have a relative worth. So, again Korsgaard can grant that her interpretation is not literally spelled out in the text:

> In one sense, it seems as if Kant is just reviewing the available options in his search for something unconditionally good: considering objects of inclinations, inclinations, natural beings or "things", and finally persons, that being the one that will serve. But it is also possible to read this passage as

---

52 People often assume that "this principle" refers to the Formula of Humanity. However, the formula has not yet been introduced, and grammatically the "this" refers to the Categorical Imperative that has been mentioned in the previous sentence; cf. Schönecker/Wood 2003, 145 note; and Chapter 3 below.

at least suggesting a regress towards the unconditioned: moving from the objects of our inclinations, to the inclinations themselves, finally (later) back to ourselves, our rational nature. (Korsgaard 1996a, 120)

But even if the argument is not openly spelled out in the passage, how much indication is there that this is what Kant had in mind? The steps of the second part were the following:

1) Non-rational things are not unconditionally valuable, but their value depends upon something else.
2) Reason seeks the unconditioned.
3) The unconditioned condition of the value of non-rational things is human (and other rational) beings' setting themselves ends.
4) Human beings can confer the value of means on things only if they themselves have an unconditional value.
5) One has to value humanity in virtue of its unconditional value wherever one finds it.

It is worth looking at each step individually to see whether it is contained in the *Groundwork* passage.

The first step clearly seems to be Kant's view: "All objects of the inclinations have only a conditional worth; for, if there were not inclinations and the needs based on them, their object would be without worth" (*GMS* 4:428; cf. *NF* 27:1319). The second step is a common Kantian theme familiar from the 'Dialectic' of the first *Critique*, but it is not mentioned in the *Groundwork* passage under consideration. The third step is roughly covered by the quote from the first step. Objects have worth because they are the means to human beings' ends: "The existence of non-rational things has no value [...] if no rational being uses them as means." (*NF* 27:1319.8–10) The end a human being sets himself is the reason why things have the value as means: "In willing, the end is a ground of why there is the means." (*NF* 27:1321.22 f.) So the Regress Argument does seem to be right in saying that, for Kant, setting ends is the condition for the value of non-rational things.

However, the capacity to set ends does not seem to be the *unconditioned* condition of the value of non-rational things, as the Regress Argument seems to claim: "regressing upon the conditions, we find that the unconditioned condition of the goodness of anything is [...] the power of rational choice" (Korsgaard 1996a, 123). This does not seem to square with Kant's text. Kant thinks that reason itself could be causally determined: "Now nature could have set up our reason entirely in accordance with natural law, that every human being learned to read of himself [...].

But in that case we would not be better than the animals." (*NF* 27:1322.8–11; cf. *KpV* 5:95) In this case the capacity to set ends would itself be conditioned by natural laws. If the capacity to set ends is the condition for the value of non-rational things, it is not the unconditioned condition.

The fourth step seems to be even less in accord with Kant's texts: "To play this role [of being the condition of the value of things], however, rational nature must itself be something of unconditional value" (Korsgaard 1996a, 123). It does not seem to be the case that the capacity to set ends can only be the condition of the value of things if it is itself of unconditional value. Kant repeatedly says that having the capacity to set ends gives human beings only an *extrinsic* value, or a value as a means: "Although a human being [...] can set himself ends, even this gives him only an *extrinsic* value for his usefulness" (*TL* 6:434; cf. *KpV* 5:61 f.; *NF* 27:1321 f.; *GMS* 4:395 f.). In the *Groundwork* passage that Korsgaard cites, where Kant leads up to the Formula of Humanity, I see nothing to suggest that Kant has in mind the inference Korsgaard draws. Kant says that everyone has to regard himself as an end in himself. For the reason for this claim he refers the reader to the Third Section of the *Groundwork* (cf. 4:429 note). There Kant argues that everyone has to regard himself as free, but the claim that one has an unconditional value in virtue of being the condition of the value of things does not appear there nor elsewhere in the *Groundwork*.

But even if the argument is not in the text, one could ask: Is Korsgaard's Regress Argument the best option for defending Kant's claim that all human beings are ends in themselves?

Evaluation of the Regress Argument

Kant's text in the passage that leads up to the Formula of Humanity is elliptical. If the Regress Argument is plausible in its own right, then it is an attractive option for a Kantian even without direct textual support. However, the argument has been heavily criticized in the literature, and it is not hard to see why Korsgaard later distanced herself from this particular version of the argument (cf. her 1998, 63 f.). There are two criticisms in particular that are levelled against the argument. One concerns the first step and the other the fourth step. I shall look at each of them in turn.

The first criticism of Korsgaard's Regress Argument objects to the view that things only have value if they are valued by human beings.[53] Are not some things good for human beings independently of whether they are appreciated by them (e. g., health, friendship etc.)? One could even object that without this independent value any choice would lack standards and would be merely arbitrary (cf. Regan 2002, 274; Christiano 2009, 113). However, these objections are not necessarily a problem for Kant. Take a view in which 'a thing has value' is not meant as a description of a distinct metaphysical property a thing has, but as saying that the thing is useful for something else (cf. Chapter 1). The objection might then run that certain things (e. g. health or friendship) are good/ useful for human beings irrespective of any specific ends human beings choose. But it seems that this objection can be softened. There could be inclinations that all human beings share, for instance, self-love is said to be a "feeling whose destination is to impel towards the furtherance of life" (*GMS* 4:422). If everyone has the same feeling, and if one sets one's prudential ends based on one's inclinations (cf. again the examples in *GMS* 4:422 f.), then everyone might – under normal circumstances – set an end based on this universal inclination and value the furtherance of life. So value could be dependent upon inclinations without making criticism obsolete. For if someone sets an end contrary to this inclination (e. g., to be reckless in battle), one can say that a different approach (to be more cautious in battle) is good for the person (given his inclination to live). Or if a chemotherapy patient suffers from his treatment and is not inclined to eat, one could still say that food is useful/good for the person given his inclination to live. So to claim that some things are good universally does not mean that they do not depend upon the person's inclinations or ends. If something that is food for human beings were the only object that exists in the world, one does not have to call it good.

One can also soften the objection that on this view one's choices would lack rational standards. It does not seem farfetched to claim that one adopts one's prudential ends prompted by inclinations (cf. again *GMS* 4:422). However, there could then still be prudential standards of a hypothetical nature ('if one wants the end, one should choose the necessary means'), and moral standards of categorical nature (e. g., 'don't lie'). One's choices would still have rational standards to conform to.

---

53 Cf., e.g., Kerstein 2002, 55–71; Regan 2002; Gaut 1997, 173 f.; Sussman 2003; Wood 2008, 92.

The second main criticism that has been levelled against Korsgaard's Regress Argument is an internal critique and is more serious. It concerns the fourth step. If a thing only has value if it is valued by human beings, then it does not follow that human beings must have an absolute value, as has often been noted.[54] In general, it does not seem to be the case that if one thing confers a property onto another, the first thing has this same property unconditionally. For instance, a university president can confer a PhD title onto a student, but this does not mean that the president has a PhD or an unconditional PhD (cf. Gaut 1997, 174; Kerstein 2002, 59). One could object that in some cases the inference does seem to hold. A stone can be warmed by holding it in one's hand. The warmth of the stone is conditioned by the warmth of the hand. Could not the act of conferring value be parallel to warming a stone?

The problem with this comparison is that the property an observer experiences as warmth would be an intrinsic property (of atoms moving) in Korsgaard's terms, while the value of things is considered to be an extrinsic or relational property between two objects (cf. Korsgaard 1996a, 257). Korsgaard uses 'intrinsic' or 'inherent' to refer to properties things have if one considers them in isolation from everything else. In this sense the extension of a thing is an intrinsic feature, while being taller than some other thing is an extrinsic property. An extrinsic or relational property is a property a thing has if it is regarded in its relation to another thing.[55] As a relational property the property of things would not be like the property (of atoms moving) an observer calls 'warmth', but more like the property of being funny or embarrassing. Here I am assuming that a line of words is not funny if it were the only thing that exists in the world. Rather it is only funny if it is funny to an observer. But if something is only funny if it is funny to human beings, then it does not follow that therefore human beings are funny in themselves.

However, could value be different from other extrinsic properties in an important respect? Could moral properties be different in this respect from non-moral examples like funniness? It does not seem to work for badness. Take the following example from Samuel Kerstein: "Suppose I

---

54 Cf. Gaut 1997, 174: Kerstein 2002, 59; Hills 2005; Martin 2006; and Langton 2007.

55 This is Korsgaard's terminology, cf. her 1996a, 250. Langton has pointed out that an intrinsic property in this sense could still be relational in another sense, e.g., if it specifies the relation of parts of the one thing that exists in isolation (cf. her 2007, 179). In this sense extension could be the relation between two points of one object, while being intrinsic to this object.

hold that what confers badness on something is that it be an object of rational disapproval. I would not thereby have to hold that rational disapproval is bad at all, let alone unconditionally bad." (Kerstein 2002, 59) If a thing is not bad in itself, but considered to be extrinsically bad, e.g. only because it is rationally disapproved, this does not make the act of rationally disapproving bad in itself. Or, to put it slightly differently, if a thing is bad because it hinders the agent's end, this does not mean that the agent is bad in himself (cf. Darwall 2006, 231 note 30).

One would have to hold that the case for moral goodness is different from the case of moral badness. If there is a law that determines what is morally bad, this does not make the law bad in itself. One could object that Kant seems to affirm such a difference in the following passage: "But the lawgiving itself, which determines all worth, must for that very reason have [...] an unconditional worth" (*GMS* 4:436).[56] If the moral law determines all worth, does not the law itself have an unconditional worth? I have already offered a more modest reading of the passage (cf. Chapter 1 above). Kant does not say that the law has value, but rather that lawgiving does. In the context of the Formula of Autonomy in which this passage occurs, 'lawgiving' refers to the requirement to universalize one's maxim. If the moral law determines all worth (i. e., what one should value), and if the law requires that one should universalize one's maxims (i. e., participate in universal lawgiving), then participating in lawgiving (for its own sake) gives one the unconditional worth of a morally good will (i. e., gives one a will one should have). There is no indication that Kant has a metaphysical conferral of a value property in mind.

Without this indication, how could one determine whether goodness would be a special case in which conditional value can only be conferred by unconditional value? It seems that there is no need to postulate an unconditional value if the value of things is considered to be extrinsic. In that case the value of the things does not require an unconditional value as its condition (see above). If one were to conceive of the value of things as intrinsic, then it might still be conditioned by something else (e. g., as the warmth of the stone is conditioned by the sun). Not every intrinsic property is unconditioned. However, not every conditioned intrinsic property is conditioned by the same property. If one folds a piece of paper into a triangular shape, the paper has the (conditioned) intrinsic property of being triangular. But this does not mean that the condition for the triangular shape (one's finger holding down

---

56 I thank Rocco Porcheddu for pressing me on this point; cf. his 2012.

the piece of paper) has the same intrinsic property. If one's finger is the condition of the paper's having a triangular shape, this does not mean that one's finger is triangular or unconditionally triangular. So one would need an independent confirmation that human beings have an unconditional value. One could not conclude that human beings have an unconditional value merely from the fact that things have a conditioned intrinsic value. Instead one would need direct confirmation that human beings have an unconditional value. This poses a dilemma. If one conceives of the value of things as extrinsic, the argument does not establish the conclusion. If, on the other hand, one conceives of the value of things as intrinsic, the argument becomes superfluous. Since there is an alternative interpretation of Kant's claim that lawgiving has an unconditional worth, I conclude that Kant does not hold the fourth step of the Regress Argument, nor is it plausible in its own right.

To put it differently: The main problem of the Regress Argument seems to be that it implicitly construes the extrinsic value of things as if it were an intrinsic property that gets added to the thing if an agent sets an end. The argument thereby violates its own assumption of the first step, that the value of things is extrinsic. Like a hand warms a stone, and thereby causes a new intrinsic property in the object (of atoms moving in the object), so one's setting of ends would bestow value on the thing: "Value in this case does not travel from an end to a means but from a fully rational choice[57] to its object. Value is, as I have put it, 'conferred' by choice." (Korsgaard 1996a, 261) However, to make a choice does not add any intrinsic feature to the object. Rather to say that a thing has extrinsic value is merely to express a relation that holds between the thing and the choice made by the agent. Kant seems to hold this view for the relation between choice and objects (cf. *GMS* 4:428). And he seems to affirm it for the relationship between means and ends, where to say that a thing has the value of means is merely to say that the thing is useful for an end set by human beings (cf. *NF* 27:1319, 1322). For instance, to say that my end of cutting bread makes a knife valuable as a means, merely says that a knife is useful for cutting bread. Setting an end merely creates the relation of utility, it does not confer a new intrinsic property on the knife. Therefore, if a knife is only useful if it is useful for human beings, it does not follow that human beings have an absolute value. The value of a knife can be

---

57 I shall consider in a moment whether the qualification "fully rational" changes the argument.

explained by its utility for human beings, whether or not they have any value 'in themselves'.

Korsgaard seems to agree with this analysis, and this problem seems to have been the reason why she disavowed this particular version of the argument: "I am aware that in early papers I made it sound too much as if value were some sort of metaphysical substance that got transferred from us to our ends via the act of choice. [...] I don't think that" (see her 1998, 64).

There is, however, one attempt to rescue the Regress Argument that needs to be addressed. One could say that the value of things needs to be objective or fully rational in order for the Regress Argument to work (cf. Korsgaard 1996a, 114–9, 261; Wood 1999, 127, 129). What is meant by 'objective' here is that what is declared to be good is held to be good for everyone (cf. Korsgaard 1996a, 115; Wood 1999, 127). Consider the following passage in Kant: "What we are to call good must be an object of the faculty of desire in the judgment of every reasonable human being" (*KpV* 5:60 f.). Maybe setting an end by reason and declaring it as being good bestows objective goodness on things. And maybe human beings can only bestow objective goodness if they themselves are objectively good.[58]

However, it has been convincingly argued that Kant does not think that in setting an end one declares it to be good for everyone.[59] Take the following quote from the passage that leads up to the Formula of Humanity:

> The ends that a rational being proposes at his discretion as *effects* of his actions (material ends) are all only relative; for only their mere relation to a specially constituted faculty of desire on the part of the subject gives them their worth (*GMS* 428; cf. Kerstein 2006, 209).

Kant does not hold that if one sets oneself an end, e.g. to support a particular sports team, one thereby is committed to holding it to be good for everyone. One adopts these kinds of ends based upon inclination (cf. again *GMS* 4:422 f.), and inclinations vary from person to person. There is therefore no reason to think that one's relative end should be valid for everyone.

---

58 This reconstruction has been suggested by Allen Wood at some point, cf. his 1999, 127, 129. I shall discuss his own version of the argument in Section 3 below.

59 Cf. Hill 2002, 262 ff., Kerstein 2006, 206–210; Timmermann 2006, 73–80; and Allison 2011, ch. 8.

The move to rescue Korsgaard's Regress Argument also does not seem plausible independently of Kant's texts. It does not seem that one has to hold one's subjective preferences to be objectively good. As Paul Guyer has put it effectively: "I may love my wife and you your husband – it certainly does not follow from that alone that I should love your husband." (Guyer 2000, 162) There is nothing wrong in reason's declaring something to be prudentially good for oneself (given one's inclinations), without claiming that it is also good for everyone else.

But why does Kant say that to declare something as good is to declare it as good "in the judgment of every reasonable human being" (*KpV* 5:60)? For Kant good is a rational concept (cf. Korsgaard 1996a, 115). I have argued in Chapter 1 above that good is a prescription of reason. The quote from the second *Critique* that declares what is good to be universal only refers to what reason declares to be necessary. Reason's judgment can come in two forms. First, if reason declares something to be necessary as a means for a given end, it produces a hypothetical imperative. It is important to note that in saying 'if you want to go to the moon, take a spaceship' one does not declare the end to be good. One does not say that everyone should go to the moon. It merely says that *if* someone wants that end, this particular means is necessary (and therefore good for everyone who shares that end).[60]

The second form in which reason commands is by categorical imperatives. And again, what reason thereby declares to be good would be good in the judgment of any reasonable being, according to Kant. This is the sense of the statement from the second *Critique*, that what reason deems necessary is thereby good "in the judgment of every reasonable human being" (*KpV* 5:60). In this context Kant distinguishes the good from prudential judgements about well-being (*Wohl*). Morality is necessary and universal (cf. *GMS* 4:389), and when practical reason deems something to be unconditionally necessary, it declares this something to be good objectively or for all (e.g., not to lie). Necessity and strict universality mutually imply each other (cf. *KrV* B4). However, by itself all this does not touch upon the question why one should respect others. Again, Kant's point here is not that in judging something to be good an intrinsic property 'goodness' is conferred onto actions that can only come from an intrinsic goodness of a human being.

In short, neither of the two senses in which reason can deem something to be good objectively – as means to a particular end or categori-

---

60 Cf. Hill 2002, 244–274; Kerstein 2006, 207–210; and Allison 2011, ch. 8.

cally in accord with the Categorical Imperative – helps the proponent of the Regress Argument to establish that human beings have an intrinsic value property and must be respected. If someone discovers that certain means are necessary for a given end, or that his reason is guided by the Categorical Imperative, this by itself does not establish that the human being has an intrinsic value property. Since the argument breaks down at the fourth step – that such a value property is needed to explain how things can have value – there is no need to discuss the fifth (that one has to respect this value wherever one finds it) or to dwell on the first three. It is therefore understandable why Korsgaard disavowed this particular version of the Regress Argument. In the following I shall look at the other prominent arguments that have been made. I shall begin with Korsgaard's modified reconstruction.

Section 2: Korsgaard's Modified Argument

Korsgaard offered a modified version of the same argument that can avoid several of the difficulties that beset the first version.[61] The argument fits better with Kant's own text, and it does not rely on the controversial fourth step that claims to establish that human beings have an unconditional value. The argument has a similar structure to the previous one, but it settles for the weaker conclusion that human beings *have to regard* themselves as valuable. Like the previous argument, the modified version has been popular in the literature and much discussed.[62] Because of its similarity to the previous one, the discussion can be shorter.

   Again the argument starts with the value of non-rational things, and it regresses upon the conditions of this goodness. The agent takes things to be good. He realizes that they are not unconditionally good, and inquires into their condition. He realizes that things are valuable because he values them, and that in valuing things he regards himself as valuable: "Kant saw that we take things to important, because they are important to us – and he concluded that we therefore take ourselves to be important." (Korsgaard 1996b, 122) In placing a value on one's own humanity,

---

61   Cf. Korsgaard 1996b, 122, 124 f., 132, 250; and her 1998, 62–64.
62   Cf. Gewirth 1978, 241 f., and his 1982, 29 ('dialectical attribution'); Prauss 1983, 126–146; and Leist 1996, 183. For critical comments see Geuss 1996, 189–199; Smith 1999, 384–394; Gibbard 1999, 140–164; Copp 1999; and Cohon 2000, 63–85.

one places a value on humanity in general: "we set a value on our own humanity and so on humanity in general" (Korsgaard 1996b, 250).

The argument can be summarized as follows:

1) Non-rational things are not unconditionally valuable, but their value depends upon something else.
2) Reason inquires into the condition.
3) Things have value because they are valued by rational beings.
4) In valuing things, one values one's own humanity.
5) In valuing one's own humanity, one values humanity in general.

Textual Basis of the Argument

The argument is another reconstruction of the passage in the *Groundwork* that leads up to the Formula of Humanity (*GMS* 4:425–9). But how exactly does it relate to that passage? To recall: After illustrating the application of the Categorical Imperative in four examples, Kant asked whether it is a necessary law for all rational beings. If so, Kant claimed, it must be a priori connected with the concept of the will. The will can be determined by ends. If ends are based on inclinations, they are relative and could not ground a Categorical Imperative. Only an end in itself could do that. Kant then considers several candidates for what could be an end in itself, and he rules out the objects of inclinations, inclinations themselves, and non-rational things. Instead, Kant affirms that human beings are ends in themselves.

How might the modified Regress Argument be said to fit the text? Again, premises 1) and 3) might be said to be contained in the following statement: "All objects of the inclinations have only a conditional worth; for, if there were not inclinations and the needs based on them, their object would be without worth" (*GMS* 4:428). Since Kant is searching for an end in itself that could be the ground of the Categorical Imperative, the exclusion of objects of inclinations, inclinations and things could be read as a regress upon the conditions of the goodness of things (premise 2). Kant's claim that everyone necessarily has to regard himself as an end in itself might be taken as an endorsement of premise 4), and his claim that the ground on which on regards oneself as an end in itself is also valid for everyone else as might be taken as Kant putting forward premise 5).

Textually, therefore, Korsgaard's modified version seems to be a better fit. This is because it accords better with Kant's claim that one has to *regard* oneself as an end in itself. He does not claim to establish that everyone is such an end, or that everyone *has* an unconditional value. For practical purposes, perhaps it is sufficient to establish that one should respect oneself and other human beings. Kant makes a similar move in the Third Section of the *Groundwork* where he argues that even if one cannot prove the reality of freedom, but only the necessity of regarding oneself as free, one is still bound by any moral laws that come with freedom (cf. *GMS* 4:448 note).

However, Korsgaard's actual claim – that it is the value of things that makes one realize that one regards oneself as valuable – is not in the text, neither in the passage leading up to the Formula of Humanity, nor in the Third Section of the *Groundwork* to which Kant refers. While one can find several bits of the premises in the text, one does not find them connected quite in the way expressed in the argument. One can find the claim that things are only valuable because they are valued by human beings (premises 1 and 3), and one can find that human beings have to regard themselves as ends in themselves (resembling premise 4), but there is no direct connection between the two. It is therefore not clear that it is Kant's view that one has to regard oneself as an end in itself because things would not have value without one's valuing them.[63] But even if the connection is not made explicitly by Kant, one could ask whether it is systematically attractive, and therefore a good option for a Kantian to put forward.

Evaluation of the Argument

One advantage of the modified version of the argument over the original Regress Argument presented in Section 2 is that the modified version does not rely on the controversial fourth step of the former. The fourth step claimed to establish that human beings *have* an unconditional value. To recall:

4) Human beings can confer the value of means on things only if they themselves have an unconditional value.

---

63 Accordingly Donagan traces the argument to Rawls rather than to Kant, cf. his 1977, 239; Rawls 1971, 440.

The problem with that step was that it construed the value of things as an intrinsic property, analogous to a hand warming a stone. The value of things was conceived of as a new intrinsic feature that it could only have received from something that conferred this feature on the thing. In contrast, the modified argument does not invoke a metaphysical transferral of features. The modified argument does not even treat the value of humanity as an intrinsic value, as a property human beings would have even if they existed in isolation (cf. Korsgaard 1998, 63). It merely concludes that, in valuing non-rational things, one implicitly *regards* oneself as being valuable:

> I don't think this reasoning need be conceived as a piece of abstruse metaphysics. Imagine it this way: "Why in the end does it matter that I achieve this end? Because it matters to me, and I matter...." (1998, 62)

But is it really the case that one has to regard oneself as valuable? The argument seems plausible for cases in which one values something for oneself: Why should one make oneself a sandwich, for instance, if one has decided to commit suicide? Conversely, if one stops valuing oneself, all other things seem to lose value: "A sense of personal worthlessness [...] can be [...] the germ from which nihilism and the rejection of all value spreads." (Korsgaard 1996b, 251)

However, does the argument work beyond cases in which one values something *for oneself*? Think about the following three cases: First, it seems that if one values something *for other* people, one is not thereby committed to valuing oneself. A case might be an anonymous donor who leaves money to a university in order to fund the education of people the donor will never know. This is not to say that donors never have (at least in part) ulterior motives, but it seems that in valuing something for other people (e.g. a good education), one is not thereby committed to valuing oneself. Second, if someone values something that even excludes all people, e.g. an ecosystem without human beings (not for the enjoyment of it, but simply), then it does not seem that one has to value oneself (cf. Gibbard 1999, 154 f.; Smith 1999). In this case one might even think that human beings are harmful, and have been the cause of the destruction of an otherwise perfect system. In this more extreme scenario there is no need to value human beings. Korsgaard seems to grant that much: "if human beings decided that human life was worthless then it *would be* worthless." (Korsgaard 1996b, 254) Third, it also does not follow that one has to value oneself if one does not value anything at all. If someone were wholly indifferent to everything that is going on, and cannot make himself do something, he too would not have to value himself.

So, the argument does not establish that one has to value oneself, nor that one has to value oneself in valuing anything at all, nor that one has to value anything. At most the argument reaches the more limited conclusion that if one values anything *for oneself,* one thereby values oneself. Does even that much follow? One has to set aside cases in which someone does things for himself instinctively. Even someone who has decided that he does not have any value might feed himself automatically, without further thought. This per se would not commit him to valuing himself. The action might be instinctive, it just happens. But what if the agent is made aware that on the one hand he holds that he himself does not have any value, but on the other values all these things for himself (food, entertainment etc.)? Would he have to give up either valuing himself or valuing something for himself? It is not clear that this is the case. After all, even if an agent did not value himself at all, this does not mean that he has to starve himself to death. Hunger is unpleasant, and he just does what it takes to avoid those unpleasant feelings. It seems that whether he commits a contradiction in denying any value of his existence but continuing to value things for himself depends on how he would react if questioned about his actions. One could ask him: "Why is it important that you eat?" If he answers: "Because I am important," then the case is closed and there is no contradiction. But if he answers: "I don't know; hunger is unpleasant, and eating takes that away," it is not clear that he is committed to valuing himself. He values being free of pain, but it is not clear that there must be a reference to his own importance. Nonetheless, I am willing to grant in the abstract that if one values something for oneself, one thereby values oneself. But how much is gained by this?

It seems that even if one grants that one has to value oneself, one has not advanced very much in an argument towards the requirement to respect others. The view that (most) people value themselves hardly needs a long argument. It fits well with psychological egoism, and can even be granted by the skeptic of the requirement to respect others. A world in which everyone aims for his own benefit and values himself is perfectly compatible with a Hobbesian state of nature, and a war of all against all. The most important premise for the requirement to respect others is still missing. If one values oneself, why does one have to value others as well?

Korsgaard's texts contain several hints as to how one might justify the fifth premise of the modified Regress Argument: 5) In valuing one's own humanity, one values humanity in general. How can one bridge the gap from valuing oneself to valuing others? First, one argument Korsgaard gives is that in valuing one's own humanity, one is thereby valuing not oneself as an individual, but humanity as such (cf. Korsgaard 1996b, 250). The idea is that Peter, in valuing something for himself, would not think that Peter as a particular individual is important, but Peter as an instance of being human. So Peter would value humanity as such, not himself in exclusion of others. This does not seem necessary though. An egoist can value himself, and he can acknowledge that others also value themselves. However, this by itself does not commit him to valuing others. The egoist does not have to value an abstract capacity in himself (e. g., the capacity to set ends as such), but he might just value himself. Second, the same thought applies if one invokes a contradiction argument to bridge the gap from valuing oneself to valuing others. A contradiction argument is basically the step previously discussed: It seems contradictory if one were to value things for oneself without valuing oneself: "If you overturn the *source* of the goodness of your end, neither your end nor the action which aims at it can possibly be good." (Korsgaard 1996a, 123) However, it is not clear how this should bridge the gap towards valuing others. What might be contradictory and self-defeating is if an agent prefers something for himself to himself, e. g. if he endangers his life to achieve minor comforts; but it is not contradictory in the same way if one disvalues other people for one's own benefit. In this example, if one endangers others for minor comforts for oneself, the minor comforts get their value from *the agent's* valuing himself. There is no contradiction in disvaluing others. The crucial question – why one should respect others – is still unanswered.

Third, Korsgaard also invokes a version of Wittgenstein's private language argument to show that one has to value others as well (cf. Korsgaard 1996b, 136–145). The idea is that having a reason to value something is not a private mental entity. Rather it is something that must be sharable and communicable to others. Likewise, valuing oneself would then not be a private affair that leaves open a gap of why one should value others. If reasons for valuing are not private but shared, then "there is no bridge to gap" (Korsgaard 1996b, 143). However, even leaving aside the question of whether this view is Kant's, the most the argument seems to establish is that one cannot have a reason (e. g., to value oneself) that is not *communicable* to others, not that another person has to aid my reasons (cf. Geuss 1996, 198). But a reason's being communicable does not as such give it normative force:

A bereaved Kwakiutl chief sets off for mass slaughter in the village across the water; 'Shall I mourn or shall they?' We find his loss no reason to slaughter the innocent, but his talk of reasons is public enough." (cf. Gibbard 1999, 163)

In short, even if a reason is not a private mental entity, it does not mean that it has normative force for everyone.

Without a stronger argument that whoever values himself also has to value others, the modified Regress Argument merely establishes a form of egoism. However, even if an argument can be found to bridge the gap from self to others, the argument contains within itself a worrisome loophole. The argument holds that if one does not value oneself, one does not have value: "if human beings decided that human life was worthless then it *would be* worthless." (Korsgaard 1996b, 254) However, what if a group of people decided that human beings do not have value? Could they treat each other as mere means? And could the group go around and treat others as if they were mere things? What would commit the group to respect others? These are worrisome implications of the argument indeed.[64]

In conclusion, the modified Regress Argument captures an important aspect of Kant's views. For Kant value is not a distinct metaphysical property 'out there'. Rather it is tied to what reason has to deem necessary. In spite of appearances, the modified argument therefore is not necessarily at odds with the account of value I have laid out in Chapter 1 above. On the other hand, I agree with the critics of the argument that its result is not strong enough. In my view the argument fails to establish why the requirement to respect others is a prescription of reason. The exact reason why one should respect others is still elusive.

Section 3: Allen Wood's Modified Regress Argument

One interesting attempt to defend Korsgaard's reconstruction is put forward by Allen Wood. The case of value might be parallel to cases of authority: "It makes sense for us to take someone's advice or prescription as authoritative only to the extent that we respect and esteem the authority itself as their ground." (1999, 130) Similarly, one can argue, it makes sense to take something as valuable (e. g., non-rational things) only to

---

64 Cf. Langton 2007, 180–5. For further objections to the argument see FitzPatrick 2005; and Darwall 2006, 234.

the extent that one respects and esteems the rational capacity determining the good:

> The act of setting an end, therefore, must be taken as committing you to represent some other act (the act of applying the means) as good. In doing all this, however, the rational being must also necessarily regard its own rational capacities as authoritative for what is good in general. For it treats these capacities as capable of determining which ends are good, and at the same time as grounding the goodness of the means taken towards those ends. But to regard one's capacities in this way is also to take a certain attitude toward *oneself* as the being that has and exercises those capacities. It is to *esteem* oneself (Wood 2008, 91).

I take it that esteeming oneself means being struck by something in oneself, a self-regard one feels if one realizes that one can set ends and choose appropriate means. In a second step one could argue that one also has to esteem the capacity to set ends of *others:* "For that capacity does belong to every rational being as such" (*ibid.* 92). If successful, the argument can remedy the two main problems of the previous argument. It could establish that one has to value one's own humanity, and that one has to value the humanity of others.

Textual Basis of the Argument

The argument can build on the same textual support as Korsgaard's arguments. Kant says that one has to regard oneself as an end in itself, but the exact reason is not clearly spelled out. Wood's reconstruction could also share the first premises (although he will give a variation of the first, see below): that the value of things is dependent upon human beings, and that reason inquires into the source of the value of things. But Wood's reconstruction offers a different explanation for why one has to value humanity: because one esteems the capacity for setting ends.

However, is there textual support for the claim that one has to esteem one's authority in choosing ends and means?[65] If anything, Kant's texts seem to speak against such an interpretation. Kant does not seem to think that one has to esteem one's capacity to find means. He famously says that reason is quite ill-suited for finding the ends and means to hap-

---

65 Wood hints that there might be a reason in the Third Section of the *Groundwork* in the claim that everyone has to regard himself as free (cf. his 2008, 92 f.). However, it is not clear how this relates to esteeming the capacity to set ends.

piness. Kant presents the following picture (which would appeal to the common moral cognition of his time) about what it would be like if nature's aim for human beings had been happiness:

> In a word, nature would have taken care that reason should not break forth into *practical use* and have the presumption, with its weak insight, to think out for itself a plan for happiness and for the means of attaining it. Nature would have taken upon itself the choice not only of ends but also of means and, with wise foresight, would have entrusted them both simply to instinct. (*GMS* 4:395; cf. *KpV* 5:61 f.).

Trusting one's reason in finding ends and means often even leads to a hatred of reason (cf. *GMS* 4:395). This suggests that Kant does not think one has to esteem one's capacity to set ends and means. But Kant also explicitly denies that the capacity to set oneself ends gives one a special value: "Although a human being has [...] something more than they [animals] and can set himself ends, even this gives him only an extrinsic value for his usefulness" (*TL* 6:434; cf. *NF* 27:1322; *KpV* 5:61 f.). In addition, Kant does not seem to think that one has to feel esteem for other people. Rather, he thinks that esteem is properly speaking just respect for the moral law of which the other may give one an example (cf. *GMS* 4:401 note; *KpV* 5:76 f., 81 note). Even more strongly, Kant explicitly says that one cannot be bound to esteem or revere others: "I am not bound to *revere* others [...]. The only reverence to which I am bound by nature is reverence for law as such" (*TL* 6:467.33–468.1).

So, if anything, Kant's texts speak against the view that one has to esteem the capacity to set ends and choose means. But setting aside Kant's texts, is this view plausible in its own right?

Evaluation of the Argument

Is there a necessary connection between setting ends and esteeming that capacity? A person with low self-esteem values things, while at the same time not having a high opinion of his capacity to do so. But his failure to esteem himself is not necessarily tied to his capacity to set ends. His judgment might in fact be bad, and he should esteem himself merely in virtue of being human. (Kant ties it more specifically to the capacity for morality which all share, cf. *TL* 6:435 f.) Similarly, the fact that others set ends and choose means does not establish that one has to think highly of their capacity to set ends. Think about politics: If you support one party, it is unlikely that you esteem the capacity to set ends of the members of the other party. While it will be often the case that people esteem their own capacities, there is no necessity to it, nor to esteeming the capacity of others.

In response, Wood could grant that one does not have to esteem any decision the other makes. To claim that one has to esteem the authority of others need not mean that the choices of others are beyond criticism. One could claim that the choice has authority only insofar as it is rational, and that the rationality of the choice must be responsive to the features of the world and the situation one is in (cf. Sussman 2003, 360). It is then not setting any end that would exact esteem from an observer, e. g., the end of counting the blades of grass on a meadow: "On the contrary, setting an end is an exercise of *practical reason* only to the extent that we think there is already *some good reason* for us to set that end." (Wood 2008, 92) This is the point where Wood's reconstruction differs from the first premise of Korsgaard's version of the argument. Things might not be good in virtue of being chosen, but the reason for choosing an end might be prior to and independent of the capacity to set ends. An agent would then be rational insofar as he discerns those independent reasons:

> Ends to be produced will usually have value, for instance, because they fulfill the needs, or enrich the lives, or contribute to the flourishing and the happiness of rational beings, and so setting and achieving these ends shows respect and concern for the value of those beings. (Wood 2008, 92)

The argument does not have to claim that one esteems the authority to set any ends, but only ends for which there are good reasons (e. g., because they promote and protect the well-being of human beings). The authority of practical reason is then a capacity for wisdom or prudence, the ability to find the means for the well-being of human beings.

This modified view does not seem to be Kant's, however. Not only does he distinguish prudence from moral practical reason (cf. *GMS* 4:415 f.), but more importantly Kant clearly distinguishes the respect owed to others from a feeling of esteem for the wisdom of another:

> **respect** shown to others. It is not to be understood as the mere *feeling* that comes from comparing our own *worth* with another's (such as a child feels merely from habit toward his parents, a pupil toward his teacher, or any subordinate toward his superior). It is rather to be understood as the *maxim* of limiting our self-esteem [...] (of not exalting oneself above others) (*TL* 6:449).

Kant does not hold that the owed respect to others is a feeling of esteem one might have for their authority regarding matters of human well-being. Rather it is a commanded maxim of not thinking oneself to be better.

But it also does not seem that Wood's argument can make a strong case on systematic grounds. So far the authority in question has been construed as a kind of expertise on questions of human well-being. It is not clear why this should create any moral reasons to respect such an authority. For instance, an attacker can admire the expertise of the castle builder who knew all about the well-being of the castle inhabitants (their safety and comfort). Nonetheless, this by itself does not give the attacker reasons not to try to take the castle.[66]

In sum, the Authority Argument seems to have some advantages over Korsgaard's versions. It does not, for instance, have to claim that any end an agent sets (e. g., grass counting) creates objective goodness. However, Wood's argument does not seem strong enough to establish that one has to value (or even esteem) oneself or others. One could argue that different contexts require different arguments, and that this is as much as one can expect from this argument (cf. Wood 2008, 93). However, the value of humanity is supposed to be the "sole fundamental and unconditional value" of morality (92). For that purpose the argument does not seem sufficient.[67]

Section 4: Guyer on the Value of Freedom

The attempts by Korsgaard and Wood to argue for the requirement to respect other human beings have been very influential, and have set the tone for the debates about the issue. However, they do not seem to fit well with Kant's text, and they do not seem to be able to establish that one should respect all others. If one follows the text, Kant seems to be saying that human beings are ends in themselves in virtue of having free will. After Kant says that every human being has to regard himself as an end in itself, he refers to the Third Section of the *Groundwork*

---

66 The example is Simon Blackburn's; cf. Christiano 2008, 116 f.
67 It is not clear whether Wood's views on the nature of value differ from my interpretation offered in Chapter 1, cf. Kain 2010. Wood sometimes seems to endorse the view that value is a distinct metaphysical property, cf. his 1999, 126, Baxley 2009, but at other times he grants that his argument only establishes how one has to regard human beings, and he contrasts it with perceiving a separate value property, cf. his 2008, 93. For further objections to his argument see Martin 2006; Darwall 2006, 229–35; Kerstein 2006, 205–212; Christiano 2008, 115–120.

for the explanation of this claim: "Here I put forward this proposition as a postulate. The grounds for it will be found in the last Section." (*GMS* 4:429 note) In the Third Section Kant argues that everyone has to regard himself as being free (cf. *GMS* 4:447 f.). From this it seems that freedom is the reason why one has to regard oneself as an end in oneself.[68] This claim also seems to fit better with Kant's explicit statements that the capacity to set ends merely gives human beings an extrinsic value of usefulness (cf. again *TL* 6:435; *KpV* 5:61 f.), and his direct confirmation that "Freedom, and freedom alone, makes it that one is an end in oneself." (*NF* 27:1322.11 f.).

However, how does freedom ground the requirement to respect others? Could not two enemies acknowledge that the other is free, without this giving them a reason to stop fighting? In a Hobbesian war of all against all, would not the awareness of the other's freedom give one even more reason to attack in anticipation? One might be able to predict the actions of a wild animal that acts according to instinct, but a free being would be even more frightful because of the unpredictability of its actions (cf. *NF* 27:1320). So how does freedom ground the requirement to respect others? Why should freedom be so central, and what might Kant's argument be?

The importance of freedom throughout Kant's works has been thoroughly documented by Paul Guyer. He presents an array of passages from different periods of Kant's writings that all seem to support the idea that Kant sees freedom as the reason why human beings are ends in themselves (and therefore should be respected).[69] He also uncovers different strands of justification that Kant put forward at different times. It is instructive to follow Guyer's analysis in order to see how freedom might ground the requirement to respect others.

The first strand of argumentation Guyer uncovers is a Stoic argument which Kant puts forth in a reflection note from around the mid-1770s. According to this argument freedom gives a special contentment, and thereby contributes to happiness:

---

68   Cf. also Mulholland 1990, 109; Schönecker/Wood 2003, 144 f.; Guyer 2000, ch. 4; and his 2007, 104–6.
69   Cf. his 2000, chs. 3 and 4 (the latter originally published in 1993), his 1998. Guyer 2006a demonstrates the importance of freedom throughout Kant's writings, moral and theoretical.

A certain basis [...] of satisfaction is necessary, which no one must lack, and without which no happiness is possible [...]. This basis [...] must 1. depend on the free will (*Refl* 7202, 19:278; tra. by Guyer 2000, 164).

However, Guyer rightly rejects this argument as one Kant could have had in mind in the *Groundwork*. For at that point Kant clearly rejects happiness as the basis of morality, and the argument would only show why one should value one's own freedom, not the freedom of others (see Guyer 2000, 164 f.). For similar reasons, Kant could not claim that freedom is what people value or desire as a matter of fact. Such a desire would be contingent in Kant's view, but he claims that everyone necessarily has to regard himself as an end in himself (cf. *GMS* 4:428; Guyer 2000, 132; Guyer 2007, 107 f.).

Another strand that runs throughout Kant's works is a teleological argument that freedom is nature's ultimate end for human beings (cf. Guyer 2000, 166–171). Guyer shows that Kant uses this language not only in the *Groundwork* while discussing our 'common moral cognition', in which case he might just repeat the common way of speaking at his time. Kant also uses this language in the later *Critiques*, in which he puts less emphasis on common cognition. For instance, in the second *Critique* Kant repeats that nature's end in giving human beings reason cannot be to bring about happiness: "reason would in that case be only a particular mode nature had used to equip the human being for the same end to which it has destined animals" (*KpV* 5:61 f.; cf. Guyer 2000, 166). Instead nature's end for human beings is said to be freedom and a moral life (cf. also *KU* 5:431; Guyer 2000, 168). According to this argument, therefore, freedom is human beings' highest purpose because it was given by nature. However, as Guyer points out, by itself this is not a justification for the value of freedom. It is merely a regulative idea, something which one can use to bring coherence into one's thought and which can serve as a motivational device, but not a constitutive idea that gives certain knowledge or a justification: "we cannot really prove that this is the ultimate purpose of nature" (Guyer 2000, 171, cf. 169). And even if one could prove it, nothing would force one to accept it. Why should one follow nature, if one is free? It cannot be forced upon human beings, otherwise they would not be free (*ibid.* 171).

Guyer's solution is that the value of freedom is "indemonstrable" (Guyer 2000, 170), a "self-evident *normative* proposition" (Guyer 2007, 112). It is immediately recognized by everyone if questioned:

> The dignity of freedom [...] will be recognized immediately by anyone as
> soon as he is asked which is more important to him, making his own choices
> or having his inclinations gratified even if he does not get to choose what
> those inclinations are or which of them should be satisfied. Anyone can read-
> ily be brought to see, I believe Kant assumes, that all his particular moral
> judgments in fact reflect his fundamental commitment to the value of pre-
> serving freedom of choice and promoting its successful exercise wherever
> freedom may be found, in himself or in others. (1998a, 30, cf. 32 & 34)

So even though the value of freedom cannot be proved by rational demonstration, Guyer claims that in Kant's view everyone is in fact committed to the value of freedom and can easily be brought to recognize that
fact.

Textual Basis of the Argument

Guyer would admit that this reconstruction is not openly in the *Groundwork* (cf. his 1998a, 32). In the *Groundwork* Kant refers to the Third Section for the reason why one has to regard oneself as an end in itself. In the
Third Section Kant argues that one has to regard oneself as free, but Kant
does not talk there about value or suggest that everyone would immediately recognize the value of freedom.[70] Guyer sees the task more in finding a coherent reading of Kant's work as a whole, since "Kant almost
never explains the deepest strategy of his arguments to us with the clarity
we would like" (1998a, 32). What is the textual evidence in favor of this
reading?

The clearest passage Guyer cites for the view that Kant held value to
be indemonstrable is from an early prize essay, *An Inquiry concerning the
Distinctness of the Principles of Natural Theology and Morality*, published
1764. The passage reads:

> Only in our times has it begun to be understood that the faculty for repre-
> senting the *true* is *cognition*, but that for sensing the *good* is *feeling*, and that
> these must not be confused with each other. Now just as there are unanalyz-
> able concepts of the true, [...] so there is also an unanalyzable feeling of the
> good [...]. But if this [good] is simple, the judgment: this is good, is fully
> indemonstrable, and is an immediate effect of the consciousness of the feel-
> ing of pleasure with the representations of the object [...]. Thus, if an action

---

70 The closest Kant comes to this is on page 4:454 f. However, there he says that
even "the most hardened scoundrel" thinks of himself a better person if he pur-
sues a good will. This refers to the value of a morally good will, not to the value
of freedom as such.

is immediately represented as good, [...] then the necessity of this action is an indemonstrable material principle of obligation. (2:299 f.; quoted from Guyer 2000, 130 f.)

This is the clearest passage because in it Kant says that value judgments are indemonstrable. Guyer is quick to point out that the particular views in this passage cannot be Kant's mature views, since he ties value judgments to a feeling of pleasure, something he would reject in the *Groundwork* and other mature writings. However, Guyer holds that the central claim that value judgments are indemonstrable has not changed (cf. 2000, 131). What is his rationale?

Guyer does not cite any other passage in which Kant directly says that the value of freedom is indemonstrable. It is more that he takes it to be the best explanation of Kant's strategy in his mature writings on moral philosophy (cf. 1998a, 28, 30). Guyer analyzes Kant's writings under the premise that "recognition and acknowledgment of the binding force of the fundamental principle of morality is readily available to every normal human being" (1998a, 28). For instance, Kant famously starts out the *Groundwork* with an analysis of common moral cognition. What this cognition more concretely consists in, according to Guyer, is "the recognition of the 'inner value, i.e., dignity' of freedom" as the "immediately evident and irreducibly normative starting point of morality" (1998a, 34). As textual evidence for this interpretation, Guyer refers to passages where Kant seems to be saying that freedom elevates us above the rest of nature, is our highest vocation and instills a respect. For instance, in the second *Critique* Kant seems to say that freedom "elevates a human being above himself" and that "a human being [...] must regard his own nature in reference to his second and highest vocation only with reverence" (*KpV* 5:86 f.; cf. Guyer 2000, 153–5). Guyer also sees these views expressed in the *Groundwork*, for instance, when Kant talks about the dignity of autonomy (4:434–6), and in the passage that leads up to the Formula of Humanity (4:427–9): "when Kant asks for a ground of a possible categorical imperative, what he is asking for is an end that could move a rational being to adopt such a constraint" (Guyer 2000, 31; cf. 34). So does Kant's ethics rest on an intuitively evident value of freedom, as Guyer argues?

Evaluation

This interpretation invites a few challenges that seem to refute it. First, if the strongpoint of the interpretation is said to be that it describes what is easily recognized by all human beings, why does Kant not lay out this view at the beginning of the *Groundwork*, where he says he starts with the 'common moral cognition'? Second, in the passage that leads up to the Formula of Humanity Kant says that everyone *necessarily* regards himself as an end in itself (cf. *GMS* 4:428 f.). This might speak against the view that Kant regards the value of freedom as indemonstrable, and rather thinks that there is a story that can be told as to why one *must* regard oneself as an end in itself (cf. Reath 2003, 154 f.). Third, without the demonstration that everyone must necessarily value freedom, it is not clear whether one could establish that all human beings value freedom (cf. Dean 2006, 127 note), or that the value of freedom "will be recognized immediately by anyone as soon as he is asked which is more important to him, making his own choices or having his inclinations gratified even if he does not get to choose what those inclinations are" (Guyer 2000, 30). The problem is that the question of whether everyone values freedom the most has now turned into an empirical question. Would all people who are constantly starving prefer their freedom over food? Have people always valued freedom the most? Do other cultures value freedom as highly as we do? Is it a truth that "every normal human being [...] would immediately acknowledge as soon as it is put to him in words that he can understand" (Guyer 2000, 30)? While Guyer admits that the question of whether freedom is valuable cannot be an empirical or contingent question for Kant (cf. 2007, 107 f.), the view that the value of freedom is indemonstrable seems to leave only empirical approaches for verification of that claim. However, empirical evidence could not yield the necessity included in Kant's claim, and even the empirical evidence one could give is doubtful.

Despite these challenges that can be leveled against this interpretation of Kant's works, I do think that Guyer's view is basically correct. I believe that Kant indeed holds that all human beings value freedom. However, I do not think that Kant takes this value to be indemonstrable, and I also think that Guyer's interpretation of value does not contradict the account I have offered in Chapter 1. Guyer does not present the value of freedom as a distinct metaphysical property (cf. 2000, 27).[71] If he understands the

---

71 Guyer confirmed this in personal conversation.

value of freedom merely to be a description of what all people (necessarily) do value, then there is not necessarily a conflict with my account offered in the last chapter. There I argued that Kant conceives of value as a prescription of what one should value or a description of what a perfectly rational being would value. This can be demonstrated. What a perfectly rational being values is described by the Categorical Imperative, according to Kant: The imperative which express an 'ought' for human beings describes what a perfectly rational being 'wills' (cf. *GMS* 4:449, 455). What a perfectly rational being wills is morality, which here includes one's freedom (cf. *GMS* 4:446 f.; *KpV* 5:29 f.). But, according to Kant, it is also the case that every normal human being values freedom. Even the hardened scoundrel wishes to be moral (cf. *GMS* 4:454 f.). This is because every human being has a feeling of respect or reverence for the moral law within. And again this motivation to be moral includes one's freedom which all value. Kant does not address abnormal cases like a psychopath. According to him, "[n]o human being is entirely without moral feeling, for were he completely lacking in receptivity to it he would be morally dead" (*TL* 6:399 f., cf. 402 f.). So Kant thinks that everyone does and should value the moral law and the freedom that comes with it. And since Kant uses 'absolute value' to say what should be valued or is valued by beings perfectly in accord with reason (cf. Chapter 1 above), one could say that freedom with its moral law has absolute value. However, this explanation does not invoke a metaphysical value property. I therefore think that Guyer's view that all human beings value freedom is correct as an interpretation of Kant, but it is not a departure from the view I have offered so far.

There would only be a conflict with my view if Guyer conceives of the value of freedom as being prior to and independent from the Categorical Imperative. It is not certain that this is his view. When Guyer says that the value of freedom is the ground of the imperative, he talks about a claim of motivation, not justification. Take again the following passage: "when Kant asks for a ground of a possible categorical imperative, what he is asking for is an end that could move a rational being to adopt such a constraint" (Guyer 2000, 31; cf. 34). However, on my reading what motivates the agent to follow the law is the law itself, aided by a feeling of respect (cf. *KpV* 5:71 ff.). This again implies that, in Kant's view, what all human beings necessarily value – freedom in accordance with the Categorical Imperative – is not independent of the imperative.

My reading of the value of freedom is also compatible with the passages Guyer cites in support of his reading. The passage Guyer quotes in which Kant seems to say that human beings revere freedom really says, in my view, that human beings have respect for the moral law. The passage starts out with a moral question: *"Duty!* [...] only holds forth a law [...] and yet gains reluctant reverence" (*KpV* 5:86). What one values is duty and the moral law. Kant then asks about the origin of duty that is worthy of the respect one has for it: "what origin is there worthy of you, and where is to be found the root of your noble descent [...]?"(*KpV* 5:86). The origin is said to be "freedom and independence from the mechanism of the whole of nature, regarded nevertheless as also a capacity of a being subject to special laws – namely pure practical laws" (*KpV* 5:87). It is the independence from nature (including one's inclinations) that accounts for the noble descent of duty. What one values or has respect for is this higher calling, as commanded by the moral law, to act for the sake of duty, free from inclinations: "it is then not to be wondered at that a human being [...] must regard his own nature in reference to his second and highest vocation only with reverence, and its laws with the highest respect." (*KpV* 5:87) This is also confirmed as the passage continues: "the pure moral law [...] lets us discover the sublimity of our supersensible existence and subjectively effects respect for their higher vocation" (*KpV* 5:88). These passages are not isolated occurrences in Kant's works – similar statements can be found elsewhere (cf. e.g. *TL* 6:435 f.: *GMS* 4:435 f.). So Kant does believe that all human beings value freedom in feeling respect for the moral law/one's moral vocation. What one feels respect for is the ability of the moral law to strike down self-conceit which is based on one's inclinations (cf. *KpV* 5:73). I therefore agree with Guyer that, according to Kant, all human beings value freedom.

My interpretation also fits the passage from the prize essay Guyer quotes. The judgment that is said to be indemonstrable is a "feeling of pleasure with the representation of the object" (2:299 f.). The indemonstrable judgment is not a necessary judgment of the value of freedom, but it is a feeling of pleasure, as Kant discusses it in connection with the paradox of method in the second *Critique* (cf. *KpV* 5:57–65). This, Kant says, is the only way one could discern the good if one wanted to put the good prior to the Categorical Imperative. But since a feeling of pleasure cannot ground a necessary moral law, Kant rules out that any good could be the ground of moral requirements (see Chapter 1 above). So the prize essay from 1764 does not seem to fully reflect Kant's mature position on this point.

But if what human beings value or feel respect for is morality and its freedom, does this mean that one should respect others because they have

a morally good will? Is the good will the foundation of moral requirements? This leads to the last question of this chapter.

Section 5: The Value of a Morally Good Will

The Kant literature, as I noted at the beginning, falls roughly within two
camps on the question why one should respect others. So far I have discussed the first camp, which holds that one should respect others because
of the value of their pre-moral capacities (e.g. freedom or the capacity to
set ends). I shall now turn to the second camp. The second camp argues
that it is a morally good will that is the reason why one should respect
others. The second reading is less popular since it seems to imply that
one only has to respect people who are morally good (cf. Denis 2010a;
Glasgow 2007). However, the reading does seem to have some textual
support, and perhaps there is a way in which it can be made consistent
with Kant's claim that *all* human beings should be respected. The reading
can rely for support on another strand in Kant's text, for instance, when
he says that only a morally good will can have an absolute value (cf. *GMS*
4:393), or that morality is the condition of being an end in itself (cf.
GMS 4:435), or that "nothing can have a worth other than that which
the law determines for it" (*GMS* 4:435). Accordingly, the reason why
one should respect others might be because they (possibly[72]) have a morally good will.

  In this section I shall look at two such attempts in the literature.
Again the question is whether they introduce a new conception of
value or a new foundation of morality that contradicts the one I have argued for in the last chapter. I shall discuss arguments presented by Richard Dean and Samuel Kerstein, two current proponents of the good
will reading of Kant.[73]

  Both rely on the opening statement of the *Groundwork* that only a
good will could be said to be good without limitation or absolutely:
"It is impossible to think of anything at all in the world, or indeed beyond it, that could be considered good without limitation except a
good will." (*GMS* 4:393) In addition, they both rely on a statement
in Kant's summary of the different formulas of the Categorical Impera-

---

72 Cf. *GMS* 4:437; Ricken 1989, 246; and Kerstein 2006, 219.
73 For earlier proponents see Paton 1947, 168 f., 177; Ross 1954, 52 f.; and Ricken
    1989, 246 f. For a critique of this view see Christiano 2008, 108–110.

tive near the end of the Second Section of the *Groundwork*. In 4:437 Kant seems to summarize his previous discussion: "We can now end where we set out from at the beginning, namely with the concept of a will unconditionally good." In summarizing the Formula of Humanity Kant then seems to specify why human beings are ends in themselves:

> Now, this end can be nothing other than the subject of all possible ends itself, because this subject is also the subject of a possible absolutely good will; for such a will cannot without contradiction be subordinated to any other object." (*GMS* 4:437)

Dean and Kerstein both base their interpretations on these passages, but present different arguments.

Richard Dean's Interpretation

Dean uses the above quoted passages to interpret the text that leads up to the Formula of Humanity. To recall, there Kant says that rational nature is the ground of the Categorical Imperative in virtue of being an end in itself. He goes on to say that one has to regard oneself as an end in itself, "so far it is thus a *subjective* principle of human actions" (*GMS* 4:428 f.). But since everyone has to regard himself as such an end, Kant proceeds, the principle is at the same time an objective one. Accordingly, Dean presents two arguments, one for a subjective and one for an objective principle.

For establishing the subjective principle that one has to regard oneself as an end in oneself, Dean offers an argument similar to Korsgaard's (cf. Dean 2006, 120–6). He describes the argument as a regress upon the conditions of the goodness of things. Unlike Korsgaard he does not hold that any setting of ends makes things valuable, but merely the setting of ends that follows from a good will and moral principles. As support he cites *Groundwork* 4:397 in which Kant says that the worth of the good will "constitutes the condition of all the rest" of the things that have worth. If this is the case, then it is contradictory to sacrifice one's good will for the merely contingent value of things: "Her subjective ends only have value if she wills the ends with her fully rational nature, so if she destroys her fully rational nature, her contingent ends will lack value when she realizes them." (Dean 2006, 125) Using a regress argument and Kant's claim that one cannot subordinate a good will without contradiction, Dean concludes that one has to value one's own humanity, understood as the good will (cf. Dean 2006, chs. 2–5).

Is this argument Kant's? The view that one should value one's own good will is certainly Kant's. And he reiterates that in saying that the absolute worth of a human being is something one can give only oneself in being morally good.[74] Throughout the First Section of the *Groundwork* Kant repeatedly says that a "good will [...] is to be valued incomparably higher than all that could merely be brought about by it in favor of some inclination" (*GMS* 4:394), that a good will "is to be esteemed in itself [...] apart from any further purpose" (*GMS* 4:396 f.), and that the worth of the good will "surpasses all else" (*GMS* 4:403). So, I think that Dean is in line with Kant regarding the view that everyone should strive to develop *his own* good will. What is less clear, however, is whether the passage leading up to the Formula of Humanity is needed to make this point, or whether this passage even supports this claim. It does not seem right to say that only a rational choice makes things good as a means: "The precepts for a physician to make his man healthy [...], and for a poisoner to be sure of killing his, are of equal worth insofar as each serves perfectly to bring about his purpose." (*GMS* 4:415) If a poisoner has an inclination to kill his victim, the poison has the value of a means. This seems to be the sense of what Kant says in 4:428: "if there were no inclinations [...], their object would be without worth." Accordingly Kant says at the beginning of the *Groundwork* that a good will is merely the condition for taking something to be *absolutely* good, not good in a derivative sense (cf. 4:394).

Dean could reply that he is not talking about the value of means or things, but of the value of ends. One's ends only have value if they follow from a rational choice. This does seem to be Kant's view if one speaks about moral value. All of one's ends are ultimately to be evaluated by the moral law: "nothing can have a worth other than that which the law determines for it" (*GMS* 4:436). Of course, a particular end might have prudential value for me (e.g., to tell a lie to gain advantage), but it would still be evaluated as to whether it is moral or not. In this sense, moral worth is the condition of all other worth (cf. *GMS* 4:397). Prudential worth is relative and contingent, while only moral worth is unconditional, and accordingly more important. Even if one end is recommended by one's inclinations (e.g., to lie), morality would

---

74 See esp. *KU* 5:443, cf. 208 f., but also, e.g., *GMS* 4:439, 449 f., 454; *KpV* 5:110 f., 147 f., 86.

be overriding for Kant in that it commands unconditionally (e.g., not to lie). According to Kant, therefore, a contradiction occurs if one were to subordinate morality to a prudential end. For since in the scheme of things the prudential end only gets its final approval from morality, a morally good "will cannot without contradiction be subordinated to any other object" (*GMS* 4:437). If prudential ends must be approved by morality, it is a contradiction that the prudential end should evaluate morality.

So I am not sure that Dean's argument is the best explanation of *Groundwork* 4:427–9, but I agree that according to Kant one should value a good will above all else, and that it would be a contradiction if one were to subordinate it to inclinations (cf. also *GMS* 4:437; *TL* 6:422 f.). But why should one value *other people's* good will? Why is valuing a good will said to be an objective principle in Dean's sense?

As a justification for the objective principle that one also has to value the good will of others, Dean refers to Kant's claim that morality has to be necessary and universal (cf. Dean 2006, 124 f.; *GMS* 4:389). For this, however, it does not seem to be enough that each universally acts on the same principle (e.g., a principle of egoism). In that case there could be strife if two people want the same object for themselves. So morality, Dean continues, requires an object that all can share, and that object is a good will:

> If morality is not a fiction, it requires an end that can be shared by all agents, and that is what justifies the move from the 'subjective principle' in the argument for the humanity formulation to the 'objective principle' that one must treat fully rational nature as an end in itself wherever one finds it. (Dean 2006, 129)

Again I think that Dean captures an important aspect of Kant's views, that morality is necessary and universal, and that egoism could not deliver that (see Chapter 1 above). However, I am less sure that it is this view to which Kant refers in the passage that leads up to the Formula of Humanity. For support of his interpretation Dean refers to the Third Theorem in the second *Critique* (*KpV* 5:27 f.). However, what Kant says there is that any material principle (e.g., happiness or pleasure) could not be the determining ground of morality, since morality has to be universal and necessary, and that *any* matter would undermine that. Instead the determining ground of morality, or the harmonious end, could only be the formal moral law (cf. *KpV* 5:27). So, Kant does not really say that there must be an object all share. He merely points out that in the pursuit of happiness, not all would share the same end and strife would result; but even if one does share the same end, there could be strife (e. g., if two women desire the same man). Instead Kant affirms that it can only be the form of the law, i.e., if everyone follows the moral law, that can yield harmony (cf. *KpV* 5:27 f.). But by itself it does not yet explain why one should respect others.

So I do not see that Dean has convincingly argued that there is an end or value that could ground the requirement to respect others. In particular, I do not see that the good will *of others* is the reason why one should respect them. As Dean agrees, the value of the good will is not a distinct metaphysical property (cf. also his 2000). A will is good if it follows the Categorical Imperative for its own sake (cf. *GMS* 4:426, 437). What about the good will generates the requirement to respect others?

One could argue that it is a feeling of respect by which one can discern the good will of another and be motivated to acknowledge it.[75] The value of the good will could be understood merely in the sense that one discerns that the other follows the moral law for its own sake (in contrast to discerning a distinct metaphysical property inherent in another). After all, Kant repeatedly claims that the respect one feels for others is properly speaking a respect for the moral law of which the other gives us an example (cf. *GMS* 4:401 note; *KpV* 5:76 f., 81 note, 87; *TL* 6:467 f.). However, Kant's ethics would then rely on a moral sense to discover what is moral rather than on pure reason, and he rejects that approach: "we no more have a special *sense* for what is (morally) good and evil than for *truth* [...]. We have, rather, a *susceptibility* on the part of free choice to be moved by pure practical reason (and its law)" (*TL* 6:400; cf. *KpV* 5:84–6; *GMS* 4:426). More importantly, Kant explicitly denies that the morally demanded respect for others is a feeling: To have a feeling cannot be commanded (cf. *GMS* 4:399; *TL* 6:399, 402 f.). Rather Kant conceives of the demanded respect for others as a maxim one should have (cf. *TL* 6:449). The reason why one should have this maxim is still elusive.

In sum, I agree with Dean that a) for Kant value is not a distinct metaphysical property, that b) Kant does not base morality on a prior or independent value (cf., e.g., 2006, 114–8, 45–9), and that c) for Kant it is one's own good will one should value above all else. However, I am skeptical that he captures Kant's justification for the requirement to respect others, especially as Kant presents it in the passage leading up to

---

75 Cf. Dean 2006, ch. 7; and Wood 1999, 141 f., 147–9.

the Formula of Humanity. Even if all human beings were to share a good will as their end, why would it be the good will of *others* one should be concerned about? In the next chapter I shall argue that the realized good will is also not *what* one should respect in others. I therefore agree with critics that for Kant the humanity one should respect in others is *not* identical with a realized good will (cf. Glasgow 2007; Denis 2010a; and Allison 2011, ch. 8). For Kant even a vicious person deserves respect as a human being (cf. *TL* 6:462 f.).[76]

Samuel Kerstein's Argument

Another scholar who interprets Kant as saying that it is a good will that should be respected in others is Samuel Kerstein. He too relies on the opening of the *Groundwork* (4:393 f.) and the passage where Kant summarizes the different formulas of the Categorical Imperative (4:437). However, his argument differs significantly from Dean's. Kerstein emphasizes the claim from the *Groundwork* that only a good will is unconditionally good, and especially preeminently good (cf. *GMS* 4:394; Kerstein 2006, 212). He then interprets the contradiction Kant mentions in 4:437 as a contradiction of the claim that the good will is preeminently good (cf. Kerstein 2006, 213): "Two different things cannot both be preeminently valuable." (Kerstein 2006, 217) So if the good will is preeminently valuable, and if one places something else above it, one fails to acknowledge the value one has attributed to the good will, and thereby contradicts oneself.

It is clearly Kant's view in the First Section of the *Groundwork* that the worth of the good will surpasses all other value, and is to be esteemed for its own sake (cf. *GMS* 4:394, 396 f., 403). And Kerstein gives a plausible explanation for why Kant holds that to subordinate a good will would be contradictory. However, does this also explain the requirement to respect others? Or does it only say that one should value one's own

---

76 Dean tries to establish that one should respect *all* human beings by arguing: a) that a good will is not rare but quite common; b) that it is hard to know whether someone has a morally good will; c) that respecting vicious human beings might be needed to give them a chance to better themselves; and d) that not respecting them could have a corrupting influence on the agent's character (cf. Dean 2006, 7). In Chapter 3 I shall argue that one should respect all human beings equally, independently of their possession of a good will. I thank Anne Margaret Baxley for pressing me on this point.

good will? Kerstein seems to be in a better position than Korsgaard or Dean to argue that what one should value is a good will as such, wherever one finds it, not just one's own good will. This is because he does not put forth a regress argument. The value of the good will is not discovered because it is the condition of things being valuable (in which case only the particular person valuing is the source of the value of things).

But what is the nature of preeminent value, according to Kerstein? He does not clearly specify what he has in mind. What could he mean? First, he could take it to be a distinct metaphysical property, but this would raise the same problems I have spelled out in Chapter 1. If the property were discerned as residing in others, heteronomy would ensue. The same seems true if this property were supposed to be something over and above one's self-awareness as it is given in introspection. How could one know that one has this property?

Second, Kerstein could argue that "an impartial rational spectator can take no delight in seeing" a good will being subordinated, whether it is one's own good will or that of another (*GMS* 4:393). The judgment would then be impartial or agent-neutral. However, is this really what Kant argues? It seems that it is not quite the same to take delight in contemplating the good will of another, and to be under the requirement to respect others. The first is an impartial judgment about which state of the world would be better, the second would be a direct demand on an agent to respect something. The one does not necessarily imply the other. One can judge one state of the world to be better than another (agent-neutrally) without endorsing what it would take to get there. The end does not always justify the means. Kant's point is more that one takes delight in seeing someone exhibiting a good will, and that one would think him deserving of happiness:

> an impartial rational spectator can take no delight in seeing the uninterrupted prosperity of a being graced with no feature of a pure and good will, so that a good will sems to constitute the indispensable condition even of worthiness to be happy. (*GMS* 4:393)

Kant's point is not that the delight one would take in seeing another exhibit a good will is the reason why one should respect them. The delight is merely a judgment about the desert of the other.

Kerstein could argue, third, that what the value of the good will amounts to is that one has a feeling of respect toward it. This would raise the same problems I have pointed out in the discussion of Richard Dean's position: A feeling cannot ground moral requirements, and it is not the commanded respect Kant has in mind, since a feeling cannot be commanded (see above). In addition, Kant is very explicit that the feeling of respect is in the first instance towards one's own will (cf. *GMS* 4:440), and towards other beings only insofar as they give us an example how we should behave (cf. *GMS* 4:401 note; *KpV* 5:76 f., 81 note). The feeling places the emphasis on how one should improve oneself, not on a duty to respect others because of their good will:

> Because we also regard enlarging our talents as a duty, we represent a person of talents also as, so to speak, an *example of the law* (to become like him in this by practice), and this is what constitutes our respect. (*GMS* 4:401 note)

So while I agree with Kerstein's claim that one should value one's own good will above all else, the justification for why one should respect others is still missing. But again, I also do not think that a realized good will is *what* one should respect in others. All human beings deserve respect, whether they have a morally good will or not (cf. Chapter 3 below).

Conclusion

In sum, while I do think that the claims about the supreme value of a good will are Kant's, there is no clear indication that he holds this value to be the reason why one should respect others. Since Kant claims that one should respect *all* other human beings, the good will arguments seem committed to claiming that all human beings have a good will. On this reading it is not enough that the other might develop it in the future (see Kerstein 2006, 219 note 26). In contrast, Kant seems to think that one should respect others even if one could know that they do not have a good will (cf. *TL* 6:462 f.). The claims about the good will are not a foundation for Kant, but rather a consequence of moral requirements: *"That will is absolutely good* that cannot be evil, hence whose maxim, if made into a universal law, can never conflict with itself." (*GMS* 4:437, cf. 426) To say that one should value a good will is to say that one should follow the moral law for its own sake. By itself this is not yet an explanation why one should respect others.

Results of this Chapter

It is a common view in the Kant literature that one should respect other human beings because of a value they possess – either a value of their pre-moral capacities (freedom or the capacity to set ends) or the value of a good will. In this chapter I have discussed the most prominent arguments put forth by Kant scholars. While one at first would most likely assume that these arguments conflict with my conclusions presented in Chapter 1, it turns out that most of the arguments employ a conception of value that is compatible with my results. A conception of value as what one is rationally committed to, or what one would agree to if one where fully rational, is in line with the account I have presented in the last chapter. To this extent I agree with these arguments, and I think that one can learn valuable lessons from them.

Korsgaard stresses rightly, I believe, that Kant does not put forward a metaphysical claim about special properties human beings have, and I think she is also right in her reading of the value of things. Wood rightly points out that the value of things is not totally arbitrary and up to a person's whim, but that many things are useful for deeply-seated inclinations human beings have. Guyer, I think, is right in emphasizing the importance of freedom and the respect one has for it; and Dean and Kerstein rightly stress the emphasis Kant places on the requirement to strive for a good will above all else.

However, I agree with the critics of these arguments that they do not ground the requirement to respect others. In the next chapter I shall offer my own interpretation of Kant's Formula of Humanity and the reason why one should respect others.

Chapter 3: Kant's Formula of Humanity

Introduction

So far I have argued that, according to Kant, the reason why one should respect others is not a value they possess. Kant has argued that there is not any prior or independent value that could ground moral requirements, as any such grounding would take away the necessary and universal nature of morality (Chapter 1). In addition, there is no non-moral activity, such as the setting of ends, that commits one to valuing others. Kant argues that one should value a good will, and that one has respect for the moral law even if it is exhibited in others (cf. *GMS* 4:401 note). However, this feeling of respect is not the morally required maxim of respecting others (cf. *TL* 6:449), and one should respect others even if one could know that they are not morally good (cf. *TL* 6:463). It is therefore neither a morally neutral capacity others have (e. g., the capacity to set ends), nor a morally good will that is the reason why one should respect others (Chapter 2).

In this chapter I shall argue that the reason why one should respect others is that it is a direct command of reason – that is, a way reason necessarily functions. According to Kant, one should respect others because it is commanded by the Formula of Humanity. This formula is said to be at bottom the same as the Categorical Imperative (cf. *GMS* 4:436, 437). Like the imperative, the command to respect others is a first normative reality, an in-built principle of reason. The claim that the requirement to respect others is already contained in the requirement to universalize one's maxim is not novel. It has been put forward by leading Kant scholars.[77] What is new is my argument that the Formula of Humanity passage (*GMS* 4:427–429) supports this claim. In the following I shall discuss the derivation, justification, and application of the Formula of Humanity. I shall first present a close reading of the passage that leads up to the Formula of Humanity (Section 1). I shall then argue that the Formula of

---

77 Cf., e. g., Ebbinghaus 1959, 216; O'Neill 1989, ch. 7; Sullivan 1989, 193–195; Hill 2000, 101–9; Engstrom 2009, 172–8; and Reath 2012b. Paul Guyer argues along similar lines that the categorical imperative is implied by the Formula of Humanity, cf. his 2006a, 194 f.

Humanity is not itself justified in reference to a value, but is a direct command of reason (Section 2). After presenting Kant's justification, I shall look at the application of the Formula of Humanity or what it means to respect humanity (Section 3). Since my interpretation brings the Formula of Humanity closer to the Categorical Imperative, I shall then address the objection that the Formula of Humanity, like the imperative, is empty and devoid of content (Section 4).

Section 1: The Formula of Humanity Passage (*GMS* 4:427–9)

So far the problem has been to find a justification for the requirement to respect other human beings, which Kant expresses in the Formula of Humanity: *"So act that you use humanity, whether in your own person or in the person of any other, always at the same time as an end, never merely as a means."* (*GMS* 4:429) The key for finding the justification is commonly thought to be contained in the following passage that leads up to the Formula of Humanity:

> The ground of this principle is: *rational nature exists as an end in itself.* The human being necessarily represents his own existence in this way; so far it is thus a *subjective* principle of human actions. But every other rational being also represents his existence in this way consequent on just the same rational ground that also holds for me;* thus it is at the same time an *objective* principle from which, as a supreme practical ground, it must be possible to derive all laws of the will. (*GMS* 4:428 f.)

Scholars who analyze this passage try to find an argument that is different from and independent of the argument for the Categorical Imperative (cf. Chapter 2 above). The key question became how one is to read the following statement of Kant's: "The ground of this principle is: *rational nature exists as an end in itself.*" (*GMS* 4:428) On the common reading of this passage, "end in itself" denotes a special moral status, e. g., a value one should always respect. When Kant goes on to say that "so far it is [...] a *subjective* principle" (*GMS* 4:429), scholars often assert that Kant is referring to the command always to regard other human beings as having this moral status, or to respect human beings, in short: the Formula of Humanity.

In the following, I shall offer a different interpretation. Two premises on which I shall rely are the results of the previous two chapters. Kant cannot refer to a value to ground the requirement to respect others (from Chapter 1), and he cannot merely have in mind that everyone has to regard himself as valuable (from Chapter 2). Instead I shall argue, first, that the principle Kant is referring to as being first merely subjective and then objective is the Categorical Imperative, and not the Formula of Humanity. Kant's question is whether the Categorical Imperative is a necessary law for all or merely a subjective principle (cf. *GMS* 4:426). Second, I shall argue that "end in itself" is foremost a descriptive, not a normative term for Kant (similarly Mulholland 1990, 108–10). It describes human beings as free, i.e., not a mere plaything of nature or the means to the will of another. The key sentence then reads: 'The ground of the Categorical Imperative is: *rational nature is free.*' This is the same justification for the Categorical Imperative Kant will give in the Third Section of the *Groundwork*, to which he explicitly refers for a fuller justification (cf. *GMS* 4:429 note). Kant does hold that free beings should be treated as if they are free (i.e., human beings treated as an end in itself), but he does not introduce a justification that is independent of the Categorical Imperative for this claim.

In the following I shall first argue for my first claim that the Formula of Humanity passage talks about whether the Categorical Imperative is a necessary law for all. I shall then argue for my second claim that 'end in itself' is primarily a descriptive concept, describing one aspect of free will. I shall then put both claims together to interpret the crucial paragraph in which the Formula of Humanity is first formulated.

The Question of the Formula of Humanity Passage

My first claim – that the passage leading up to the Formula of Humanity examines whether the *Categorical Imperative* is a necessary law for all – becomes clear if one looks at the question Kant sets himself. To understand the passage in which Kant first states the Formula of Humanity, one has to start as early as 4:425, right after Kant discussed examples for the application of the Law of Nature Formula: *"act as if the maxim of your action were to become by your will a* **universal law of nature."** (*GMS* 4:421) Kant concludes the discussion of this formula by emphasizing that he has not yet justified the Categorical Imperative. So far he has only argued for a conditional: If there is moral duty, it can only be expressed in a categorical imperative. "But we have not yet advanced so far as to prove a priori that there really is such an imperative, […] and that the observance of this law is duty." (*GMS* 4:425) Kant warns again that one cannot answer these questions in referring to a special

property of human nature, as morality should be valid for all rational beings; and he reiterates the question that has not yet been answered: "is it a
necessary law *for all rational beings* always to appraise their actions in accordance with such maxims as they themselves could will to serve as a
universal law?" (*GMS* 4:426)

It is this question that Kant seeks to answer in the pages that follow.
He goes on to say that if there is necessary Categorical Imperative, "it
must already be connected (completely a priori) with the concept of
the will of a rational being as such" (*GMS* 4:426). The reason presumably
is that only an a priori inquiry can yield necessity: "Necessity and strict
universality are therefore secure indications of an *a priori* cognition,
and also belong together inseparably." (*KrV* B4) If one wants to show
that the Categorical Imperative is a necessary law for all, one must
show that it is already connected a priori with the concept of a being
for whom it should be a law. Kant goes on to say that in order to discover
the connection between the concept of a rational being as such and the
Categorical Imperative, "we must, however reluctantly, step forth, namely
into metaphysics" (*GMS* 4:426). By this he does not mean the speculative
metaphysics he combats in the first *Critique*, e. g., a metaphysics that tries
to give answers beyond the realm of possible experience. The step required is merely into a "metaphysics of morals" (*GMS* 4:427). What
he means by this is a "system of a priori cognition from concepts
alone" (*RL* 6:216; cf. *GMS* 4:412). In order to show that the Categorical
Imperative is a necessary law for all rational beings, Kant therefore seeks
to show that the imperative is connected a priori with the concept of a
rational being as such.

Accordingly, in the next paragraph Kant turns to the concept of a (rational) will: "The will is thought as a capacity to determine itself to acting
in conformity with the *representation of certain laws*." (*GMS* 4:427) In
saying that a law is connected to the concept of a will, Kant anticipates
his conclusions of the Third Section of the *Groundwork*. There he argues
– without invoking a value property – that freedom is connected to the
concept of a will, and that freedom is the ground of the imperative, since
"a free will and a will under the moral law are one and the same" (*GMS*
4:447; cf. Section 3 below).[78] In 4:427 Kant does not yet talk about the

---

78 This view does not change in the *Critique of Practical Reason*. There Kant con-
    firms: "Thus freedom and unconditional practical law reciprocally imply each
    other" (*KpV* 5:29), and he calls freedom the *"ratio essendi"* of the moral law
    (*KpV* 5:4 note).

requirement to respect others. But it is important to note that he also does not do so in the sentences right before he states the Formula of Humanity for the first time. In order to conclude my first claim – that the passage leading up to the Formula of Humanity examines whether the *Categorical Imperative* is a necessary law for all – I shall for now skip the rest of page 427 and the bulk of page 428. But I shall come back to it for my second claim – that for Kant 'end in itself' is primarily a descriptive concept.

In the paragraph in which Kant first states the Formula of Humanity he is still talking about the question whether the Categorical Imperative is a necessary law for all (or is objective). The paragraph starts out:

> If, then, there is to be [...] a categorical imperative, it must be one such that, from the representation of what is necessarily an end for everyone [...], it constitutes an *objective* principle of the will [...]. The ground of this principle is: *rational nature exists as an end in itself.* (*GMS* 4:428 f.)

In this passage Kant talks about the Categorical Imperative, and he spells out a condition under which it can be necessary or objective. When he talks about *"this* principle" (my emphasis), he therefore talks about the Categorical Imperative (not the Formula of Humanity) of which he spells out the ground (cf. Schönecker/Wood 2003, 145 note 70).

This concludes my first claim. The passage leading up to the Formula of Humanity is about the question whether the Categorical Imperative is a necessary law for all. However, by itself the first claim does not show that Kant does not ground the Categorical Imperative in any prior and independent end. To the contrary, the passage seems to assert that there must be an end underlying the Categorical Imperative. I shall therefore turn to my second claim, that Kant uses 'end in itself' as the ground of the imperative in a descriptive sense. An end in itself is not by itself a normative entity.

Kant's Usage of 'End in Itself'

In order to conclude my first claim I had left the discussion of the passage leading up to the Formula of Humanity on page 427, right after Kant turns to the concept of a will. I shall now return to the passage that begins: "The will is thought as a capacity to determine itself to acting in conformity with the *representation of certain laws.*" (*GMS* 4:427) In specifying the concept of a rational will, Kant treats of ends. Ends, he says, serve to determine the will. If those ends follow from reason (like the ends that are also duties: one's own perfection and the happiness of others) they are objective and the same for every rational being. Ends that one adopts because of an inclination could not ground the Categorical Imperative; for these ends are relative to one's faculty of desire, and therefore cannot ground a *universal* moral law: "Hence all these relative ends are only the ground of hypothetical imperatives." (*GMS* 4:428) These claims have been basic tenets throughout the *Groundwork*. They do not introduce a new justification of morality.

The crucial passage comes in the next paragraph. Kant sets up a parallel: Relative ends ground hypothetical imperative, while an end in itself grounds the Categorical Imperative:

> But suppose there were something the *existence of which in itself* has an absolute worth, something which as *an end in itself* could be a ground of determinate laws; then in it, and in it alone, would lie the ground of a possible categorical imperative, that is, of a practical law. (*GMS* 4:428)

This parallel, however, does not mean that an end in itself is similar to a relative end or functions in quite the same way. To understand in which sense an end is the ground of the Categorical Imperative, one has to clarify Kant's usage of 'end in itself'. What does Kant mean by an 'end in itself' [*Zweck-an-sich*]?

The next paragraph (*GMS* 4:428) contains a few hints, but does not fully specify what the expression is meant to signify. Kant starts out by asserting that human beings exist as an end (in contrast to being merely a means), and that human beings should be regarded as an end:

> Now I say that the human being and in general every rational being *exists* as an end in itself, *not merely as a means* to be used by this or that will at its discretion; instead he must [...] always be regarded *at the same time as an end* (*GMS* 4:428).

So the expression 'end in itself' is often used in normative statements: A human being (as an end in himself) "must [...] always be regarded *at the same time as an end*" or "may not be used merely as a means" (*GMS* 4:428). However, as such these specifications merely state how one should treat something that is an end in itself; they state normative requirements connected with ends in themselves. But they do not clarify in virtue of which feature something is an end in itself, and why one should treat ends in themselves this way: What is the descriptive component of 'end in itself'? And what is the justification for the normative requirements?

Adding that an end in itself has "an absolute worth" (*GMS* 4:428) does not clarify anything. For, as I have argued in Chapter 1, 'absolute worth' is merely a shorthand for the prescription of what one should value independently of one's inclinations. Nothing Kant says here contradicts that account. Therefore, to say that an end in itself has absolute worth is merely to reformulate the normative requirements associated with 'end in itself' – that is, that one should value human beings independently of whether one wants to. (I shall look more closely at Kant's usage of 'worth' in this passage below.) The key to understanding the descriptive aspect of 'end in itself' must be found elsewhere.

In order to find the descriptive component of the concept of 'end in itself' one has to go beyond the *Groundwork*. Kant gives a clear description of it in the lectures *Naturrecht Feyerabend* (*NF* 27:1319–22), which he gave at the same time as he published the *Groundwork*. The same view can be traced through his published writings, if only less clearly. I shall first look at the Feyerabend lectures, and then turn to the published writings for confirmation. In short: The lectures suggest that Kant uses the expression 'end in itself' to describe one aspect of free will. In virtue of freedom human beings are not a mere plaything of nature, or the means to the end of another (e. g., nature's ends). Rather it is only in virtue of freedom that one is not merely a means to another's end, but in oneself an end. What is important to note is that this claim by itself does not justify any moral claim or any normative connotation of 'end in itself'. It says only that in being free, one is not causally determined by an outside ground. This is merely a descriptive sense of 'freedom' and the descriptive sense of 'end in itself'.

In the lectures Kant says: "A thing in nature is a means to another; that goes on and on" (*NF* 27:1321.18). "The human being is an end in himself, and never mere means; that is against his nature." (*NF* 27:1321.36 f.) "If only rational beings can be an end in themselves, they can be such an end not because they have reason, but because they have freedom. Reason is a mere means." (*NF* 27:1321.41–3) "Freedom, only freedom alone, makes it that we are an end in ourselves." (*NF* 27:1322.12) "Here we have a capacity to act according to our own will." (*NF* 27:1322.12 f.) "If our reason were set up according to natural laws, my will would not be my own, but rather the will of nature." (*NF* 27:1322.13–5) "If the actions of the human being lie in the mechanism of nature, the ground of them would not be in himself but rather outside him." (*NF* 27:1322.15–17)

What Kant refers to in using the expression 'end in itself' is that human beings are not fully determined by causal laws. In virtue of freedom human beings are not merely a link in the chain of natural causes. They are not merely means to the ends of external causes, but in themselves an end. 'End in itself' is a technical term that gets its meaning from its contrast to 'mere means'. This is also the case in the *Groundwork* passage where Kant says that a "rational being *exists* [...] *not merely as a means*" (4:428). However, what is important is that this concept by itself does not yet provide a justification for the normative component. It is in the first instance merely descriptive. It aims to describe a metaphysical fact, that human beings are not causally determined by external forces. By itself, to say that human beings are ends in themselves, is to say that human being are free. (Kant will later – in the Third Section of the *Groundwork* – argue that freedom comes with the moral law, and I will suggest that the justification for the normative component of 'end in itself' has to be sought there.) The same conclusion – albeit more indirectly – can be reached if one looks at Kant's usage of 'end in itself' in his published writings.

Throughout his published writings Kant uses the phrase 'end in itself' only 26 times.[79] Where he does specify the meaning of it, he equates it with "final end" (see *TP* 8:279 note; *KU* 5:429). What he means by speaking about a final end depends on the context. In an Aristotelian sense he calls happiness the final end of one's (pre-moral) strivings (cf. *RGV* 6:6 note). He talks about the highest good as the final moral end (*TP* 8:279 note); and he talks about freedom as the final end of nature (*KU* 5:448 f.). In the *Groundwork*, where Kant says that an end in itself is the ground of morality, the first two candidates for 'final end' cannot be what Kant means. Kant repeatedly says that happiness cannot be the ground of morality, and the highest good *follows* from morality (cf. *TP* 8:279). There is then only one specification of 'end in itself' in Kant's published writings that could be the sense in which he talks about 'end in itself' in the *Groundwork*. But what is a final end of nature?

Kant talks about 'final end of nature' in the *Critique of the Powers of Judgment*. There Kant argues at length that, in order to unify one's cog-

---

79 In his published writings he uses the exact phrase only 22 times: see *GMS* 4:428–431, 433–435, 438; *KpV* 5:87, 110, 131; *TL* 6:345, 423, 435; and *RGV* 6:13. Four times he uses the plural (*GMS* 4:433, 462; *KpV* 5:87; *KU* 5:429). In addition, he talks three times about something being "in itself an end [*an sich selbst Zweck*]": *GMS* 4:391, 4:428; and *TP* 8:289.

nitions about the natural world, one is justified in regarding the world as if it has a final end (cf. *KU* 5:425–434). While one does not have certainty of the truth of the proposition, reason necessarily conceives of nature this way. It is a regulative, not a constitutive principle (cf. *KU* 5:396, 403 f.). The final end of nature is rational beings, i.e., beings that have free will, in virtue of which they are "under the moral law" (*KU* 5:448 f., cf. 436). To be under the moral law does not mean that one follows the moral law or actually is morally good. It merely means that one is addressed by the law, and accordingly could follow it. One has the capacity to be moral. The descriptive element in virtue of which human beings are final ends of nature or ends in themselves is freedom and the capacity for morality (cf. *KU* 5:448 note).

The way to trace what Kant means by 'end in itself' in his published works is more indirect than the clear passages from the lecture *Naturrecht Feyerabend*; however, his published usages of the term confirm the same result. Kant uses 'end in itself' to express that human beings are not completely determined by external causes, but are free. The support from Kant's other writings does not mean that the understanding of 'end in itself' as freedom is not in the *Groundwork*. It can be discovered if one follows Kant's link from the footnote on page 4:429, but there is also a direct explanation, for instance, in the following passage:

> his own nature as an end in itself [...] – as free with respect to all laws of nature, obeying only those which he himself gives and in accordance with which his maxims can belong to a giving of universal law (*GMS* 4:435).

The *Groundwork* also makes the claim that someone is an end in himself in virtue of freedom and the capacity for morality.[80] This establishes my second claim, that for Kant 'end in itself' is in the first instance not a normative expression. With this in mind, I shall now interpret the paragraph in which the Formula of Humanity first appears.

The Passage on the Formula of Humanity

So far I have argued that Kant's question in the passage leading up to the Formula of Humanity (*GMS* 4:427–9) is whether the Categorical Imperative is a necessary law for all. Kant had said that such a law must

---

80 Similarly Schönecker/Wood 2003, 144 f.; Guyer 2007, 104–6; and Engstrom 2009, 169.

spring a priori from the concept of a will (cf. *GMS* 4:426), and he therefore analyzed the concept of a will in regard to ends. He then set up a
parallel: Subjective ends ground hypothetical imperative, an end in itself
grounds the Categorical Imperative. I have also argued that Kant uses
'end in itself' as an expression for freedom. If one puts these views together, the paragraph that first states the Formula of Humanity appears in a
new light. The paragraph begins:

> If, then, there is to be [...] a categorical imperative, it must be one such that,
> from the representation of what is necessarily an end for everyone because it
> is an *end in itself*, it constitutes an *objective* principle of the will and thus can
> serve as a universal practical law. The ground of this principle is: *rational na-*
> *ture exists as an end in itself.* (*GMS* 4:428 f.)

As I have already pointed out, Kant begins the passage by talking about
the Categorical Imperative. He repeats his claim that the imperative must
be connected a priori or necessarily with the concept of a rational will (its
necessary end). The end that is the ground of the imperative is said to be
necessary for everyone, because it is an end in itself. Kant is still interested
in the question whether the Categorical Imperative is an objective principle for all, and he grounds the imperative in an end in itself. When
Kant says "[t]he ground of this principle is", he is talking about the Categorical Imperative. When he says *"rational nature exists as an end in it-*
self", I have argued that this is to be read as saying: 'rational nature is
free'[81]. Therefore freedom is the ground of the Categorical Imperative.
(In the next Section I shall try to present how this works without invoking a prior value.)

Kant is not giving a new justification for the Formula of Humanity in
this passage, rather he foreshadows the justification he will give in the
Third Section of the *Groundwork*. Kant makes one and the same
claim, when he (in the paragraph that first states the Formula of Humanity) says that an end in itself is the ground of the Categorical Imperative,
and when he (in the Third Section of the *Groundwork*) says that freedom
is that ground. Human beings are free (ends in themselves), or at least
everyone has to represent himself thus; and since freedom is the ground
of the Categorical Imperative, the imperative is a necessary law for all,
i.e., an objective principle. Kant himself refers to the Third Section in
making his claims. If one reads 'end in itself' as freedom, one can also
make sense of the difficult passage that follows:

---

81 For Kant's usage of 'rational nature' see Timmermann 2006, 71 f.

> The human being necessarily represents his own existence in this way; so far it is thus a *subjective* principle of human actions. But every other rational being also represents his existence in this way consequent on just the same rational ground that also holds for me;* thus it is at the same time an *objective* principle from which, as a supreme practical ground, it must be possible to derive all laws of the will. (*GMS* 4:428 f.)

If it is taken as an argument that one has to regard other human beings as valuable, this passage seems unpersuasive (cf. Chapter 2). From the fact that I have to regard myself as valuable it does not follow that I have to regard others as valuable too. However, the passage makes sense and becomes consistent with Kant's other passages if one reads it under the premises I have outlined above: Everyone has to regard *himself* as free or an end in itself. As freedom is the ground of the Categorical Imperative, the imperative is therefore a subjective principle, valid for oneself. In virtue of being free I am under the Categorical Imperative. But everyone else also has to regard himself as free. In the footnote Kant explicitly refers to the Third Section of the *Groundwork* for a justification of this claim. There he argues that everyone has to regard himself and others as being free in virtue of having reason (cf. *GMS* 4:447 f.). This means that everyone else also has to regard himself as being free and as being under the Categorical Imperative. The imperative is therefore not just a subjective law, valid only for oneself. "It", that is the Categorical Imperative (cf. again Schönecker/Wood 2003, 145 f. note 70), is also an objective principle, valid for everyone else. This answers the original question Kant had asked at 4:426, whether the Categorical Imperative is a necessary law for all. The imperative is a necessary law for all rational beings, because it springs from a rational will in virtue of freedom which all share.

Accordingly, Kant's claim in the context of the Formula of Humanity, that an end in itself is the ground of the Categorical Imperative, merely anticipates the conclusions he reaches elsewhere about the justification of the imperative. However, this means that the derivation of the Formula of Humanity is not explained at 4:427–429. Kant states:

> The practical imperative will therefore be the following: *So act that you use humanity, whether in your own person or in the person of any other, always at the same time as an end, never merely as a means.* (*GMS* 4:429)

In this translation "therefore" gives the impression that the previous sentences are like premises to the Formula of Humanity as its conclusion. However, this is misleading. Kant uses the German *"also"*. There is a discrepancy between the German of Kant's time and contemporary usage of '*also*'. Kant's '*also*' is equivalent to a current '*so*': so[82]. The transition to the Formula of Humanity should read: "So the practical imperative will be the following". This clarification is important because the Formula of Humanity is not a strict consequence of what has come before. Kant has not yet explained why the Formula of Humanity is a moral requirement.

Kant still has to explain why one should respect others. To put it differently: So far, I have argued that the expression 'end in itself' has a descriptive and a normative component. The descriptive component is freedom; the normative component is that one should treat free beings never merely as a means, but always at the same time as ends in themselves (i. e., as being free). Kant's text has not yet stated a justification for the normative connotation of 'end in itself'. Freedom is the *metaphysical* ground of the Categorical Imperative, the "*ratio essendi*" (*KpV* 5:4 note). Without freedom there would be no Categorical Imperative, but by itself this does not yet justify why one should respect others. The reason for that requirement has not yet been spelled out. So far I have only argued for the negative claims that it is not a distinct metaphysical value property human beings possess (in Chapter 1), nor a value internal to one's will (in Chapter 2). So how does Kant derive the Formula of Humanity, and why does he raise the question whether the Categorical Imperative is a necessary law for all?

The Derivation of the Formula of Humanity

At *Groundwork* 4:427–429 Kant does not spell out the justification for the requirement to respect others. However, he states it clearly in the summary of the Formula of Humanity he gives a few pages later in the *Groundwork* (cf. 4:437 f.). Kant says that the requirement not to treat others as mere means is already contained in the main formulation of the Categorical Imperative (cf. *GMS* 4:421.7 f.). The Formula of Humanity is "at bottom the same" (4:437) as the Formula of Universal Law. That is, the requirement to respect others is "tantamount" to the requirement to universalize one's maxims. The reason Kant gives is this:

> to say that in the use of means to any end I am to limit my maxim to the condition of its universal validity as a law for every subject [Formula of Universal Law] is tantamount to saying that the subject of ends, that is, the ra-

---

82 I thank Jens Timmermann for pointing that out to me.

tional being itself, must be made the basis of all maxims of actions, never merely as a means but as the supreme limiting condition in the use of all means, that is, always at the same time as an end [Formula of Humanity]. (*GMS* 4:438)

In other words, the requirement to universalize one's maxim for every subject contains also the requirement to respect those over whom one universalizes.

Kant states this point more explicitly in the *Critique of Practical Reason*. In the chapter on the incentives of pure practical reason (*KpV* 5:71–89) Kant explains how the Formula of Humanity is contained in the Categorical Imperative in the following way: The main formulation of the Categorical Imperative requires that one can universalize one's maxim. This means that one should not act on maxims that could not also be adopted by others or spring from the will of others. However, this also means that in not acting on the improper maxim one already respects others as equals and as limiting conditions for one's maxims:

> every will […] is restricted to the condition of agreement with the *autonomy* of the rational being, that is to say, such a being is not to be subjected to any purpose that is not possible in accordance with a law that could arise from the will of the affected subject himself; hence this subject is to be used never merely as a means but as at the same time an end.[83]

One would treat others as mere means if one acted on a maxim that could not be adopted by them. The requirement to respect others is already contained in the main formulation of the Categorical Imperative, which is "the principle of equality" (*TL* 6:451.15).

This is not to say that there is no difference between the main formula of the Categorical Imperative and the Formula of Humanity. Kant famously says that the different formulas "are at bottom only so many formulae of the same law" but that "[t]here is nevertheless a difference among them" (*GMS* 4:436). So far I have focused on the respect in which both principles are the same; a way to make sense of the difference among them, given what I have just said about the equivalence, is the following: The principal moral requirement is that one's maxim could be (willed as) a universal law: *"act only in accordance with that maxim through which you can at the same time will that it become a universal law"* (*GMS* 4:421.7 f.). Kant then gives three main formulas of the basic law:

---

83 *KpV* 5:87.21–7; cf. *GMS* 4:437 f.; and Hill 2000, 101–9.

Formula of Law of Nature [FLN]: "act as if the maxim of your action were to become by your will a **universal law of nature"** (*GMS* 4:421)

Formula of Humanity [FH]: *"So act that you use humanity, whether in your own person or in the person of any other, always at the same time as an end, never merely as a means."* (*GMS* 4:429)

Formula of Autonomy [FA]: *"act only so that the will could regard itself as at the same time giving universal law through its maxim"* (*GMS* 4:434)[84]

The three different formulas (FLN, FH, FA), on my interpretation, are three different ways one can test whether a maxim could be universal, or three different ways one can detect when universality breaks down. FLN uses a contradiction test: If in universalizing a contradiction would occur, the proposed maxim could not be a universal law for all. FH requires that the proposed maxim could be adopted by others as well: If others could not adopt the maxim, it could not be a universal law. FA requires that one's selection of maxims not be distorted by inclinations (cf. *GMS* 4:431 f.): If a law is conditioned by inclinations, it cannot be a universal moral law (see Chapter 1). The respect in which FH is different, therefore, does not destroy the equivalence with the main Categorical Imperative. It merely looks at the same requirement from a different perspective: According to the Categorical Imperative the agent should test whether his maxim can be universalized, which – if looked at from the perspective of the recipient of one's actions (cf. O'Neill 1989, 141–4)[85] – means that one should reject a maxim that could not spring from the will of the person affected. The reason why one should respect others is accordingly still that it is commanded by the Categorical Imperative.

Clarifications

In order to clarify my position further I shall compare it with a self-referential reading of the Formula of Humanity passage.[86] One way of explaining why Kant introduces the formula is that the will might have a self-referential structure: 'the will wills itself'. There are different versions

---

84 I have left out the Formula of Kingdom of Ends. Kant treats it as part of the Formula of Autonomy (cf. Chapter 5). Paton accordingly classifies it as a sub-formula to FA, cf. his 1947, 129.

85 Similarly Engstrom 2009, 172–8; Reath 2012b.

86 I thank Günter Zöller, Heiner Klemme, Houston Smit and Günter Stoltzenberg for pressing me on this point.

of this reading, but the basic idea is that the end of a rational will is the will itself or its own proper exercise. Humanity, here understood as one's own rational will, is then the end for which one acts. This does not mean that every action is selfish, for the proper exercise of a rational will might be to follow its law, the Categorical Imperative as the law of universality. The will wills itself only insofar as it is "self-consciously guided by [...] the formal end of satisfying its own internal norm (the conditions of universality)" (Reath 2012a, 41). However, this formal end might be needed to motivate the agent. In this sense humanity might be said to be the ground of the Categorical Imperative (cf. *GMS* 4:428 f.): "the representation of the end leads to active interest in its actuality" (Reath 2012a, 41 note; cf. 43). This is one version of this line of interpretation.[87]

My interpretation is not necessarily in conflict with this reading. Insofar as the will is said to have the Categorical Imperative as its guiding norm, there is no essential disagreement with my view. I merely read 'end in itself' and Kant's account of willing in a different way. First, I do not read 'end in itself' as 'what is valued for its own sake' (cf. Reath 2012a, 41 note; Engstrom 2009, 74 f.). I think this is an older usage of 'end in itself' to which Kant sometimes refers, but which is not his well-considered usage.[88] Kant seems to employ the older usage when he contrasts his position with that of the ancient Greeks (cf. *GMS* 4:393 f.; *Vigil* 27:482 ff.). However, in the context of the Formula of Humanity I do not read Kant as using 'end in itself' in this way. Rather humanity is represented as an end because it really is not merely a means in the clockwork of nature, but free. Humanity "is necessarily an end for everyone because it is an *end in itself*" (*GMS* 4:428). Humanity's "nature as an end in itself" is being "free with respect to all laws of nature" (*GMS* 4:435). In this sense an end in itself is an *"independently existing* end [*selbständiger Zweck*]" (*GMS* 4:437). It is an end (i.e., free) independently of anyone's willing it. Human beings really are free and ends in themselves, according to Kant. One difference therefore is that I do not read 'end in itself' as 'valued for its own sake', but as 'not merely a means to the will of another'.

A second minor difference between my interpretation and the self-referential reading is that I do not claim that one would need the self-refer-

---

87 Cf. also Prauss 1983, 126–146; Löhrer 1995, 269–298; Engstrom 2009, 167–183; Herman 2010; Flikschuh 2010; Uleman 2010, 111–143; and Porcheddu 2012.

88 I thank Thomas Hill for suggesting this way of putting it.

ential structure in order to be motivated to act morally. When Kant talks about the proper motivation (in *GMS* section 1, and *KpV* 5:71 ff.), he suggests that one could be moved by the Categorical Imperative alone (cf. also *KpV* 5:30), aided by a feeling of respect. I am not denying that one can construe this as the will willing its proper exercise, but phenomenologically this seems to be an extra level of reflection that Kant does not mention in his usual accounts of moral motivation.

However, both of these differences are minor. The self-referential reading does not introduce 'end in itself' as a distinct metaphysical value property, and it is still the Categorical Imperative that justifies moral requirements. So there is no fundamental disagreement. But why then does Kant introduce the Formula of Humanity, according to my interpretation? If his reference to 'ends in themselves' is not needed for moral motivation, but merely a different way of stating the universality requirement, why does Kant introduce the formula? Is it one possible perspective on universality one can take, or is it a necessary perspective to mention? And why is the discussion of the formula tied to the question of whether the Categorical Imperative is a necessary law for all?

The exact reason why Kant used the Formula of Humanity is a matter of speculation. There are several possible explanations in the literature for why Kant introduces the Formula of Humanity. For instance, Klaus Reich has argued that Kant introduces the different formulas of the Categorical Imperative to show that his imperative can account for and give the proper reading of the three principles of Stoic ethics which Kant found in Cicero's *De Officiis* and which were made popular at the time by Garve's translation and commentary.[89] The Formula of Humanity would then be the equivalent of the Stoic principle that human beings deserve respect simply because they are human. However, as Kant does with the Biblical principle to love thy neighbor (cf. *GMS* 4:399), here too Kant interprets the principle as following from his account of morality. The Stoic principle is then incorporated into Kant's account, but at the same time subordinated and reinterpreted in light of Kant's account of morality.

In contrast, Henry Allison has pointed out that there is also a systematic reason for including the Formula of Humanity. According to Allison, Kant uses the different formulas of the Categorical Imperative to spell out the imperative in relation to an analysis of rational agency (cf. Allison

---

89 Cf. Reich 1939, 458 f.; Allison 2011, ch. 2; Duncan 1958, 173 – 8; and Timmermann 2007, xxviif. For a critical note see Wood 2006, 361 – 4.

2012). The Formula of Humanity, accordingly, relates to the fact that rational agency includes acting on ends.

Both interpretations seem right to me. Kant first says that he introduces the different formulas to bring the Categorical Imperative "closer to intuition" by a "certain analogy" (*GMS* 4:436, 437). He then says that the three formulas (FLN, FH, FA) mark a progression of unity, plurality and totality (*GMS* 4:436). There are signs therefore that Kant both wanted to incorporate an idea close to intuition, and he thought that it is part of a comprehensive progression. Kant explains the sense in which the Formula of Humanity brings the Categorical Imperative closer to intuition in that every maxim and every action has an end (cf. *GMS* 4:436; *TL* 6:385), and "in this respect the formula says that a rational being, as an end by its nature and hence as an end in itself, must in every maxim serve as the limiting condition of all merely relative and arbitrary ends" (*GMS* 4:436). The Formula of Humanity expresses what the Categorical Imperative says in relation to ends or using the language of ends. Ends are an important and familiar part of action, and with the Formula of Humanity Kant brings the imperative closer to intuition.

At the same time, using the language of ends is not just a way to bring the Categorical Imperative closer to intuition, but ends are also one aspect of actions, "the plurality of the matter (of objects, i.e., of ends)" (*GMS* 4:436). The Formula of Humanity therefore picks out one aspect of a fuller conception of agency, as Allison has argued.[90] In addition to these two explanations from the Kant literature by Reich and Allison, there is of course Kant's own admission that it was Rousseau who taught him to honor humanity:

> I am an inquirer by inclination. [...] There was a time when I believed this constituted the honor of humanity, and I despised the people, who know nothing. Rousseau set me right about this. [...] I learned to honor humanity [...]. (20:44)[91]

So there are different explanations as to why Kant introduces the Formula of Humanity, although he does not conceive of it as a wholly separate principle from the Categorical Imperative. One can mention reasons why he introduced the formula, but it remains a matter of speculation.

To summarize this Section: On a close reading the passage leading up to the Formula of Humanity (*GMS* 4:427–9) confirms my argument

---

90 Cf. Allison 2011, ch. 9; and his 2012.
91 Remarks on *SE* 20:44; the translation is from Wood 1996, xvii. Cf. Schneewind 1998, 487–92.

from Chapter 1 that Kant does not ground the requirement to respect others on a prior and independent value. Instead, this requirement is already contained in the command of the Categorical Imperative. Kant uses the Formula of Humanity to bring this command closer to intuition.

However, if there is no independent justification of the Formula of Humanity, its justification depends on the validity of the Categorical Imperative. How is the imperative itself justified? To conclude my argument that the requirement to respect others is not based on a value, I shall therefore address Kant's justification of the Categorical Imperative.

Section 2: The Justification for Respect

The Formula of Humanity expresses that what is an end in itself should also be treated as such, or – what amounts to the same thing – that a free being should be treated as being free. This claim has to be argued for. As I noted in Chapter 2, in a Hobbesian war of all against all one can recognize that the other is free, but this is a reason to be especially cautious of him (cf. *NF* 27:1320). The reason Kant gives for this requirement is that it is commanded by the Categorical Imperative. It is a direct command of reason. But how is this command itself justified?

This question is ambiguous. What are we looking for in a justification? What does it mean to justify the Categorical Imperative? For Kant, there are two questions. The first question is whether there is such an imperative (cf. *GMS* 4:425, 431, 445). The second question is whether such a law is binding. This question is not the same as the one of contemporary ethics: "Why be moral?" Rather it is the question why the moral law appears as necessitating to human beings. I shall treat both questions in turn.

First Question: Is There Such an Imperative?

The first justificatory question Kant is concerned with is whether there is a Categorical Imperative: "we have not yet advanced so far as to prove a priori that there really is such an imperative" (*GMS* 4:425; cf. 431; 445). In the Third Section of the *Groundwork* Kant first tries to establish the existence of this imperative. It is important to note again that Kant does not refer to a prior and independent value to establish the existence of the imperative (for the arguments that that cannot be Kant's view see again Chapter 1 above).

Instead Kant conceives of the imperative as the causal law of freedom. Freedom is in the first instance not a normative property for Kant, but a form of causality (see *GMS* 4:446 f.; *KpV* 5:28–30; cf. *Vigil* 27:481). Every form of causality needs a law, and the moral law would describe the actions of a purely free being. The moral law only appears as an imperative to beings that are not completely free (cf. *GMS* 4:414, 449). But the imperative is not derived from a normative fact (e.g., a value), but follows from freedom in a descriptive sense (see Timmermann 2007, 122, 130 f.; and Johnson 2010). Kant had hinted at this form of justification in the passage leading up to the Formula of Humanity. The ground of the Categorical Imperative was said to be the fact that human beings are ends in themselves (i.e., that they are free). In the Third Section of the *Groundwork* Kant now explicitly states this grounding. Just as natural causality works according to laws, so human freedom is governed by a law:

> Since the idea of causality brings with it that of laws in accordance with which, by something that we call cause, something else, namely an effect, must be posited, so freedom, although it is not a property of the will in accordance with natural laws, is not for that reason lawless but must instead be a causality in accordance with immutable laws but of a special kind (*GMS* 4:446).

The law of freedom is the Categorical Imperative: "hence a free will and a will under moral laws are one and the same" (*GMS* 4:447). This view has not changed in the second *Critique:* "Thus freedom and unconditional practical law reciprocally imply each other." (*KpV* 5:29) It seems that Kant merely gives different arguments in the two works for the view that one has to regard oneself as being free, but in both works Kant maintains that freedom yields the moral law, or is the *"ratio essendi"* (*KpV* 5:4 note) of the law.

> Thus the question, how a categorical imperative is possible, can indeed be answered to the extent that one can furnish the sole presupposition on which alone it is possible, namely the idea of freedom, and that one can also see the necessity of this presupposition, which is sufficient for the *practical use* of reason, that is, for the *validity of this imperative* and so also of the moral law; but how this presupposition itself is possible can never be seen by any human reason (*GMS* 4:461).

For Kant, the reality of the moral law is shown under the condition of freedom. My aim here is not to evaluate this claim systematically. It seems fair to ask why every form of causality needs a law, and whether this might only be valid for natural causality. Again the skeptic would have to engage Kant's arguments in the first *Critique*, and work out a very thorough alternative to Kant's views on causality. I shall indicate an additional line of defense for arguing that there really is a Categorical Imperative at the end of Chapter 5 below. For now it is just important to note that for Kant the imperative is a causal law. It describes actions that are governed by the causality of freedom. Kant does not invoke a value in order to explain why the Categorical Imperative is real and a valid command. Rather the moral law is an in-built principle of a reason that has the property of freedom. The moral law is an operating principle of reason, so to speak. Reason automatically functions in accordance with this law. As the principle of non-contradiction guides one's thinking in theoretical matters, the moral law guides one's reason in moral deliberation. One can say that the moral law is constitutive of rational willing (cf. Reath 2006, 4, 176–80). It describes how pure reason operates. However, even if the Categorical Imperative really is a principle that guides our thought, why is it binding in the sense that it is not one principle among others, but is necessitating and a constraint regarding one's inclinations? This is the second justificatory question.

Second Question: Why Is the Imperative Binding?

The first question does not yet explain why the moral law is necessitating or constraining. It is one thing for there to be a moral law, but it is another for it to be an imperative that necessitates the will to act in accordance with it. Kant asks: "But why, then, ought I to subject myself to this principle and do so simply as a rational being, thus also subjecting to it all other beings endowed with reason?" (*GMS* 4:449) The question – I shall argue – is not the same as the prominent question: "Why be moral?" Kant's concern is not why one should follow the moral command over one's inclinations in case of conflict. Rather the question is why the moral law appears to human beings as a command at all. Kant's answer is simple:

> this "ought" is strictly speaking a "will" [*dieses Sollen ist eigentlich ein Wollen*] that holds for every rational being under the condition that reason in him is practical without hindrance; but for beings like us – who are also affected by sensibility, by incentives of a different kind, and in whose case that which reason by itself would do is not always done – that necessity of action is

called only an "ought," and the subjective necessity is distinguished from the objective. (*GMS* 449; cf. 413; 454 f.)

The moral law would describe the actions of a purely rational being. Such a being – who does not have sensibility (e. g., God or angels) – would naturally do and will what the moral law says. The law appears to human beings as an imperative because such beings also have inclinations which often pull them in a different direction from what the law commands. Kant uses this explanation to answer the question how a categorical imperative as an *imperative* is possible (cf. *GMS* 4:453), i. e., how a law can appear as a categorical 'ought'. The imperative appears as binding or constraining because it opposes one's selfish inclinations.

But again, Kant's question is not why one should be moral rather than following one's inclinations. For Kant there is not a neutral standpoint from which one can weigh one's inclinations against the command of duty. Morality is not one demand among others that is felt. Rather for Kant one's standpoint is already colored – so to speak – by the moral ought.[92] The concern is not why one should be moral; even the "most hardened scoundrel" wishes to be moral (*GMS* 4:454). In addition, the moral command is an unconditional one, and should be recognized as such. For Kant the incomprehensible point is why one sometimes does not follow the moral command. This is why Kant refers to immorality as a lack of an ability to follow the command rather than in itself an ability (cf. *RL* 6:227). Kant does address the question "why the *universality of a maxim as a law* and hence morality interests us" (*GMS* 4:460). But Kant argues that this is impossible to explain:

> This much only is certain: it is not *because the law interests* us that it has validity for us (for that is heteronomy and dependence of practical reason upon sensibility, namely upon a feeling lying at its basis, in which case it could never be morally lawgiving); instead the law interests because it is valid for us as human beings, since it arose from our will as intelligence and so from our proper self (*GMS* 4:461).

The law interests us because it is valid. It is valid because it has a genuine source that is not external; an external source could not ground a necessary and universal law (see again Chapter 1). Again, the reason that one should take an interest in the law cannot be that it is a value (as I have argued in that chapter). If it is not a value, then Kant cannot hold a view according to which acting freely (independently of being command-

---

92   Cf. Esser 2004, 183–92; Timmermann 2003, 199.

ed by the Categorical Imperative) is more valuable than acting from desire; and it can also not be that freedom is our end by nature, as in the Stoic view (cf. Guyer 2000, ch. 4). Rather, in realizing that the moral law is genuine (i. e., not conditioned by a subjective inclination), one is interested in it, according to Kant. Is Kant too optimistic on this point? Again my aim is not to defend him systematically. Kant himself does not seem to argue for the claim that even the most hardened scoundrel wishes to be moral (cf. *GMS* 4:454; and *TL* 6:400, 382 note). Without Kant's explanation, one would have to find some independent support for the view that everyone does think along the lines of the Categorical Imperative. I shall point to such a defense at the end of Chapter 5.

In sum: Kant justifies the Categorical Imperative in two steps. He first argues that there really is a moral law, and he then reflects on how it can be binding. Kant does not think that one needs to be persuaded that one should follow the law – even the scoundrel wishes to be moral – but why this is the case one cannot explain further (since this goes beyond experience, cf. *GMS* 4:460 f.). For our purposes what is important to note is that Kant does not ground the moral law in a prior and independent value, and that he does not invoke a value in order to explain why one should follow the Categorical Imperative for its own sake.[93] The moral law is the descriptive law of freedom, and one takes an interest in it in virtue of its being genuine.

For Kant, then, the Categorical Imperative is a direct command of reason. It is an operating principle of a reason that has freedom. As reason tries to overcome contradictions or seeks the unconditioned, so it is under the moral law or Categorical Imperative. The imperative does not have to be grounded in a normative reality (e. g., a value). Rather it is the first normative reality. One can say that ancient Greek philosophy insisted that the good is more fundamental for human beings than the right or the moral law. However, in the Judeo-Christian tradition the law was taken to be the first normative reality (cf. Ricken 1998a, 215 f.). The primacy of laws was maintained in the natural law traditions of, for instance, Grotius and Pufendorf. As J.B. Schneewind has argued convincingly, Kant's emphasis on law can be seen as a reaction to their views (cf. his 1998, chs. 22 and 23). For Kant too the first normative reality is a law. This he has in common with, for instance, divine command theories.

---

93 *Pace* Langton, who seems to hold that in order to explain why one should do something whether one wants to or not, one would need a Moorean value attribute; cf. her 2007, 184.

However, Kant is quick to argue that this law cannot be a law that comes from an external source, e. g., from God, the state or other human beings. For such a command would be heteronomy in the sense described in Chapter 1 above. One would only discover the law and be motivated by it via a feeling of pleasure which would undermine its absolute bindingness. Instead, Kant conceives of the moral law as a direct command of reason.

If the Formula of Humanity shares the same justification as the Categorical Imperative, and if it means to express the same requirement – that one's maxim should be able to be willed as a universal law – this still means that one can use the Formula of Humanity (instead of the stricter method of the Categorical Imperative) to *derive* concrete duties. The application of the Formula of Humanity for deriving concrete duties is my next topic.

Section 3: The Application of the Formula of Humanity

So far I have argued that the Categorical Imperative and the Formula of Humanity share the same justification, and that Kant considers the two principles to be at bottom the same and tantamount to one another. But how is the Formula of Humanity applied to determine what is morally right and wrong? So far I have talked about the justification and derivation of the Formula of Humanity. In the following, I shall turn to the application of the formula. I shall: 1.) examine how Kant conceives of the respect that one owes to every other human being. 2.) I shall then look at how the formula can determine concrete duties. 3.) Finally, I shall discuss who should be respected, according to Kant.

1.) Kant's Conception of Respect Owed to Others

If the Formula of Humanity is tantamount to the Categorical Imperative, then one can use the formula rather than the imperative to derive concrete duties. I am not here interested in the full application of the Formula of Humanity, i. e., in all the duties that can be derived from it.[94] Rather I am merely interested in the question of why one should respect others. Kant describes this as a negative duty, i. e., a duty *not* to treat others in a

---

94   For such a discussion see Timmons/Smit 2012.

certain way (cf. *TL* 6:449 f.). And he says that this requirement is already contained in the Formula of Humanity and its command never to treat others as mere means: "The duty of respect for my neighbor is contained in the maxim not to degrade any other to a mere means to my ends" (*TL* 6:450.5–7). So what exactly is the respect one owes to others, and how does it follow from the Formula of Humanity?

To begin, it is important to realize that for Kant the respect one should have is foremost an attitude one should adopt. In the first instance, the owed respect is not something one does to the other, but rather something that characterizes the agent. But it is not a *feeling* the agent has (e. g., a feeling of admiration or esteem), but rather a *maxim* the agent adopts. The particular maxim is one of not exalting oneself above others:

> **respect** to be shown to others [...] is not to be understood as the mere *feeling* that comes from comparing our own *worth* with another's (such as a child feels merely from habit toward his parents, a pupil toward his teacher, or any subordinate toward his superior). It is rather to be understood as the *maxim* of limiting our self-esteem by the dignity of humanity in another person, and so as respect in a practical sense (*TL* 6:449.23–30).

So Kant conceives of the respect owed to others as a maxim one should adopt to limit one's self-esteem by the dignity of others. I shall look at Kant's understanding of dignity in the next two chapters. However, Kant immediately clarifies what he means: "a duty of free respect toward others is, strictly speaking only a negative one (of not exalting oneself above others)" (*TL* 6:449.31 f.). The requirement to respect others consists in adopting the maxim of not exalting oneself above other people, of not thinking that one is something better (cf. *Vigil* 27:610).

The respect owed to others is therefore different from a feeling of esteem one might have for the achievements or rank of another, but it is also different from the moral feeling of respect that can motivate everyone to follow the moral law. To have a feeling cannot be commanded (cf. *TL* 6:399, 402 f.), but the respect one owes others is commanded. So Kant seems to use 'respect' in at least three different ways: 1) the esteem one might have for the other's appearance or non-moral achievements (*TL* 6:449), 2) the moral feeling of respect for the Categorical Imperative (*KpV* 5:71–89), and 3) a commanded maxim of not exalting oneself above others (*TL* 6:449). This means that the morally required respect one should have for others is different from both of what Stephen Darwall has called 'appraisal' and 'recognition respect' (cf. Darwall 2008, 179). Appraisal respect is the first kind I have listed, a feeling of esteem that responds to merit. Recognition respect recognizes an existing authority, e.g., the authority of the moral law (or of a value or authority in others). However, the commanded respect one should have for others is different from both forms of respect. It is not the appraisal of any merit. All human beings should be respected independently of their merit, moral or otherwise (cf. *TL* 4:463). But it is also not recognition respect. The morally required respect is not a recognition of a value or authority in others (cf. Chapter 1). Rather it is a direct command of reason, implied in the demand of the Categorical Imperative (see Section 1 above).

It is worth elucidating further Kant's conception of the respect owed to others. First, there is one aspect of the common notion of 'treating someone with respect' that seems different from Kant's notion. Consider Derek Parfit's example of the highway robber.[95] The highway robber takes the money from his victim, but he might otherwise treat him with respect: He greets the victim, holds open the car door for him after the robbery, and wishes him all the best as they depart. One could say that according to one aspect of the common notion the highway robber treats his victim with respect. Nonetheless one would say that the robber does the wrong thing (taking the money from his victim). This aspect of the common notion of respect does not seem to refer primarily to the moral rightness of actions towards others. But it is not what Kant is concerned about in the first instance. His question would be whether the act of robbing would use the other as mere means.

Second, as paradoxical as it sounds, the duty to respect others is for Kant in the first instance a duty to oneself. This means that initially one can determine in isolation (without knowledge of the actual wishes of others) whether one does respect others. Respecting others is a maxim one adopts. Empirical knowledge (including the actual reaction and wishes of others) comes in later in determining whether one really has the right maxim and how one should implement it in action. To explain: Kant's question concerning respect is whether one adopts a maxim of exalting oneself above others. This adoption is prohibited by one's own reason, and can be tested in isolation. In this sense Kant's ethics is not second-personal – he does not ground the requirement in the recognition of another's authority to demand respect, despite the advantages of such an approach (see Darwall 2009). Rather for Kant every duty towards others is subordinate to a duty to oneself to follow the Categorical Imperative. If another makes a claim on oneself, one still has to be bound by this claim, which in Kant's view can only be in virtue of the moral law:

---

95 Used by Parfit in a class at Harvard University.

I can recognize that I am under obligation to others only insofar as I at the same time put myself under obligation, since the law by virtue of which I regard myself as being under obligation proceeds in every case from my own practical reason; and in being constrained by my own reason, I am also the one constraining myself. (*TL* 6:417.25–418.1).[96]

Making a claim on an agent does not by itself generate an obligation for the agent. For Kant the bindingess arises through the qualification of the claim as a universal law, as commanded by the Categorical Imperative: "since our self-love cannot be separated from our need to be [...] helped in case of need [...], we therefore make ourselves an end for others; and the only way this maxim can be binding is through its qualification as a universal law" (*TL* 6:393; cf. *Vigil* 27:580). Accordingly, another can claim what is owed to him by reminding the agent of *his duty*, expressed in the imperative. For Kant, duties are prior to rights:

But why is the doctrine of morals usually called [...] a doctrine of *duties* and not also a doctrine of *rights* [...]? – The reason is that we know our own freedom (from which all moral laws, and so all rights as well as duties proceed) only through the *moral imperative*, which is a proposition commanding duty, from which the capacity for putting others under obligation, that is, the concept of right, can afterwards be explicated. (*RL* 6:239)

Someone can claim a right in reminding the other that he has a duty to follow the Categorical Imperative. Kant confirms this view at other places throughout his writings. For instance, he says in the *Doctrine of Virtue* that "to revere the law [...] is a human being's universal and unconditional duty toward others, which each of them can require as the respect originally owed to others" (*TL* 6:467 f.). The other can require that I follow the moral law. Kant repeats this point also in the *Lectures on Ethics:* "he who puts me under obligation does so by virtue of the law of freedom", which is the "ground of his right" (*Vigil* 27:580).

In Kant's view obligations arise from the first-person standpoint, not the second- or third-person (e.g., claims about distinct value properties). Everyone is under the Categorical Imperative in virtue of the freedom of one's reason. Even a hermit or a person who lives in complete isolation from everyone else (e.g., Robinson Crusoe on an island) would be under the Categorical Imperative and the Formula of Humanity. (I shall consider the plausibility of this claim at the end of Chapter 5.) Even a hermit could test whether he has the maxim of exalting himself

---

96 On this point see Schönecker 2010; Denis 2010b; and Timmermann 2012.

above other rational beings *were he to encounter any.* At this point the actual wishes of others do not yet enter the moral question.

This does not mean that empirical knowledge and the knowledge of others' wishes is wholly irrelevant. Respect towards others can differ depending on their condition and wishes: "The different forms of respect to be shown to others in accordance with differences in their qualities or contingent relations [...] cannot be set forth in detail [...] in the *metaphysical* first principles of a doctrine of virtue." (*TL* 6:468, cf. 468 f.) Depending on the circumstances, refusing or offering a particular help to others could be exalting oneself above them. However, these considerations only come in later, for the application of the general maxim of respect to concrete situations; they are not Kant's concern in the *Doctrine of Virtue.*

In sum: When Kant says that one should respect others, he means by it that one should adopt a maxim of not exalting oneself above others. One should not think of oneself as something better than others (in a moral sense). But this also means that in the first instance one can determine whether one is acting in accord with duty without considering the specifics of each case – one does not have to look at what the other is like or what his wishes and demands are. One merely has to check whether one thinks of oneself as something better than others. Only later does the question arise whether there might be circumstances or different cultural settings in which the same action would be interpreted as exalting oneself. But this is different from really having that maxim – which is Kant's concern. (I shall look at the question what exactly one should do in respecting others under a separate heading below.) But how does the requirement to respect others follow from the Formula of Humanity, and does the formula yield the same duties as the Categorical Imperative?

Respect and the Categorical Imperative

So far I have tried to determine what Kant means by 'respect'. Before I discuss in the next section which concrete duties are connected with respect, I shall pause for a moment to clarify how Kant's notion of respect – the requirement not to exalt oneself above others – can be said to be commanded by the Categorical Imperative. I had argued that Kant conceives of the Formula of Humanity as already being implied in the imperative, and at bottom the same as the imperative (cf. Section 1 above). In which sense is the requirement to respect others tantamount to the Categorical Imperative?

What I have said already should make less surprising the claim that the imperative and the requirement of respect are the same and get at the same thing. I argue for a strong equivalence between the two (cf. also Engstrom 2009, 167–183; Reath 2012b). I have argued that both share the same justification (cf. Section 1 above), and now I shall argue that they are not only extensionally equivalent (i.e., they would determine the same actions as wrong), but that they are also intensionally equivalent: They express one and the same requirement, merely in different ways. First, one can test for oneself in isolation whether one's maxim can be universalized – as the Categorical Imperative demands – and whether one has a maxim of exalting oneself above others – as the requirement to respect others demands. In both cases the initial test does not involve the actual maxims and demands of others. But I shall also argue, second, that both requirements get at the same thing. In requiring that one's maxim can be universalized the imperative demands that a law can be adopted by everyone. This, I shall argue, is also what the demand not to exalt oneself aims at.

Kant explains the Categorical Imperative as follows:

> If we now attend to ourselves in any transgression of duty, we find that we do not really will that our maxim should become a universal law, since that is impossible for us, but that the opposite of our maxim should instead remain a universal law, only we take the liberty of making an *exception* to it for ourselves (or just for this once) to the advantage of our inclination. (*GMS* 4:424.15–20)

The central idea behind the Categorical Imperative in its main formulation is that one should not make an exception for oneself (or in the case of duties towards self: not this once). The central idea behind duties of respect as described in the *Doctrine of Virtue* is that one should not exalt oneself above others: "a duty of free respect toward others is, strictly speaking only a negative one (of not exalting oneself above others)" (*TL* 6:449.31 f.). One can see why Kant does not have to think that the Categorical Imperative and the requirement to respect others differ essentially. If one makes an exception for oneself, one thereby exalts oneself over others who do have to follow the law. And if one thinks of oneself as being above others, one considers oneself to be an exception, and is likely to act accordingly. The Categorical Imperative and the requirement to respect others can therefore be seen as one command put in different ways.[97] They can be conceived of as two ways of expressing the same command. A maxim is not universal if one aims to be an exception, or if one tries to exalt oneself with it.

Kant's requirement to respect others – like the Formula of Humanity – can therefore be read as being tantamount to and at bottom the same as the Categorical Imperative, as Kant claims. But which concrete duties follow from the requirement to respect others? This is my next question.

2.) The Requirement Not To Exalt Oneself Above Others

The *Doctrine of Virtue* is the work in which Kant gives the most elaborate treatment of duties of respect (cf. *TL* 6:462–8), and therefore I shall focus on that work here. Duties of respect emphasize a negative aspect of one's duty. They are limiting conditions, admonishing one to keep to certain limits with regard to others. Everyone owes these duties to everyone else without putting the other person under a further obligation (of gratitude etc.). They are analogous to duties of right as presented in Kant's *Doctrine of Right*, "not to encroach upon what belongs to anyone" (*TL* 6:449.33; cf. 6:448–450).

Since the *Doctrine of Virtue* passage is the main place where Kant discusses negative duties towards others, one would expect a substantive and thorough account of those duties. This makes it more puzzling which particular vices Kant discusses, and how little room he devotes to duties from respect. Among negative duties towards others one would expect the prohibition of much serious offences (such as murder, rape, deception). One would also expect a longer discussion, maybe even divided into duties towards others as natural beings (e. g., the prohibition of murder, mutilation, intoxication), and as moral beings (e. g., the prohibition of deception, the use of others as mere means, and contempt for others) – corresponding to the division Kant gives for negative duties towards self (cf. *TL* 6:421–37; cf. *Vigil* 27:595). Instead, Kant specifies the vices that violate duties of respect for other human beings as: a) arrogance [*Hochmut*], b) defamation [*Afterreden*], and c) ridicule [*Verhöhnung*] (cf. *TL*

---

97 This is why in the second *Critique* Kant can use the main formulation of the imperative to rule out self-conceit (as an inflated self-esteem or *Eigendünkel*), cf. *KpV* 5:73 f.; Darwall 2008, 184–7.

6:464 f.). Why does Kant merely put forth arrogance, defamation, and ridicule as vices of disrespect? Why not others?

Arrogance, Defamation, and Ridicule: Why Not Others?

In order to answer the question why Kant puts forth these particular three vices, one first has to see why he does not propose other more obvious duties (e. g., the prohibition of murder etc.). This can be explained by looking at the particular level to which the imperative is applied at this stage of the *Metaphysics of Morals*. There are at least four different aspects one could evaluate in regard to any given action (cf. Baron, 2002, 401–5).

1.) One could merely test whether the type of action, as observable by an outsider, could be universalized. In this connection Kant says that "Ethics does not give laws for *actions* (*ius* does that), but only for *maxims* of actions" (*TL* 6:388.32 f.; cf. 6:410).

2.) Instead of evaluating the outer behavior, the imperative could evaluate the motivation from which one acts. This is the second half of Kant's famous distinction between the *legality* and *morality* of actions (cf. *KpV* 5:71 f.; *RL* 6:214): "in the case of what is to be morally good it is not enough that it *conform* with the moral law but it must also be done *for the sake of the law*" (*GMS* 4:390.4–6). This is a requirement about the proper motivation for moral actions, "of doing such actions not from inclination but *from duty*" (*GMS* 4:398.19 f.; cf. 432).

3.) However, one might distinguish further aspects of maxims. The imperative can command that one adopt a maxim with a certain end: one's own perfection and the happiness of others. This seems to be different from the requirement of moral motivation: If one adopts the end to help others pursue their happiness, one could do it from different motivations: e. g., for one's reputation, out of love, or simply out of duty.[98]

4.) Duties of respect do not seem to fit into any of the three previous categories. They are not one of the ends that it is a duty to have (cf. *TL* 6:385 f.), nor are they in the first instance a requirement of the right motivation. Duties of respect are similar to duties of right in that they are

---

98 I am side-stepping the question whether helping others for one's own self-interest or simply out of duty are the same end pursued out of different motivations, or two different ends; cf. Baron 2002, 402. I am merely distinguishing different aspects to clarify what exactly duties of respect require.

negative, stricter, and concerned with not encroaching upon others. However, they differ from duties of right in that for the latter only an external lawgiving is possible – one can coerce someone to the outward fulfillment of the duty, but not to the inner free adoption of the maxim of respect. The lawgiving for duties of respect is "an inner one [...], since they are derived from the concept of freedom through the law of non-contradiction" (*Vigil* 27:587; cf. *TL* 6:380). So duties of respect concern the internal determination of one's will to adopt a maxim of respect (cf. *TL* 6:449).

This answers the question why Kant does not talk about particular types of action (e.g., murder, mutilation, deception). The reason is that these are already dealt with in the *Doctrine of Right* (e.g., under civil independence and contract laws). They would be outer violations of one's innate right to freedom (cf. *RL* 6:230), and coercion can be used to prevent violations (*ibid.* 230–2). However, it is important to note that the prohibition of holding maxims of disrespect will rule out any action that would be used to express that inner disrespect. A maxim of contempt would "contain a general determination of the will, having under it several practical rules" (*KpV* 5:19.7 f.). The prohibition of maxims of disrespect rules out any means of implementing these vices, as well as any "outward manifestation" or action on these maxims (*TL* 6:463.6). But even if one can explain why Kant confines himself to *maxims* of disrespect at this point, why does he put forth the particular three of arrogance, defamation and ridicule?

Arrogance, Defamation, and Ridicule: Why these Three?

As far as I can see, this particular classification of three vices of respect is Kant's own. It is not in Baumgarten's *Introduction to Practical First Philosophy* or his *Philosophical Ethics*, the textbooks for Kant's lectures on moral philosophy. Accordingly the classification is not in the Collins notes on Kant's lectures on practical philosophy and Baumgarten (1784–5). Comments on arrogance, defamation, and ridicule are scattered throughout the Vigilantius notes on Kant's lecture on the metaphysics of morals (1793–4), but Kant does not treat duties of respect as a separate category (cf. *Vigil* 27:600, 611, 666, 687, 705, 708 f.). Is there a good reason why Kant should list these particular three?

The reason – I think – is that the maxims of arrogance, defamation and ridicule form a *progression* on the vice of disrespecting others. To disrespect others, I have argued, means to adopt a maxim of exalting oneself above others. The three particular maxims are three ways one can intend to exalt oneself and put others down: Regarding arrogance as "an inclination to be always *on top* [...] we demand that others think little of themselves in comparison with us" (*TL* 6:465.10–3). "By defamation [...] I mean only the immediate inclination, with no particular aim in view, to bring into the open something prejudicial to respect for others." (*TL* 6:466.10–4) "But holding up to ridicule a person's real faults [...], in order to deprive him of the respect he deserves [...] has something of fiendish joy in it; and this make it an even more serious violation of one's duty of respect for other human beings." (*TL* 6:467.10–5)

There is a progression in the forms of contempt the three vices display. Arrogance makes one *regard* others as lower. Defamation reveals an intent to lower the other in *public* or in the open. Ridicule attaches to this a *joy* in the lowering of others. Kant cites three vices and these three vices because they are the possible expressions of the vice of disrespecting others.[99]

Kant lists vices and not corresponding virtues because the duty is only a negative one: "I am not bound to *revere* others [...]. The only reverence to which I am bound by nature is reverence for law as such" (*TL* 6:467.33–468.1). The ultimate reason for respect is the moral law or Categorical Imperative: "to revere the law [...] is a human being's universal and unconditional duty toward others" (*TL* 6:468.1–4). The imperative also explains why Kant regards arrogance, defamation, and ridicule as the vices concerning the respect owed to others.

But who are these others? Whom should one respect? Why does Kant talk merely about humanity and not, for instance, about animals? What does he mean by 'humanity'? These are the questions to which I shall now turn.

3.) Humanity as an End in Itself

I shall now briefly look at Kant's usage of 'humanity' to determine what should be respected or never be treated as mere means. This includes the

---

99 In discussing defamation Kant also cites the indirect bad consequences defamation has. However, the real reason is that it would make "contempt the prevalent cast of mind" (*TL* 6:466), and contempt is ruled out by the imperative.

questions why only humanity (or rational nature) should be respected and not non-rational nature, e. g., non-rational animals.

To clarify Kant's usage of 'humanity', the literature often refers to a distinction which Kant draws in the *Doctrine of Virtue* and the *Religion*. In these later writings Kant famously distinguishes between a human being's animality, humanity, and personality (cf. *TL* 6:434 f.; *RGV* 6:26–8). According to this distinction, animality is the aspect of human beings which they have in common with non-rational living things. Humanity involves reason and the capacity to set ends, but it is a reason that might be merely a slave of the passions in that it is governed by inclinations. Finally, personality is the human being under the moral law. Personality involves a reason that can be practical by itself, i. e., it is not conditioned by inclinations but free (cf. *RGV* 6:28).

However, this does not mean that in the *Groundwork* Kant has in mind the humanity of the later writings, which he characterizes as the "capacity to set oneself an end – any end whatsoever" (*TL* 6:392[100]). For in the *Groundwork* Kant does not yet draw the threefold distinction (cf. Ricken 1989, 236–41), and in the later writings he explicitly says that the capacity to set ends "gives him only an *extrinsic* value for his usefulness" (*TL* 6:434; cf. *KpV* 5:61 f; *NF* 27:1321 f.). But, one also cannot infer that he uses 'humanity' to mean a morally good will, for he says that all human beings should be respected, even the "vicious man as a human being" (*TL* 6:463). Kant's point is not that a vicious man may be morally good after all (for all we know), or that he is good deep down, but that even if he is not morally good, he still should be respected as a human being (cf. also Denis 2010a). I shall argue that in the Formula of Humanity Kant conceives of 'humanity' as freedom. As freedom brings with it the moral law, what should be respected is freedom or the *capacity* to be morally good.[101] In the later writings Kant calls this 'personality', but he also characterizes it with a different distinction throughout his writings, the distinction between *homo phenomenon* and *homo noumenon* (cf. Ricken 1989, 236–241; Denis 2010a).

Kant elaborates this distinction within humanity in his *Lectures on Ethics* which – I shall argue – also appears in the *Doctrine of Right* as well as the *Doctrine of Virtue*, the *Religion* and more importantly in the *Groundwork*. In the *Lectures* Kant distinguishes two forms of humanity.

---

100 Cf. Korsgaard 1996a, 110–4; Wood 1999, 118–120; Wood 2008, 88.
101 Cf. Allison 2011, ch. 8; Guyer 2007, 104–6; Ricken 1989, 236; Schönecker/ Wood 2003 144 f.; Mulholland 1990, 104–110; and Engstrom 2009, 169.

Kant calls the one *"homo phenomenon"* and the other *"homo noumenon"* (*Vigil* 27:593). However, this is not a metaphysical distinction of two separate entities. Rather, the *homo phenomenon* is "man in the state of sensibility", that is a human being as he experiences himself in introspection. In contrast, the *homo noumenon* is not a separate being, but merely man "as an ideal, as he ought to be and can be, merely according to reason" (*Vigil* 27:593). The second form of humanity is the idea one can have of oneself as being morally good. It refers to oneself as following

> the moral law, which in respect of its definition is identical with humanity and the Idea thereof; it is rendered practical, if we conceive thereunder a person adequate to the Idea, or an ideal (*Vigil* 27: 610).

This second concept of humanity does not imply that one actually *is* morally good. It is merely the *idea* of how one could be. This idea is possible because one is under the Categorical Imperative in virtue of freedom. The second conception of humanity therefore refers to one's moral capacity. The lectures make explicit two conceptions of humanity: the human being as he is given in experience, and the *idea* of a human being as following the moral law for its own sake, as free and moral.

Humanity in one's person is therefore what Kant elsewhere calls personality, or the capacity for freedom under the moral law. In the *Lectures* Kant also calls it 'personhood' and equates it with humanity in one's person:

> Personhood, or humanity in my person, is [...] that which distinguishes man in his freedom from all objects under whose jurisdiction he stands in his visible nature. It is thought of, therefore, as a subject that is destined to give moral laws to man, and to determine him: as occupant of the body, to whose jurisdiction the control of all man's powers is subordinated. There is thus lodged in man an unlimited capacity that can be determined to operate in his nature through himself alone, and not through anything else in nature. This is freedom (*Vigil* 27:627; cf. 579).

'Humanity in one's person' is the expression Kant uses in the Formula of Humanity. The *Vigilantius* passage summarizes key elements of Kant's account of humanity. Kant distinguishes man (or the *homo phenomenon*) from the humanity in one's person (the *homo noumenon*). This is one aspect of a human being: freedom.

This understanding of humanity, and the distinction between *homo phenomenon* and *noumenon*, is not confined to the *Lectures*, but can be traced throughout Kant's writings. A clear instance can be found in the introduction to the *Doctrine of Right*:

> In the doctrine of duties a human being can and should be represented in terms of his capacity for freedom, which is wholly supersensible, and so too merely in terms of his *humanity*, his personality independent of physical attributes (*homo noumenon*), as distinguished from the same subject represented as affected by physical attributes, *a human being* (*homo phaenomenon*). (*RL* 6:239)

This passage confirms the interpretation I have offered above. Humanity has two aspects, the *homo noumenon* and *homo phaenomenon*. The *homo noumenon* is the capacity for freedom or one's personality.

Kant also uses this understanding of humanity to explain duties towards self in the *Doctrine of Virtue*. Kant grants that the notion of duties towards self is paradoxical, since it seems to presuppose two persons, one who obligates and one who is obligated. Kant's solution is that the human being is taken in two senses when he is thought to be under a duty to himself:

> When a human being is conscious of a duty to himself, he views himself, as the subject of duty, under two attributes: first as a *sensible being*, that is as a human being (a member of one of the animal species), and secondly as an *intelligible being* [...] this latter aspect of a human being [...] can be cognized only in morally practical relations, where the incomprehensible property of *freedom* is revealed by the influence of reason on the inner lawgiving will. (*TL* 6:418)

Kant calls the second aspect of a human being "his *personality*, that is, [...] a being endowed with *inner freedom* (*homo noumenon*)" (*TL* 6:418). There is one human being that can be viewed under two attributes: as a being affected by inclinations, and as a free being that can be morally good. Similarly, in the *Religion* Kant clearly calls personality "the idea of humanity regarded intellectually" (*RGV* 6:28).

In sum: These passages make clear that Kant has two notions of humanity. One refers to the human being as observable in experience (*homo phenomenon*). The other is the idea of a human being as being morally good. It is a moral ideal that might not be observed in experience, but that is prescribed by reason (*homo noumenon*). Which of the two should one respect, according to the Formula of Humanity?

Respecting Humanity

In the following I shall argue that it is the *homo noumenon* that one should respect in others (and oneself). The phrase that Kant uses in the Formula of Humanity *"humanity, whether in your own person or in the person of another"* (*GMS* 4:429) is the same expression Kant specifies explicitly as the *homo noumenon* (see *TL* 6:423.5; *Vigil* 27:593). To say that one should respect the *homo noumenon* is just another way of saying that one should respect freedom. In virtue of freedom one is under the moral law. But this is not the same as saying that what one should respect in others is a morally good will. The *homo noumenon* is freedom or the *capacity* for morality. In virtue of the *homo noumenon* a human being is *under* the moral law, he does not necessarily follow it (see *KU* 5:448; cf. Ricken 1989, 246 f.). What one should respect in others is therefore their freedom and their *striving* for morality.

Kant states this in the *Doctrine of Virtue* passage that deals with the respect owed to others (cf. *TL* 6:462 f.). As the passage makes frequent use of the term 'dignity', I shall treat it in detail in Chapter 5 below. For now I shall merely focus on the question of what one should respect in others. Kant explains it in the following way:

> But just as he cannot give himself away for any price (this would conflict with his duty of self-esteem), so neither can he act contrary to the equally necessary self-esteem of others, as human beings (*TL* 6:462.26–29).

This passage is not an argument for why one should respect others. By itself it would not be able to breach the gap that exists between oneself and others. If everyone has to esteem himself, it does not follow that one has to esteem others. As I have argued above, the argument is provided by the Categorical Imperative in the Formula of Humanity (see Section 1 above). Rather this passage explains *what* one should respect in others. What one should respect in others is their self-esteem. As one is under a duty to esteem oneself, so everyone else is under this duty also. This self-esteem is said to be necessary. In which sense is self-esteem necessary? Kant explains this in §11, where he discusses the vice of servility or false humility (*TL* 6:434–6).[102]

He says that the vice would be "belittling one's own moral worth merely as a means to acquiring the favor of another" (*TL* 6:435.37–436.2). In contrast, true humility relates to the Categorical Imperative: "True humility follows unavoidably from our sincere and exact comparison of ourselves with the moral law" (*TL* 6:436.5–7). The idea is that everyone is subject to the Categorical Imperative. In following it, one is capable of achieving a good will, and with it a worth that is beyond price

---

102 For a full commentary of that section see Bacin 2012a.

(in the sense specified in Chapter 1 above). As this is the only worth that is of prime importance, one does not have to lower oneself to anyone, but one should "revere the (moral) human being within his own person" (*TL* 6:436.8 f.). Therefore one has a duty of self-esteem, and a duty not to fall into servility or false humility. For "as the subject of a morally practical reason", the human being "can measure himself with every other being of this kind and value himself on a footing of equality with them" (*TL* 6:434.32 f., 435.3–5; cf. *Vigil* 27:609 f.).

I shall connect this thought back to the claim that one should respect the *homo noumenon* with further support from different texts: The reason why one should not adopt a servile spirit is that "every man must have cause to believe that in regard to moral worth he can vie with every other man" (*Vigil* 27:609 f.). One can achieve this worth in respecting the moral law: "simply respect for the law is that incentive which can give actions a moral worth" (*GMS* 4:440). Respecting the law is the same as respecting the idea of oneself as being morally good, i.e., the *homo noumenon*: "Our own will insofar as it would act only under the condition of a possible giving of universal law through its maxims – this will possible for us in idea – is the proper object of respect" (*GMS* 4:440). Kant can explain certain duties with respect to the fact that their opposites violate the Categorical Imperative, i.e., the law of the *noumenon*: "suicide violates the law of the noumenon, and respect for the latter" (*Vigil* 27:594). The requirement that one should strive for a good will and the Categorical Imperative for its own sake can now, without introducing a new justification, be expressed as saying that one should not "dispose of a human being in my own person" (*GMS* 4:429). Take the following passage:

> A man cannot dispose over his own substance, for he would then himself be master over his personality, his *inner freedom*, or humanity in his own person. These, however, do not belong to him; he belongs to them, and as phenomenon is obligated to the noumenon. (*Vigil* 27:601)

This is not a new justification (in the sense that the *noumenon* has a higher value than the *phenomenon*). Rather a human being owes respect (and feels respect) for the *noumenon*. This – as I have argued – merely refers to one's freedom and its moral law. One has a duty of self-esteem towards the moral law. So, if one should respect others – as is required by the Formula of Humanity – then one should respect their freedom in virtue of which they have a duty of self-esteem (as expressed by freedom's moral law):

But just as he cannot give himself away for any price (this would conflict with his duty of self-esteem), so neither can he act contrary to the equally necessary self-esteem of others, as human beings (*TL* 6:462.26–29).

In sum: What one should respect in others is their freedom. As freedom entails the moral law, one should respect others who are under the moral law and capable of morality. The reason why one should respect the freedom of others – I have argued (cf. Chapter 1) – is not because freedom is a normative property, e.g., a prior value. Rather it is the Categorical Imperative that demands that one's maxim can be a universal law. A maxim could not be universal if others could not adopt it. Why could others not adopt the agent's maxim of murder, torture or deception? For Kant, the idea is not just that one is not inclined to be murdered or tortured, but that the other also has a duty to preserve his life, health and self-esteem. It is therefore the Categorical Imperative that specifies that one should respect the other's duty of self-esteem, and thereby the other's moral capacities.

However, this view raises new questions: Why does the imperative not demand respect for non-rational beings (e.g., non-rational animals[103])? If, as I have argued, the imperative does not rest on a value of rational natures, is the requirement to respect other rational beings arbitrary? Is Kant a speciesist?

Respect for Animals

In the *Groundwork* Kant is as brief about the status of non-rational beings as he is elsewhere.[104] Kant says: "Beings the existence of which rests not on our will but on nature, if they are beings without reason, still have only a relative worth, as means, and are therefore called *things*" (*GMS* 4:428). The idea seems to be that non-rational beings do not possess freedom, and are therefore mere playthings of nature (cf. *KU* 5:426). But why does this lack of freedom give things the *normative* status of means? Why do human beings not have a direct duty to respect them?

The key point in answering these questions seems to me to be a matter of burden of proof (cf. O'Neill 1998, 222 f.). Kant rejects the view

---

103 Kant is not concerned with hard human cases, e.g., young infants or elderly demented. Since one cannot experience freedom, even in one's own case, one cannot rule it out in others, cf. *RL* §28.

104 Cf., e.g., *TL* 6:442–444; *Collins* 27:458–460; *Reflection* 7305, 19:307.

that there is a value property 'out there' (in heaven or earth) on which one can then base the requirement to respect either humans or non-rational beings: "we see philosophy put in fact in a precarious position, which is to be firm even though there is nothing in heaven or on earth from which it depends or on which it is based." (*GMS* 4:425; cf. *Vigil* 27:545) If there is no value property that could justify the requirement to respect non-rational things, then the burden of proof is on the defender of such requirements. Kant does not arbitrarily give human beings a status that he should also attribute to non-rational beings; rather, the only requirement that he can find is that one should universalize one's maxims and thereby respect others, which as such only extends to beings which are able to act on maxims. Kant then uses this requirement to extend respect as far as he can to non-rational beings. One has an indirect duty to respect animals because cruelty to them would jeopardize the maxims needed for being morally good (cf. *TL* 6:442–444). The question is what effect cruel behavior has on the agent himself, rather than whether one respects an existing value property.

As a result Kant's protection of animals is quite strong. One simply should not behave cruelly toward them.[105] Nonetheless, one might think that animals are still not protected properly, because one does not owe the duty *to* the animals. Instead one owes it to oneself, so to speak, not to torture animals. While animals are not to be tortured, according to Kant, one might still think that Kant's view does not protect them properly: for their own sakes. But this is not a charge that is particular to Kant's views on animals. Even duties towards other human beings rest on a duty to oneself, not on a *factum* (e. g., a value) the other possesses: "the existence of man is not by itself a *factum* that produces any obligation" (*Vigil* 27:545). Rather the duty to respect others rests on the Categorical Imperative. Since it is the imperative that commands respect for others, one first has to be constrained to follow the law springing from one's own reason:

> For I can recognize that I am under obligation to others only insofar as I at the same time put myself under obligation, since the law by virtue of which I regard myself as being under obligation proceeds in every case from my own practical reason; and in being constrained by my own reason, I am also the one constraining myself. (*TL* 6:417.25–418.1)

---

105 In this respect Kant's views seem to be stronger than a utilitarian could guarantee. For a utilitarian the suffering of an animal could in principle be outweighed, e. g., if a group of people would get a lot of pleasure out of torturing one animal.

Here too the Categorical Imperative is the only requirement Kant can find. The burden of proof would be on someone who claims that a duty towards others is generated from a feature the other has (e.g., a value property). However, even if one could establish such a value, this would still only be heteronomy for Kant (cf. Chapter 1), and could not ground a necessary moral law.

Another implication of Kant's views is that the question whether some of the higher mammals (e.g., chimpanzees, elephants, dolphins) do have freedom and reason does not change much as to how one should treat them for Kant. In any case, one should not be cruel to them or let them suffer. But it is nothing about the other in virtue of which one should respect them. Kant asks in the abstract whether one's maxim could be adopted by all free beings or whether one aims to exalt oneself above them. This can be determined in a thought experiment independently of who exactly these others are.[106]

Section 4: The Emptiness Objection

The interpretation of the requirement to respect others I have offered has been described as a thin reading of the Formula of Humanity (cf. Hill 2000, 146–151). It is contrasted with a thicker reading that assumes that the formula rests on a substantive value claim that would violate Kant's own views about value as sketched in Chapter 1 above.

The thin reading I have offered has many advantages. For instance, it can account for the fact that Kant never refers to value when he wants to justify moral requirements. It also avoids attributing to Kant an implausibly inconsistent view in that he puts a value at the basis of a moral requirement, while he explicitly argues that there cannot be such a basis for these requirements. My reading can furthermore explain the paradox that only a good will is said to have absolute value, while at the same time all human beings should be respected, whether they have a good will or not. Last but not least my reading can also explain the paradox that Kant in the *Groundwork* says that all human beings are ends in themselves (*GMS*

---

106 One could object that if higher mammals turn out to have freedom, one could have duties towards them one would otherwise not have (e.g., not lie to them). However, for this and related duties (e.g., to uphold contracts) one would also need to be able to communicate with them. As long as one cannot do it, one's concrete duties towards higher mammals do not seem to change.

4:428) *and* that morality is the condition of being an end in itself (*GMS* 4:435). The paradoxical claims – how can even immoral human beings be ends in themselves while morality is the condition for being such an end? – can be explained if one keeps in mind how Kant uses 'end in itself'. I have argued that 'end in itself' in its descriptive component refers to freedom. But there are two stages of freedom. All human beings have the *capacity* for freedom. As such they are not just a means to an end or a link in the chain of events. They are in this sense ends in themselves and should be treated as such (as commanded by the Categorical Imperative). However, there is a second stage. One could fail to use one's freedom and let oneself be pushed around by natural forces. Only if one acts morally does one realize one's freedom (in that one determines oneself in accordance with one's own law independently of the forces of nature). So only in being morally good does one fully become free and an end in itself in Kant's second sense. Morality is then a condition for someone's actually being an end in himself in the full sense (but this realized sense is not a condition for being treated as an end in itself). The thin reading can therefore make Kant's texts coherent. This alone should be a major advantage of this reading.

The main reservation against a thin reading is an old worry that the Categorical Imperative by itself is empty and cannot yield concrete duties.[107] If – as I have argued – the Formula of Humanity repeats the same demand as the Categorical Imperative (only in a different way), then is the formula not equally an empty formalism? Can the thin formula deliver the content that one wants for a moral theory? In the following I shall not visit the old debate whether one can reliably and correctly derive concrete duties from the Categorical Imperative.[108] Instead I shall briefly discuss whether one can determine any duties from the thin reading of the Formula of Humanity. I shall also confine myself to the requirement to respect others, i.e., negative duties towards others.

Against the emptiness charge I want to point out three things: The first thing to note is that a thick reading of the Formula of Humanity is not in a better position to determine any concrete duties. If one claims that the requirement to respect human beings is based on a substantive value they possess, this does not by itself make it any easier to determine

---

107 This echoes Hegel's charge that the imperative is empty and unable to derive specific duties; cf. Hegel, 1820, §135. On this objection cf. Stern 2012.
108 For a defense see O'Neill 1989, ch. 5; Höffe 1992, ch. 3.

when one respects this value.[109] Many opposing duties could with equal
plausibility be derived from a value of human beings. For instance, in
case of conflict should one not hurt the feelings of the other or is it
more important to tell the naked truth? Does one's value imply that
one can decide for oneself when to end one's life, for instance, or does
it imply that it is to be preserved regardless of all wishes? A thick reading
therefore does not necessarily provide a clearer guide as to what one
should do more concretely. In addition, it is not clear why such a value
would not lead into a form of consequentialism. It seems to be contrary
to Kant's view that one could sacrifice one human being for the sake of
saving more (esp. if one were to use the one as a mere means). However, it
is not clear how this would follow from a view that all human beings have
a substantive value. In that case one might be justified to sacrifice one and
required to maximize such a value.[110] A thick reading of the Formula of
Humanity is therefore not more specific when it comes to deriving concrete duties than a thin reading. The difference between the two readings
is mainly a matter of the justification of the Formula of Humanity.

Second, it seems that the emptiness charge misrepresents Kant's aim
and intention for the application of the moral law. It is a common assumption that the Categorical Imperative should yield duties a) by itself,
and b) give a full moral theory. Take, for instance, the following summary:

> Reason [...] lays down principles which are universal, categorical and inter-
> nally consistent. Hence a rational morality will lay down principles which
> both can and ought to be held by all men, independent of the circumstances
> and conditions, and which could consistently be obeyed by every rational
> agent on every occasion.[111]

On this view reason can generate laws by itself that might be quite specific. Kant's derivation of duties has often been discussed as a rival for
utilitarianism, and an implicit assumption is that Kant's imperative
should be able to lay down exactly what to do in each situation. I believe
there is good reason to deny this assumption.

Kant can readily admit that *by itself* the moral law is empty and without content. As such the moral law merely gives the form of obligation,
not any particular duty. It says what obligation or moral normativity is
(its essence so to speak), not which particular maxim one is obliged to

---

109 See Christiano 2008; Timmons 2012; Parfit 2011, 233–5; Mohr 2007, 22–5.
110 Cf. Hill 1992, 48–50; and Cummiskey 1996.
111 MacIntyre 1981, 43. For a discussion of this passage see Timmermann 2000, 45.

hold (cf. *RL* 6:225; *Vigil* 27:578). This purely formal principle "needs anthropology for its *application* to human beings" (*GMS* 4:412). This means that there are not any specific duties derived from the moral law by itself; rather the moral law is applied to an existing matter, and merely tests whether this matter is permissible (cf. Oberer 2006; Seel 2009, 75).

This comes out in the examples Kant gives about how to apply the Categorical Imperative in the *Groundwork* (4:421–3). The examples always have the same structure: Someone has an inclination to do something, and is about to adopt a maxim to act accordingly. However, "he still has conscience enough to ask himself: is it not forbidden or contrary to duty [...]?" (*GMS* 4:422). Whether the maxim passes the test or not, the resulting action or inaction has its matter from the original maxim. The matter comes from the initial projects and ultimately from inclinations that have been adopted as ends and maxims. In the *Doctrine of Virtue* Kant's position seems to have changed when he claims that one's own perfection and the happiness of others are ends that follow from the imperative (*TL* 6:382). This seems to suggest that the imperative by itself can yield duties. However, on a second look these two ends involve anthropological knowledge. They would not be commanded if human beings were self-sufficient and already perfect at birth. These two ends are therefore not contained in the imperative as such, but are grounded in anthropological knowledge "in accordance with moral principles" (*TL* 6:382). The textual evidence therefore speaks against the claim that the Categorical Imperative is meant to yield specific duties by itself.

And even the duties Kant does derive in his moral philosophy using anthropological knowledge have to stay quite general, and are very few in number. Kant's aim is not to give a full moral theory, laying down once and for all generations what exactly should and should not be done (similarly Esser 2004, 389 f.). Even in the *Doctrine of Virtue*, in which he presents the fullest account of ethical duties in his published writings, the list he gives is quite minimal (of not undermining one's freedom, but perfecting oneself, of not thinking of others as worthless, but helping them in their pursuit of happiness). Kant's aim is to give a very general framework in which a more particular moral system would have to be worked out according to the specifics of the situation:

> The different forms of respect to be shown to others in accordance with differences in their qualities or contingent relations – differences of age, sex, birth, strength or weakness, or even rank and dignity, which depend in part on arbitrary arrangements – cannot be set forth in detail and classified

in the *metaphysical* first principles of a doctrine of virtue, since this has to do only with its pure rational principles. (*TL* 6:468.6–13)

Even in the *Doctrine of Virtue* Kant deliberately stays at a very general level. Moral metaphysics is a system of a priori insights (cf. *RL* 6:216). There are only a few general guidelines that the concept of a finite rational agent who is subject to inclinations can yield a priori. This does not mean that one cannot determine what is right or wrong. But one needs a particular maxim to be tested. The general requirement regarding respect for others is merely that one does not exalt oneself above others, "not to demand that another throw himself away in order to slave for my end" (*TL* 6:450). This requirement has to be applied to a particular maxim in order to generate a restriction. Therefore neither the Categorical Imperative nor the Formula of Humanity is meant to yield duties by itself, but merely to test existing maxims that one is prompted to adopt by inclinations.[112]

Third, if one accepts the thin reading of the Formula of Humanity, it does not mean that one has to derive duties using the non-contradiction-test of the Categorical Imperative in the Formula of Law of Nature (cf. *GMS* 4:421–4). One can still use the Formula of Humanity if one finds it more accessible (cf. *GMS* 4:436 f.). Again the difference between a thin and a thick reading of the Formula of Humanity does not necessarily affect the question of how to apply it. If one finds this formula more attractive than the Categorical Imperative, one can still use it to determine one's duties, according to Kant.[113]

In sum, a thin reading of the Categorical Imperative does not mean that one has to use the non-contradiction-test to test one's maxims. Furthermore, the thin reading does not seem to be less fruitful than a thick reading would be. For Kant the moral law does not by itself contain any particular duty. It is always applied to a given matter (anthropology and concrete maxims). It therefore does not seem that the emptiness objection that has been leveled against the Categorical Imperative has to damage the thin reading of the Formula of Humanity.

---

112 Similarly Allison 2012; Oberer 2006; Seel 2009, 75.
113 For examples in the literature see Hill 2000, 87–118; his 2003; and Timmons/ Smit 2012.

Conclusion

In this chapter I have argued for a thin reading of the Formula of Humanity. The reason why one should respect others is that it is commanded by the Categorical Imperative, a direct command of reason. In asking whether one's maxim could be a universal law, one also asks whether the maxim could be adopted by all others (and thereby be universal). This, Kant says, is what treating others never merely as a means amounts to. The thin reading has the advantage that it makes Kant's texts coherent. Kant says that the Formula of Humanity is tantamount to and at bottom the same as the Categorical Imperative; and where he says he justifies moral requirements he does not talk about a value of humanity, nor does he do so when he summarizes his own position in various writings. In addition, the thin reading fits better with Kant's overall philosophy. The key role Kant assigns to a priori principles is familiar from the first *Critique*, and the thin reading fits well with Kant's epistemology. Finally, the main passage that is often read as speaking in favor of a thick reading (the passage leading up to the Formula of Humanity in the *Groundwork*) can more adequately be read as supporting the thin reading, as I have argued above.

Many people will want more from a moral theory than the thin reading provides. However, this goes against the spirit of Kant's moral philosophy, as I see it. Kant's morality is all about freedom. It is grounded in freedom, and requires the protection of freedom. One should treat free beings as if they are free. This minimal requirement is an advantage, not a defect. Why should one expect an 18th century Prussian to have the answer for all societies from now on forever more? Instead, his account leaves a lot of freedom for individuals and individual societies to pursue their conception of a good life. Different accounts of the good life are permitted, as long as one's freedom "can coexist with everyone's freedom in accordance with a universal law" (*RL* 6:231.11 f.), and does not violate duties towards self. In a diverse world, where different traditions coexist, Kant's moral framework does not prescribe one uniform way of life, but merely demands respect for humanity in all of its manifestations. I regard this as a strength, rather than a weakness.

Part II
Kant's Conception of Dignity

I began this book with the popular view that dignity is an absolute inner value all human beings possess and a value that grounds the requirement to respect others. In the first part of the book I examined whether Kant has such a conception of value. My conclusion was that Kant employs a different conception of value, and gives a different reason for why one should respect others. Kant argues directly against the view that value could ground moral requirements (Chapter 1), and he grounds the requirement to respect others on a direct command of reason (Chapter 3). My interpretation makes Kant's text coherent, but it leads to the question how does Kant conceive of dignity? If he does not have a conception of value as the ground for respecting others, it is hard to see how he could use 'dignity' in this way. The aim of the second part of this book is to give a positive account of Kant's conception of dignity.

How could Kant conceive of dignity? In accordance with the conception of value outlined in Chapter 1, 'dignity' still could be a name for value as a prescription that follows from the moral law. This would fit with passages where Kant *seems* to define 'dignity' as a value, for instance, when in the *Groundwork* he uses expressions like "inner worth, that is, dignity" (*GMS* 4:435) and "dignity, that is, an unconditional, incomparable worth" (4:436). It could be that 'dignity' is another way of saying what should be valued unconditionally. But it would also fit with passages in which Kant says that human beings have dignity because they should be respected rather than the other way around (cf. *TL* 6:435; 462).[114]

However, I shall argue that Kant's usage of 'dignity' is more complicated than that. The equation of 'dignity' with a morally relevant 'absolute inner value' does not square nicely with Kant's talk about the 'dignity of mathematics' (cf. *KrV* 3:323.09), the 'dignity of a minister' (*ZeF* 8:344.06–08), or 'the dignity of a teacher' (cf. *RGV* 6:162.19).[115] In these instances Kant is not talking about something that should be pursued unconditionally. Rather I shall present evidence that Kant uses a fundamentally Stoic conception of dignity. (I call it 'Stoic' because Cicero was the first who used *'dignitas'* in this sense based on Stoic teachings, and Kant directly refers to the Stoics for his understanding of dignity, cf. *RGV* 6:57 note.) For Kant 'dignity' is then not the name for a value – irrespective of whether one conceives of value as a distinct met-

---

114 For further skeptical points against the view that Kant adheres to the popular view of dignity cf. Klemme 2010; and von der Pfordten 2009.
115 For further skeptical points that 'dignity' is a 'value' cf. Meyer 1989.

aphysical property or with Kant as a prescription to value something. Rather I shall argue that Kant uses 'dignity' to express that something is raised above something else. This explains why he can ascribe dignity to such different objects as mathematics, humanity and morality at the same time. In each case he expresses a similar relation, that one object is elevated or higher on a specific scale: Mathematics is more a priori than other sciences, humanity is special in nature in virtue of possessing freedom and reason, morality is raised above all price in that it is more important (only morality should be valued unconditionally). What all these usages have in common is that they express the relation of being elevated or higher. An expression 'dignity, i.e., an absolute inner value' is therefore not necessarily a definition of 'dignity' as a specific kind of value. In this context it is used to express that something – morality – has an elevated standing, not merely a relative value, but a *higher* absolute inner value (i.e., it alone should be valued unconditionally).

This fundamentally Stoic conception allows one to make sense of all usages of 'dignity' in Kant's published writings. Kant uses the expression 111 times. Of these there are only eight times when 'dignity' appears in conjunction with 'worth' or 'value'. One cannot plausibly substitute 'value' for 'dignity' in all 111 passages,[116] but one can explain the eight value passages in terms of an elevation. The fundamentally Stoic conception also explains why Kant does not talk about dignity at all in key passages of his writings. It is striking that dignity plays no role where Kant addresses the justification of morality, e.g., in the Third Section of the *Groundwork*, in the derivation of the Formula of Humanity (*GMS* 4:427–429), in the second *Critique*, in summaries of his position in the introduction to the *Metaphysics of Morals*, in his essay 'Theory and Practice', nor in his *Lectures on Ethics*. Dignity does not play a role in these passages because by itself it is not a notion that carries any justificatory weight. It expresses the special standing of something, but it depends on the context for an explanation of what is elevated and in which respect. This differs, as in the case of mathematics or humanity.

This does not mean, however, that the concept of dignity is useless or does not play any role whatsoever. In the following I shall first explain the basic Stoic conception of dignity, and give general evidence

---

116 Cf., e.g., *TL* 6:468: "differences of […] rank and dignity"; or *TL* 6:467: "conduct it with dignity and seriousness".

that Kant used this conception (Chapter 4). I shall then look more closely at the passages in which Kant seems to define dignity as a value in the *Groundwork* and *Doctrine of Virtue*, and reflect on the role dignity plays in Kant's ethics (Chapter 5).

Chapter 4: Three Paradigms of Dignity

Introduction

I have argued that Kant does not have a conception of value as an independent property that grounds the requirement to respect others (cf. Chapter 1). On my view, therefore, this cannot be his conception of dignity. But how else could he understand it? What else could dignity be but an inherent value of human beings that commands respect? There is another way of conceiving of dignity that in a way is more deeply engrained in our ordinary language than the dignity of human rights debates. When we talk about a 'dignitary', 'undignified behavior', something's being 'below one's dignity', or 'dying or behaving with dignity' we are using it not as a synonym for a distinct value property. Rather in usages like these 'dignity' refers to a rank and the behavior appropriate to it. In the first instance, 'dignity' refers to the higher standing of its bearer. In the second instance, it refers to the behavior and esteem appropriate to such standing.

This other way of conceiving dignity has many facets, which I shall try to describe later. The most important feature, however, is that dignity refers to a rank or elevated position. It expresses that something is raised above something else. What is raised above and why depends on the context. It can refer to a rank one person occupies over others, but it does not have to be exclusive in this sense. As I shall argue, in the past it has often been used to describe the place of all human beings in the universe. Thinkers like Cicero, Leo the Great, or Pico della Mirandola argued that human beings have a special standing in nature because they have superior capacities: reason and intelligence, or a free will. Dignity is a status, but not necessarily a moral one or one properly expressed in terms of value. The scale on which something is higher can be a moral one, but does not have to be. A dignitary can have a higher standing in society without having more moral authority or being morally good himself.

My aim in this chapter is to clearly distinguish different conceptions of dignity, and illustrate them by using historical examples. In the following I shall first characterize the influential *contemporary* view of human dignity, using UN documents as an illustration (Section 1). I shall then introduce the other paradigm of dignity that has been prominent historically. I shall refer to the views of Cicero, Leo the Great, and Pico della Mirandola as illustrations of this paradigm (Section 2). I shall then spell out the contrast between what I call the *contemporary* and the *traditional* patterns of thought[117] (Section 3). Finally, I shall give some general evidence that Kant knew and adhered to the *traditional* paradigm of dignity (Section 4).

In this chapter the aim is not yet to give a full account of Kant's usage of dignity, but to introduce another way of thinking about dignity, and to indicate that it is important to understand Kant's position. In the next chapter I shall then look at passages in which Kant is often taken to put forth the *contemporary* paradigm of dignity.

Section 1: The *Contemporary* Paradigm of Dignity

I shall start with a fuller description of the conception of dignity that is often thought to be Kant's, but which – I shall argue – he does not hold. In contemporary usage, dignity – when it is thought to be more than a mere ascription or convention – is often conceived of as a description of an inherent value of human beings. Accordingly, the German dictionary *Duden* describes dignity [*Würde*] as a "worth inherent in human beings that commands respect."[118] Human dignity is understood to be a concept with strong moral implications; in particular, it is often said that one should respect other people because of their dignity.[119] In justifying why one should respect others, the good (here understood as an inherent value of the individual) is seen as prior to the right (the principle that demands respect for others), and the rights of those affected are seen as being prior to the duty of the agent. Accordingly, Josef Seifert expresses the contemporary view as follows:

> When we speak of the dignity of human life, we mean an objective and intrinsic value. We speak of a value and intrinsic goodness greater than, and different from, a modest aesthetic value of an ornament or the intellectual value of a chess player [...], which do not directly impose *moral* imperatives

---

117 Throughout the chapter I shall use 'pattern of thought', 'paradigm' and 'conception' interchangeably.

118 "[*Achtung gebietender Wert, der dem Menschen innewohnt*]" (*Duden* 1997, 821; my translation).

119 Cf. again Wood 1998b, 189; Jones 1971, 130; Paton 1947, 171; Ross 1954, 52–4; Hutchings 1972, 287, 290; Lo 1987, 165; and Löhrer 1995, 124, 34–36.

on us. Instead, when we speak of human dignity, we speak of *morally relevant value*, one which evidently imposes on us a moral call and an obligation to respect it. (Seifert 1997, 97)

That is, human beings possess the objective and inherent value property called 'dignity', and because of this they can make claims on others to be respected. Not many proponents of human dignity reflect on the ontological status of this value. However, scholars who do, such as Seifert, typically consider the value to be a distinct metaphysical property,[120] that is, a property that does not change according to the different circumstances or relations in which a human being finds himself. The distinguishing feature of this property is a moral importance: Each human being has an "intrinsic and objective preciousness". Dignity is said to be a value that is "incommensurably higher" (Seifert 1997, 98) than other values (e.g., things one values for pleasure or use). This view of dignity as an ontologically distinct value property is a stark form of value realism, such as one might find in G.E. Moore and Max Scheler.[121] The way one can detect such a value is often said to be by intuition as direct recognition. For instance, Seifert writes:

> As life, and human life, this value called 'dignity' is an ultimate and irreducible phenomenon which cannot be defined properly speaking but can only be unfolded and brought to evidence. (Seifert 1997, 98)

Seifert's view that the inherent value property cannot be defined is based on his interpretation of G.E. Moore's intuitionism (cf. Seifert 1997, 95). Not every proponent of the contemporary paradigm of dignity holds an intuitionist epistemology, however. For instance, a number of contemporary Kantians provide arguments for an absolute value of human beings (cf. Chapter 2 above). For now it is only important to note the main structure or pattern of thought characteristic of the contemporary conception of dignity. Today dignity is widely conceived of as an inherent

---

120 Cf., e.g., Seifert 1997, 98; Langton 2007; Schönecker 1999, 387–389.

121 Cf. Moore 1903; and Max Scheler 1913/16. Not all forms of value realism postulate an ontologically distinct property. More modest forms of realism might, for instance, hold that value statements have a truth value, or that they refer to something independent of human beings, cf. Gibbard 1999, 142 note 3. For some disadvantages of the Moore-style realism cf. John Mackie 1977, ch. 1. The ontological and epistemic nature of this value might seem 'queer' in comparison with natural objects. In addition, one who holds this view would be powerless to argue against relativism, and – from a Humean perspective – it fails to give an account of how this value could be motivating. For a more recent defense see Shafer-Landau 2003.

value property on the basis of which one can claim respect from others: One is justified in making this claim because of one's intrinsic and objective preciousness. In justifying moral claims, the good (dignity) is prior to a principle stating what is right; and one's claims as entitlements – which are justified by the good – are prior to the duties of the agent.

The character and importance of this contemporary conception of dignity can be illustrated by the usage of 'dignity' in United Nations documents. In UN documents human dignity is currently said to be *the* justification for human rights. However, there is one important limitation to using the UN documents as an example that has to be noted at the beginning. In documents like these key terms are deliberately kept vague, since one can only secure an agreement among so many different parties at the price of a certain ambiguity.[122] If one were to specify the meaning and grounding force of human dignity, it might be at odds with some parties' deeply entrenched opinions and beliefs. In this case the whole project might fail. Accordingly, there is no explicit attempt to clarify or justify human dignity in these documents. However, the language that is used is perfectly in line with the contemporary paradigm, and can to this extent be used as an illustration: The two UN Covenants state that human rights derive from an inherent dignity of the human person, and the UN Charter links dignity and worth.

In 1947, in the wake of the Second World War and only two years after the founding Charter of the United Nations, the decision was made to draft an 'International Bill of Rights'. This Bill was intended to serve as the basis of freedom, justice, and world peace, and it was to consist of three parts: a non-binding declaration of a general nature, a convention of more limited scope, and a document of methods of implementation (see Craven 1995, 16 f., 1). Human dignity plays an important role in all of these UN documents: the founding Charter of 1945, the Universal Declaration of Human Rights of 1948, and the two Covenants on Rights, drafted in 1966.[123] In all of these documents human dignity is central to justifying human rights, or is explicitly said to be the basis for them.

As scholars point out,[124] the role of dignity as *the* basis for human rights is not unambiguous in the 1945 Charter and 1948 Declaration,

---

122 Cf. Glendon 1999, 10; Ibsen 1990, 642; Wetz 1998, 75 f.
123 For further examples see Griffin 2001, 6 note. For a brief overview of human dignity in international law more generally, see Frohwein 2002, 121–135.
124 See Wetz 1998, 51; Glendon 1999, 2.

as 'dignity' and 'rights' are listed in them side by side. However, the view of dignity as the ground of rights is made explicit in the Covenants of 1966.

The Introduction to the founding Charter of the UN (1945) reads:

> We the peoples of the United Nations determined [...] to reaffirm faith in fundamental human rights, in the dignity and worth of the human person, in the equal rights of men and women and of nations large and small [...] and for these aims [...] have resolved to combine our efforts to accomplish these aims.[125]

In this document human rights and dignity are listed together, but neither of them is said to depend on the other; dignity is more closely associated with the "worth of the human person".

Similarly, the first sentence of the Preamble of the UN Universal Declaration of Human Rights (1948) places rights and dignity side by side:

> Whereas recognition of the inherent dignity and of the equal and inalienable rights of all members of the human family is the foundation of freedom, justice and peace in the world [...] now therefore the General Assembly proclaims this Universal Declaration of Human Rights [...].[126]

So, in both the 1945 and 1948 documents, human dignity is presented hand in hand with rights, implying an important connection between them, but dignity is not yet made the explicit basis for rights. However, in the 1948 Declaration dignity is already strengthened in its importance, as it is now named before rights.

It is also noteworthy that the framers of the 1948 Declaration had more confidence in the existence of human dignity.[127] Whereas the parties to the 1945 Charter express their faith in dignity, the members to the Declaration present dignity as an "inherent" fact or property that can be "recognized". As I indicated above, this way of conceiving of dignity suggests that human beings are equipped with dignity as a distinct (value[128]) property, in virtue of which one is justified in demanding one's rights

---

125 (1946) *Charter of the United Nations.* New York: United Nations Publications, p. 2.
126 (1949) *Universal Declaration of Human Rights.* New York: United Nations Publications, 'Preamble'.
127 For an account of the history of the drafting process see Glendon 2001; and Dicke 2002, 111–120.
128 The UN Charter lists dignity and worth together (see above), thereby associating dignity and worth or value.

from others. The Declaration, though, does not give an account of what this "inherent" (value) property is, nor of how one is able to know or "recognize" it.

The two Covenants on rights adopted in 1966, the International Covenant on Civil and Political Rights, and the International Covenant on Economic, Social and Cultural Rights, give human dignity an even more important role: Their preambles explicitly state that dignity is the basis for human rights. Both Covenants begin their preamble with these words (my emphasis):

> The States Parties to the present Covenant,
> *Considering* that, in accordance with the principles proclaimed in the Charter of the United Nations, recognition of the inherent dignity and of the equal and inalienable rights of all members of the human family is the foundation of freedom, justice and peace in the world,
> Recognizing *that these rights derive from the inherent dignity of the human person* [...],
> *Agree* upon the following articles: [...].[129]

Accordingly, in both Covenants human dignity is presented as the main foundation of rights: Rights "derive" from inherent dignity. The Covenants are more important than the 1948 Declaration insofar as the Declaration is a non-binding statement of intent (cf. Craven 1995, 7), while the Covenants put some requirements on their parties – even if they include no sanctions.[130]

---

129 (1967) *International Covenants on Human Rights*. New York: United Nations Office of Public Information, 'Preamble'.

130 Parties of both covenants regularly write reports to the UN about measures of implementation and their progress in these measures, and the relevant committees can then make recommendations. However, it is up to the individual states whether they heed these recommendations. The International Covenant on Civil and Political Rights has two further control mechanisms (see Ibsen 1990, 647–649). Member States of the Covenant can complain about the progress of other members in front of the Human Rights Committee, which can ask for clarification and ultimately seek to mediate between the two states. However, state parties first have to declare in general that they recognize the competence of the Committee (see articles 41 f., 28). In 1989 24 member states out of 87 which had signed the Covenant had also recognized the Human Rights Committee (see Ibsen 1990, 648, 641). Additionally, in signing an Optional Protocol members to the Covenant on Civil and Political Rights can further authorize the Human Rights Committee to accept complaints from individual citizens about their state. The Committee will then give its views on the matter (see article 5 of the Optional Protocol). By 30 June 1995 83 states had signed the Optional Protocol out of 113 parties to the Covenant (see *Encyclopedia of Human Rights*

To sum up, UN documents serve as an illustration of the contemporary paradigm of human dignity and its prominence. Although in these documents 'dignity' is neither defined nor justified, the UN documents associate human dignity with worth and specify dignity as being inherent. In the following section, I shall characterize the traditional paradigm of dignity. In Section 3 I shall then bring out the most important differences between the traditional and the contemporary paradigms of human dignity.

Section 2: The *Traditional* Paradigm of Dignity

There is a historically prominent way of thinking about human dignity that is distinct from the contemporary paradigm. Because of its prominence I shall call it the traditional paradigm of human dignity. It can be argued that this traditional paradigm was dominant throughout most of the history of philosophy, and that the contemporary paradigm virtually did not exist before the twentieth century.[131] While I believe this claim to be true (and to give further credence to the view that Kant did not hold the contemporary view), my aim here is not to present a history of ideas.[132] Rather my aim is to bring out more clearly the structure of a prominent alternative conception of dignity. I shall then illustrate the traditional paradigm in reference to the views on human dignity of Cicero, Leo the Great, and Pico della Mirandola – three prominent thinkers spanning classical antiquity, the Christian middle ages, and the Renaissance. In doing so, the primary aim is not to provide a detailed or novel reading of the thinkers in question, but to bring to light the

---

1996, 1672 f.). The International Covenant on Economic, Social, and Cultural Rights does not have these additional control mechanisms. For detailed information about the Covenant on Economic, Social, and Cultural Rights see Craven 1995. For a thorough analysis of different aspects of the Covenant on Civil and Political Rights see the essay collection edited by Henkin 1981.

131 See Pöschl 1969, 55 f.; Wetz 1998, ch. 3; and Dicke 2002, 111. One exception might be G.W.F. Schiller's *Don Carlos*, Act III, Scene 3 (1787), although he does not characterize dignity as value. Whitman, Appiah and Waldron even argue that the prominence of dignity in contemporary political documents results from what I call the traditional paradigm, cf. Whitman 2003, 243–266; Appiah 2001, 107; and Waldron 2007.

132 Several scholars have attempted to trace the history of the idea of human dignity; cf., e. g., Baker 1947; Dürig 1957; Pöschl 1969; Horstmann 1980; Bayertz 1996; Forschner 1998; Wetz 1998, ch. 2; and Kretzmer/Klein 2002.

broad similarities in their views of human dignity, and to formulate the traditional paradigm more clearly. After contrasting the contemporary and the traditional paradigms in the next section, I shall then argue that Kant was a proponent of the traditional paradigm in the modern age.

To begin with a brief overview: Human dignity, in the traditional conception, is in the first place the answer to the theoretical question of the place of human beings in the universe. According to this paradigm, human beings are distinguished from the rest of nature in virtue of certain capacities they have, particularly reason and freedom. The term 'dignity' is used to express this special position or elevation. Only in a further step does human dignity gain *moral* relevance: Through the introduction of a further moral premise, one is said to have a *duty* to realize fully one's initial dignity. This second stage I shall therefore call 'realized dignity', and the first stage 'initial dignity'. The traditional paradigm then uses a two-fold conception of dignity.[133]

The Origin of the Traditional Paradigm

The traditional paradigm of human dignity is related to a third and older *aristocratic* paradigm of 'dignity'. The aristocratic usage is familiar from common parlance if, for instance, one speaks of a 'dignitary' or a 'baroness who carries herself with dignity'. The aristocratic paradigm of 'dignity' can be seen in the ancient Roman *dignitas*[134], according to which dignity is an elevated position or rank. In ancient Rome *dignitas* was a concept of political life: It expressed the *elevated position* of the ruling class. In the aristocratic usage 'dignity' is not ascribed to all human beings but is a term of distinction; it was an aristocratic conception in that it applied only to a few, for instance to a consul or senator. The elevated position could be gained, lost, or regained. It could be gained through the political office which itself could be gained through merit, birth, or wealth. In virtue of this rank one had certain powers and privileges, but one also had duties to behave appropriately to one's rank.

---

133 However, I do not mean to suggest that all of the thinkers who follow the traditional paradigm of dignity conceived of these as two separate stages.

134 Cf. Wegehaupt 1932; Drexler 1944, 231–255; Pöschl 1969; Gadamer 1988. For a sociological description of Roman society cf. Alföldy 1986. The *archaic* conception has much in common with Aristotle's conception of 'magnanimity' (cf. his *Nicomachean Ethics*, bk IV, 1123b-1125a).

The Roman *dignitas* is a complicated notion that has further connotations than rank, e.g., excellence, worthiness, and esteem. The *Oxford
Latin Dictionary* gives four groups of translations: 1.) worthiness or suit-
ability for a task, 2.) visual impressiveness or the quality of being worthy
(excellence), 3.) rank, office, or a position conferring high rank, 4.) standing, esteem (and its enjoyment), or honour.[135] The Latin conception of
dignitas has many facets. One can have a high rank in society, one can
be worthy of it, one can be excellent at it, and one can be esteemed
for it. To say that a Roman senator has dignity can mean all these things
at the same time. But several elements could also be missing. One can
have the high office without being excellent, worthy, or esteemed. (On
the other hand, one could be elevated in ability, worthiness and esteem,
and not have the office.) In the late Roman Empire there was the *Notitia
dignitatum*, a list ranking the highest offices in the empire (cf. Pöschl
1969, 36). To have dignity in this sense neither presupposes excellence,
nor high esteem. One simply has to have the office, which was given
out by the emperor.

This is the same with our notion of a 'dignitary'. It's a notion that has
many facets. It refers to a certain rank based on titles. The dignitary
might be excellent, worthy and esteemed. But here too these are not necessary. The person is a dignitary as long as he occupies the rank. The additional connotations are not essential to *dignitas* or 'dignitary'. The essential component is that dignity expresses a *relation*, an elevated standing
of something over something else. I shall argue below that this is the same
for Kant. When he uses 'dignity' in the *aristocratic* sense, he explicitly
specifies it as rank (cf., e.g., *RL* 6:328.33; *TL* 6:468.09; *Anth* 7:127.09).

What this paradigm therefore brings out – and this will be crucial for
understanding the contrast between the contemporary and the traditional
patterns of thought – is that one does not have to understand dignity as a
distinct metaphysical value property human beings possess. Rather dignity can merely refer to rank or an elevated position. To say that something
is elevated over something else therefore does not necessarily refer to a
moral order, or an order in value. One can be a dignitary (or have dignity)
without being worthy (morally or otherwise) of the rank. And one can be
elevated in political ability or popular esteem, without being morally bet-

---

135 Number 1.) seems to be the oldest connotation, as *dignitas* is believed to derive
    from *dignum* (worthy). For an etymology of the Latin *dignitas* cf. Wegehaupt
    1932, 5 and Drexler 1944, 233.

ter. The sense in which something is elevated over something else will therefore have to be specified with each usage of 'dignity'.

Cicero and the Traditional Paradigm

The most important illustration of both of the older paradigms of dignity is Cicero. His work is full of examples of the aristocratic usage of the Roman *dignitas*,[136] but he was also the first to use the term *'dignitas'* to express the idea of human beings' elevated place in the universe. He thereby universalized *'dignitas'* to apply to *all* human beings: All human beings have a rank or elevated position in nature. His thought therefore provides a clear and important example of the traditional conception of dignity, as one can see by considering his discussion of the superiority or dignity of human beings over animals in chapter XXX of book I of *De officiis.*[137] In paragraphs 105 to 107 he says that animals are governed only by instinct and their sensual pleasure, while human beings have reason. Because of this superiority it would be unworthy of humans to live a life of pleasure:

> But it is essential to every inquiry about duty that we keep before our eyes how far superior man is by nature to cattle and other beasts: they have no thought except for sensual pleasure and this they are impelled by every instinct to seek; but man's mind is nurtured by study and meditation. (I 105)[138]

Cicero concludes the paragraph by saying that human beings are ashamed if they are caught in living a life of pleasure. He continues:

> From this we see that sensual pleasure is quite unworthy of the dignity of man and that we ought to despise it and cast it from us; [...] And if we will only bear in mind the superiority and dignity [*excellentia et dignitas*] of our nature, we shall realize how wrong it is to abandon ourselves to excess

---

136 The *Oxford Latin Dictionary* illustrates all four usages of *dignitas* with examples from Cicero. Before Cicero there is extant only one usage each in Plautus and Terence, cf. Wegehaupt 1932, 9.

137 Scholars believe that this is the earliest passage in which the Latin term *dignitas* is used to refer to *all* human beings, see Pöschl 1969, 37–41; Wetz 1998, 20; and Cancik 2002, 19–40. While a similar pattern of thought was common in Greek philosophy, there was no direct equivalent for the Latin *dignitas* in the Greek language, cf. Pöschl 1969, 9 f. For a thorough commentary on *De officiis* cf. Dyck 1996.

138 Translated by W. Miller in Cicero 1913.

and to live in luxury and voluptuousness, and how right it is to live in thrift, self-denial, simplicity, and sobriety. (I 106)

From the fact that one would be ashamed if one were caught indulging in pleasure, Cicero argues, one can see that living a life of pleasure is unworthy of the elevated position human beings occupy. One's superiority and elevated position demand a life in which one's lower desires are governed in accordance with reason. According to Cicero, all human beings are endowed with reason:

> We must realize also that we are invested by Nature with two characters, as it were: one of these is universal, arising from the fact of our being all alike endowed with reason and with that superiority which lifts us above the brute. From this all morality and propriety are derived, and upon it depends the rational method of ascertaining our duty. The other character is the one that is assigned to individuals in particular. (I 107)

This is a clear example of the traditional pattern of thought. Human beings are said to be elevated over animals in virtue of having reason. Because one is elevated over animals, one should not behave like animals, but live a life of reason. Cicero's derivation of *duty* from the fact that one possesses reason is implicitly based upon a teleological premise: Nature has given one reason, and one should act according to nature. Therefore, the superiority or elevation of human beings over animals is at first only a factual description: Human beings possess the capacity for reason, while animals do not (cf. I 13). It is only by adding a further premise that this fact yields an obligation (even if Cicero did not introduce them as two separate premises, they are logically distinguishable). It is because nature gave one the end of self-control and restraint that one should act this way: "nature has endowed us with the role of steadfastness, restraint, self-control, and modesty" (I 98).[139] As to the reason why one should behave in accordance with nature, Cicero claims that it would be pointless to go against it:

> It is pointless to go to war with nature and to aim at something which we cannot achieve. This is a truth which lends greater clarity to the nature of the fitting; for nothing is fitting if it flies in the face of Minerva, as the saying goes, in other words if nature confronts and conflicts with it. (I 110)

---

139 Cf. also I 100: "If we take nature as our guide, we shall never go astray"; or I 103: "Nature has not fashioned us to behave as if we have been created for fun and games. Rather, we are moulded for self-discipline and for more sober and important pursuits."

Nature, then, circumscribes the lives open to human beings, and it points them toward the life that is fitting for them. That life is one that accords with the dignity or elevation of human nature: "the fitting is what is consistent with man's excellence in the respect in which his nature differs from all other living creatures." (I 96)

To sum up, Cicero gives a clear example of the traditional paradigm of dignity, according to which human beings are special in nature in virtue of possessing a certain capacity, namely reason. Being elevated, or having dignity, in this way was said to yield a duty to behave in a way that is worthy of this dignity. For Cicero, human beings have this duty because nature endowed them with reason, and it would be pointless to go against nature. The duty to use one's reason appropriately is justified with a teleological premise.

Leo the Great

Among Christian thinkers, an important example of the traditional twofold conception of dignity is found in the sermons of Pope Leo I (or St. Leo the Great, reigned 440–461 A.D). His sermons are thought to contain the earliest known usages of the Latin *dignitas* by a Christian thinker (cf. Pöschl 1969, 48 f.). In one famous passage, he says: "Realize [*agnosce*], o Christian, your dignity. Once made a 'partaker in the divine nature,' do not return to your former baseness by a life unworthy [of that dignity]."[140] This passage is still used today as the opening sentence of the section on moral questions in the Catholic Catechism (cf. *Catechism* 1999, §1691). Leo also expresses the view that one is made a "partaker in the divine nature" by saying that one is created in God's image: "Wake up then, o friend, and acknowledge the dignity of your nature. Recall that you have been made 'according to the image of God.'"[141]

For Leo, then, human beings have dignity, which is to say that they are elevated over the rest of nature in being created in the image of

---

140 *Sermons* 21, ch. 3; from Leo 1996. To the following cf. Pöschl 1969, 42–50; Dürig 1957; and Bruch 1981.

141 *Sermons* 27, ch. 6 (p. 114). Cf. *Sermons* 94, ch. 2 (p. 392): "People should acknowledge their own dignity, and see themselves as 'made in the image and likeness of' their Creator." The idea that human beings are created in the image of God is likely meant to be a reference to the *Bible*; cf. the *Book of Genesis* 1:26, cf. 1:27 f, and *Psalms* 8:5–10.

God.[142] The respect in which human beings are an image of God is that they have a soul, which is what elevates them above animals, and over the body more generally: "let the soul, which properly is constituted as ruler of the body under the direction of God, retain the dignity of its mastery."[143] And this dignity, Leo says, consists in the soul's capacity to govern itself independently of bodily desires by the use of reason – that is, in not being determined by bodily desires:

> If [...] the desires of the body are stronger, the soul will shamefully lose dignity proper to it, and it will be calamitous for it to be a slave to what it ought to govern. But if the mind, submissive to its Ruler and to heavenly gifts, tramples on the lures of earthly indulgence and does not allow "sin to reign in its own body," reason will hold a well-ordered leadership.[144]

So while Leo explicitly conceives of dignity in reference to God, he would agree with Cicero's view that human beings are elevated over the rest of nature in virtue of reason and the capacity to rule bodily desires.[145] Leo goes on to say that one ought to imitate God:

> If we reflect upon the beginning of our creation with faith and wisdom, dearly beloved, we shall come to the realization that human beings have been formed according to the image of God precisely with a view that they might imitate their Designer. Our race has this dignity of nature, so long as the figure of divine goodness continues to be reflected in us as in a kind of mirror.[146]

A human being lives up to the dignity of his nature as long as he remains an image of God.

To sum up, Leo provides another example of the traditional two-fold conception of dignity.[147] According to this conception, to repeat, human beings are distinguished in nature in virtue of having certain capacities

---

142 Some scholars have claimed that this is a general feature of Christian views on dignity; cf. Pöschl 1969, 42; and Bruch 1981, 140.

143 *Sermons* 42, ch. 2 (p. 180).

144 *Sermons* 39, ch. 2 (p. 167 f.).

145 Cf. Pöschl 1969, 44, 46; Bruch 1981, 141. The *Catechism of the Catholic Church* indicates that this is still the view of the Catholic Church today: "By virtue of his soul and his spiritual powers of intellect and will, man is endowed with freedom, an 'outstanding manifestation of the divine image.'" (1999 §1705, cf. §§ 1934, 1730, 306). In addition, Leo holds the view that human beings are an image of God in being able to do justice and be merciful, see *Sermons* 95, ch. 7 (p. 398 f.).

146 *Sermons* 12, ch. 1 (p. 49).

147 Some scholars argue that the two-fold structure is a general feature of Christian thinkers; cf. Bruch 1981, 148 f.; and Glendon 1999, 13 f.

that animals and non-rational nature lack, specifically reason and freedom from the determination of bodily desires. Because human beings
are distinguished in possessing these capacities, it is said that they *should*
make a proper use of them, and thus realize their initial dignity. Leo's
views are similar to Cicero's in this respect, but in Leo's thought a prov-
idential God takes the place of a teleological nature.[148] Leo expresses this
duty by emphasizing that God commands human beings to imitate divine works: "justly does God demand from them the 'imitation of himself,' for he has made them 'in his image and likeness.'"[149]

Pico della Mirandola

Human dignity emerged as a topic of particular prominence among Renaissance thinkers; it even appears in the titles of several famous books
from the period.[150] This prominence is often seen as a reaction to a
work called *De Miseria Humane Conditionis* by Cardinal Lotario dei
Conti (or Segni), later Pope Innocent III, that emphasized the misery
of man.[151]

In the following I shall focus on the most salient of the writers treating dignity in this period, Pico della Mirandola (1463–1494),[152] whose
thought provides another example of the traditional paradigm of dignity.
In his *Discourse on the Dignity of Man* (1486) Pico considers the place of
man within the "universal order" or the "chain of being"[153] that stretches

---

148 However, in *De Legibus* I, 24 Cicero too holds that the soul was created by God,
and that humans have a likeness with God in being virtuous; cf. Pöschl 1969, 42.
A clear difference is that Leo holds that the dignity of humans was forfeited in
Adam's fall and restored in Jesus' death: "This nature, although it had been cor-
rupted in Adam, has nevertheless been re-fashioned in Christ." *Sermons* 27, ch. 6
(p. 114), cf. 25, ch. 5 (p. 102 f), 72, ch. 2 (p. 316). Pöschl 1969, 48 holds that
this view was a general feature among Christian thinkers.

149 *Sermons* 45, ch. 2 (p. 194).

150 Apart from Pico's discourse *De Dignitate Hominis*, cf. also Bartolommeo Fazio
(1450) *De Excellentia et Praestantia Hominis*, and Giannozzo Manetti (1452)
De Dignitate et Excellentia Hominis.

151 Cf., e.g., Murchland 1966, vi. The prominence is probably a reaction to a similar emphasis in the Christian Middle Ages more generally, cf. Machiavelli, *Dis-
courses on Livy*, II 2.9

152 For a brief biography see Kristeller 1964, ch. 4.

153 Cf. *Discourse* §3.6. Pico refers to the place of man *"in universi serie"*. Translations
of Pico are taken from the joint research project by Brown and Bologna Univer-

from God to the lowest animals, and he concludes that the initial dignity
of man consists in having no *fixed* place in that chain. Rather, the dignity
of human beings lies in their capacity to choose their own place on that
chain. At the beginning of his *Discourse* Pico relates a story of creation in
which he has God address Adam as follows:

> Constrained by no limits, you may determine it for yourself, according to
> your own free will, in whose hand we have placed you. [...] It will be in
> your power to degenerate into the lower forms of life, which are brutish;
> you shall have the power, according to your soul's judgement, to be reborn
> into the higher orders, which are divine. (*Discourse* §4.20 & 23)

On Pico's view, human beings are special because they were given freedom and reason: Human beings have the freedom to live like brutes,
but their souls also possess reason, through which they are able to grow
toward the divine. What lifts human beings up above the rest of nature
is that they can choose their fate themselves: Even human beings who live
like animals are – unlike mere animals – free to choose a different course.
In this passage the other elements of the traditional conception of dignity
are briefly touched upon. Being placed in this special position is suggested to yield a duty to oneself to realize fully one's initial dignity. Realizing
that dignity or falling short of it is presented as being equivalent to moving 'upward' or 'downward' in the chain of being:

> The Father infused in man, at birth, every sort of seed and sprouts of every
> kind of life. These seeds will grow and bear their fruit in each man who will
> cultivate them. If he cultivates his vegetable seeds, he will become a plant. If
> he cultivates his sensitive seeds, he will become brutish. If he cultivates his
> rational seeds, he will become a heavenly animal. If he cultivates his intellec-
> tual seeds, he will be an angel and a son of God.[154]

Accordingly, it is through the cultivation of reason and intellect that
human beings realize their dignity. Pico's claim, in short, is that human
beings are *free* to choose their path in life, and that this is what lifts
human beings up above the rest of nature, or gives them a dignity. Yet
this freedom entails the chance to rise high or fall low. That is, human
beings are superior to animals in the *capacities* they possess, though not
necessarily in how they choose to *exercise* those capacities. The reason

---

sities on the *Discourse on the Dignity of Man*, see: http://www.brown.edu/Depart-
ments/Italian_Studies/pico/index.html. For the idea of the chain of being more
generally cf. Lovejoy 1961.

154 *Ibid.* §6.28–30. For similar themes in Leo cf. his *Sermons* 24, ch. 2; 71, ch. 2;
and 73, ch. 4.

why one should choose to live according to one's superior capacities is explained by Pico as follows:

> It is in order for us to understand that, because we were born with the option to be what we want to be, we must take most care of this; lest people say of us that, being held in honor, we did not realize that we reduced ourselves to brutes and mindless beasts of burden. Let us rather remember the saying of Asaph the prophet: "You are all gods and sons of the most high," unless abusing the most indulgent liberality of the Father, we turn from beneficial to harmful the free choice he bestowed on us. Let a holy ambition pervade our soul, so that, not satisfied with mediocre things, we strive for the loftiest and apply ourselves with all our strength to pursue them. (*Discourse* §10.48–50)

That is, striving for the highest is what God intended one to do, what is to one's advantage, and what is the ambitious or excellent thing to do. Pico's talk of "higher" and "lower" can therefore be explained against the background of the chain of being. He does not refer to a value property as it is used in the contemporary paradigm.[155]

To sum up, the conceptions of human dignity found in Cicero, Leo and Pico all share the same basic structure. On the traditional paradigm dignity has two levels. First, all human beings are said to be elevated over the rest of nature in virtue of possessing a capacity for freedom or reason (initial dignity). Second, morality is tied to a duty to realize fully one's initial dignity. In the next section I shall try to bring out more clearly the differences between the traditional and the contemporary paradigms.

Section 3: The Differences Between the Two Conceptions

There are four main respects in which the traditional conception of dignity I have sketched differs from the contemporary one. In the traditional conception: 1.) dignity is not conceived of as a distinct metaphysical value property; 2.) there are two stages of dignity; 3.) dignity by itself

---

155 While the claim that one should strive for a higher level of being can be expressed in terms of 'being better' or 'having more worth', this does not imply a separate value property in the sense of G.E. Moore 1903 or Max Scheler 1913/16. Ontologically, a higher level only has more being, cf. Ricken 1998b. Pöschl traces this view back to Plotinus' *Enneads*, cf. Pöschl 1969, 51.

is not the basis of rights, and 4.) dignity is primarily about duties to *oneself*.[156]

1.) Dignity not a value

In the traditional conception, 'dignity' refers to an elevated position of human beings in the universe, not an inherent value property. 'Dignity' therefore expresses a relative standing of one thing over another (i.e., that human beings are higher), not the possession of an intrinsic feature (even if the elevated status is based on an intrinsic feature like freedom or reason). Also the reference to 'higher' and 'elevated' does not imply a hierarchy of value. It was a common thought throughout much of the history of philosophy that there is a hierarchy in being (cf. Lovejoy 1961). The special standing of human beings within this hierarchy is not based on the possession of a distinct metaphysical value property in a strong moral realist sense. Rather, it is based on the fact that different kinds of beings possess different capacities.[157]

To understand this aspect of the traditional paradigm it is important to keep in mind its origin from the *aristocratic* conception of the Roman *dignitas*. A Roman senator is elevated in society by his merit, rank, wealth or esteem. While in the aristocratic conception one human being has an elevated status over others – without reference to a distinct metaphysical value property – Cicero took the conception of *dignitas* and he *universalized* it, applying it to the status of all human beings within nature – again without invoking a distinct metaphysical value property. In the traditional pattern of thought human beings are elevated over the rest of nature in virtue of having certain capacities like reason and freedom.

2.) Dignity is a two-fold notion

An important second difference is that in the traditional pattern of thought there are two stages of dignity. While in the contemporary paradigm 'dignity' refers to a value human beings possess, and therefore one either has or does not have dignity, in the traditional pattern of thought

---

156 This way of putting the differences is my own. I have, however, been greatly helped by the works in the history of the idea of dignity mentioned earlier, esp. Pöschl 1969.

157 For instance, plants are capable of nutrition and growth; animals possess those capacities and also the capacity for perception and motion, and human beings possess not only these, but also the capacity for reason and choice; cf. Aristotle: *On the Soul* 414a29–415a13; Plotinus: *Enneads* V 2, 1–2; Ricken 1998b, 137–140.

one's initial dignity can be realized but also wasted.[158] On this account everyone has an initial dignity in having certain capacities (e. g., reason, freedom). But only if one makes a proper use of one's capacities does one fully realize one's initial dignity. In the traditional paradigm there are therefore two stages of elevation, which are both referred to with the term 'dignity'.

3.) Dignity does not yield rights

In the traditional conception of dignity, the prime emphasis is on *duties*, not on *rights*. The thought is not that one can make claims on others because one has freedom and reason. Instead, having reason or freedom is said to yield the duty to make a proper use of one's capacities. As I spelled out above, one's duty to behave in a proper way does not immediately follow from having the capacities of reason or freedom. Rather proponents of the traditional paradigm of dignity use a further premise: for instance, a teleological view that one ought to use the specific human capacities with which nature (or God) endowed human beings. (It could also be a separate principle like Kant's Categorical Imperative.) If the traditional paradigm justifies human rights in the sense of entitlements, then they are grounded on the further normative premise, not on dignity itself.

   This is an important contrast to the contemporary paradigm. In the contemporary pattern of thought human rights are based on an inherent (value) property of human beings. One can claim one's rights in pointing to one's absolute value. The traditional paradigm, in contrast, does not rest rights on a distinct metaphysical value property of human beings. In the traditional paradigm it is therefore not dignity as an elevated position that grounds rights, but the further normative premise that is used to derive any duties, e. g., to fully realize one's initial dignity. This point is further supported by the observation that rights in the sense of entitlements do not figure prominently in thinkers who use the traditional paradigm of dignity.[159] One reason might be the perfectionism that is commonly connected with this paradigm.

---

158 For a characterisation of the two-fold aspect of the traditional paradigm cf. again Bruch 1981, 148 f.; and Glendon 1999, 13 f.

159 Richard Tuck has argued that the concept of a right in the sense of entitlement originated in twelfth century property law, and that it had its breakthrough only in the seventeenth century, cf. his 1979, 9, 11; cf. Schneewind 1998, 93; Glendon 1999, 6.

4.) Perfectionism

The fourth main difference in the general structure of the traditional and the contemporary conception of dignity is that, in the traditional pattern of thought, the primary focus is not on the dignity of others, but on the realisation of *one's own* dignity (similarly Pöschl 1969, 55 f.). When Cicero, Leo, and Pico talk about human dignity, they emphasize that the agent should realize his or her own initial dignity. In talking about human dignity, they highlight a privilege or capacity human beings have been given, and their emphasis is on how one should use that capacity. This emphasis stems from an underlying perfectionism. The *main* concern of these three thinkers in questions of moral philosophy is how one should perfect oneself, not how one should treat others.

In short, in the traditional paradigm it is *one's own* realized dignity or perfection that is of prime concern. I shall now argue that Kant endorses all four features of the traditional paradigm when he talks about dignity. My aim is a positive exhibition. Only in the next chapter shall I argue why Kant's conception of dignity is not an instance of the contemporary pattern of thought.

Section 4: Kant and the Traditional Paradigm

Throughout his writings Kant often uses 'dignity' in the aristocratic sense of the term, for instance, when he talks about the dignity of a teacher (*RGV* 6:162.19), of mathematics (*KrV* 3:323.09) or of a minister (*ZeF* 8:344.08). In this final section my aim is to give some general evidence that Kant foremost uses the traditional paradigm when he talks about dignity. My claim that Kant too adheres to the traditional paradigm of dignity will be somewhat controversial. Kant is perhaps the most famous modern philosopher to talk about human dignity. He is often read as adhering to what I have called the contemporary paradigm. Many scholars allege that for Kant dignity is an absolute inner value all human beings possess, and that this value is the reason why one should respect others.[160] Accordingly, people often refer to Kant as an inspiration for what I have called the contemporary conception of dignity.[161] In the following my

---

160 Cf. again Paton 1947, 171, 189; Ross 1954, 52–4; Löhrer 1995, 124, 34–44; Wood 1998b, 189; Wood 1999, 115; and Schönecker/Wood 2003, 142.

161 See, for instance, Gewirth 1982, 28; Seifert 1997, 98; Wood 2008, 94; and Dürig's object formula in German constitutional law.

aim is not to prove that Kant does not hold the contemporary paradigm. I have already argued in Part I of this book that Kant does not have a conception of value that grounds the requirement to respect others (see Chapters 1–3). My aim is merely to point out that Kant's writings display the four key features of the traditional pattern of thought about human dignity. In the next Chapter I shall then analyze closely the passages in the *Groundwork* and *Doctrine of Virtue* to argue that even they are an instance of the traditional paradigm of dignity.

To begin, Kant was familiar with what I have called the traditional conception of dignity and mentions it approvingly:

> These philosophers [Stoics and others] derived their universal moral principle from the dignity of human nature, from its freedom (as an independence from the power of the inclinations), and they could not have laid down a better or nobler principle for foundation. They then drew the moral laws directly from reason, the sole legislator, commanding absolutely through its laws. And so was everything quite correctly apportioned (*RGV* 6:57 note[162]).

Kant, then, both knew and approved of what I have called the traditional paradigm of dignity. But in addition there are passages that indicate that he adhered to each of the four elements of the traditional conception himself: 1) that dignity refers to an elevation rather than a value per se, 2) that his conception of dignity allows for two stages: an initial and a fully realized conception of dignity, 3) that he connects dignity with duties, not in the first instance with rights, and 4) that he uses 'dignity' primarily in reference to duties towards self.

1.) For Kant dignity refers to an elevation, not a value per se
The first respect in which Kant's view of dignity turns out to be more in line with a Stoic conception is in the way he specifies dignity. Throughout writings on different topics and from different periods, Kant conceives of dignity as rank or sublimity (*Erhabenheit*).[163] By this I mean

---

162 For the relation between Kant and the Stoics cf. also Reich 1939; Schneewind 1996; Allison 2011, ch. 2; Timmermann 2007, xxviif.; Wood 2006; and Nussbaum, 1997, 5. Reich argues that Kant's *Groundwork* was (partly) a direct response to Cicero's *De Officiis*.

163 It appears in such different writings as: "The Only Possible Argument in Support of a Demonstration of the Existence of God" (1763); "Attempt to Introduce the Concept of Negative Magnitudes into Philosophy" (1763); "Observations on the Feeling of the Beautiful and Sublime" (1764); *Groundwork of the Metaphysics of Morals* (1785); *Critique of Practical Reason* (1788); *Doctrine of Right* (1797); *Doctrine of Virtue* (1797); *Lectures on Logic* (1800). Cf., e.g., *BDG* 2:117.35,

that Kant often uses 'dignity' to express that something is elevated or up-lifted over something else. In this usage 'X has dignity' is another expres-sion for 'X is elevated over Y' or 'X is higher than Y'. In particular, Kant specifies sublimity as the highest form of elevation (cf. *KU* 5:248[164]), so that to say 'X has dignity' is to say 'X is raised above all else'. What it is raised above, and why, depends on the context in which Kant uses 'dig-nity'. For instance, Kant uses expressions like "dignity of a monarch" (*SF* 7:19.26) to refer to the elevated position a king has in the state; when he talks about the "dignity of humanity"[165] he is expressing the view that human beings are elevated over the rest of nature in virtue of being free. When he talks about dignity in connection with morality[166] he is saying that morality is raised above all else in that morality alone should be valued unconditionally. I shall analyze and illustrate these different usages more fully in the next chapter.

What is important for now is that Kant typically uses 'dignity' to ex-press an elevation of something over something else. Sublimity is not a concept that appears much in the Kant literature (for an exception see Guyer 2000, 167, 169, 171). Sublimity is mostly discussed in the context of the feeling of the sublime as Kant treats it in the essay "Observations on the Feeling of the Beautiful and Sublime" (1764).[167] However, the sublimity at issue here is not a feeling.[168] Kant does not always have a feel-ing in mind when he talks about sublimity [*Erhabenheit*]. Take, for in-stance, the following passage:

> [I]t is now easy to explain how it happens that, although in thinking the con-cept of duty we think of subjection to the law, yet at the same time we there-by represent a certain sublimity and *dignity* in the person who fulfills all his

---

NG 212.01, 215.20, *GSE* 241.18; *GMS* 4:425.28, 440.01; *KpV* 5:71.21; *TL* 6:435.20; *Log* 9:30.12.

164 Kant characterizes sublimity or *Erhabenheit* as that which is absolutely great or great without comparison, cf. *KU* 5:248.05 – 10. Another translation could be exaltedness. When Kant uses the adjective *erhaben* though, as in his work on physical geography, he does not necessarily use it in the absolute sense as being the highest form of elevation, cf. *PG* 9:169.05, 191.14, 342.10.

165 For instance, in: *GMS* 4:439.04, 440.11; *KU* 5:273.13 f.; *RGV* 6:80.18, 183.24; *TL* 6:420.16, 429.16, 436.16, 449.28 f., 459.23, 462.30; *Päd* 9:488.36, 489.01.

166 Cf. *GMS* 4:440.01, 11; *KpV* 5:147.17 f.; *TL* 6:464.18 f., 483.03.

167 For different connotations of Kant's account of 'dignity' as 'sublimity' cf. Santeler 1962, 65 – 70; Shell 2003, 60, 73; and Denis 2000. On Kant's notion of the sub-lime cf. also Clewis 2009.

168 I thank Susan Shell for pressing me on this point.

duties. For there is indeed no sublimity in him insofar as he is *subject* to the moral law, but there certainly is insofar as he is at the same time *lawgiving* with respect to it and only for that reason subordinated to it [...] and the dignity of humanity consists just in this capacity to give universal law, though with the condition of also being itself subject to this very lawgiving (*GMS* 4:439 f.).

In this passage Kant elucidates dignity as sublimity, and contrasts it with subordination. What is elevated is a morally good person and humanity as the capacity to be moral (I shall come back to these two elements under heading 2) below). But here sublimity is not a feeling. It merely expresses that something (e. g., a person who fulfills all his duties) is elevated over something else (namely, a being which is not lawgiving) on a certain scale – specifically, in terms of morality.

Similarly in the *Critique of the Powers of Judgment* sublimity is not just a feeling. At the beginning of his discussion of the mathematical sublime (i. e., the sublime in terms of quantity) Kant defines sublimity as that which is great beyond comparison: "We call *sublime* that which is *absolutely great*." (*KU* 5:248) Kant then elucidates 'absolutely great' as "that *which is great beyond all comparison*" (*ibid.*). Accordingly, sublimity here refers not to a feeling, but to infinity as an idea of the mind (cf. *KU* 5:250). Likewise for the dynamical sublime (i. e., the sublime in terms of quality) the sublime is not merely a feeling. The truly sublime in this sense is the power to overcome nature and sensible impulses: "Thus sublimity is not contained in anything in nature, but only in our mind, insofar as we can become conscious of being superior to nature within us and thus also to nature outside us (insofar as it influences us)" (*KU* 5:264; cf. 260 f.).[169] The fact that true sublimity is only in the mind (as the idea of infinity or the power to overcome sensible impulses) does not mean that it is a feeling. Otherwise expressions like "a feeling which is itself sublime" (*KU* 5:246) would become a tautology and make little sense. Rather Kant uses 'sublimity' to express that something is elevated above something else. Contemplating such a state can then be connected to a feeling of the sublime.

My claim that Kant typically conceives of dignity as elevation is further supported by passages in which Kant directly equates it with rank (cf. *RL* 6:328; *TL* 6:468; *Anth* 7:127). So far I have not argued that Kant does not also sometimes understands dignity as an inherent value property. However, I have already argued that Kant did not put forth and

---

169 On the different forms of the sublime see Clewis 2009; and Höffe 2009.

did not even envision such a conception of value (cf. Chapter 1). In the next chapter I shall look more closely at the passages where Kant uses 'dignity' in conjunction with 'worth'. For now I conclude that Kant – in line with the traditional paradigm – often uses dignity as elevation or sublimity.

2.) Kant's conception of dignity allows for two stages: an initial and a realized one

Kant's usage of 'dignity' also shares the second feature of the traditional paradigm of dignity. There are two stages of elevation open to all human beings. *All* human beings are said to have dignity in virtue of freedom, but only one who uses his freedom in a certain way has the second form of dignity too. The clearest passage is a reflection note from the mid-1770's where Kant refers to both stages side by side: "The dignity of human nature lies only in its freedom [...]. But the dignity of one human being (worthiness) rests on the use of his freedom"[170]. On a first level all human beings are uplifted over the rest of nature in virtue of being free. Kant calls freedom "the innate dignity of a human being" (*TL* 6:420), and he refers to the first stage as "initial dignity" [*ursprüngliche Würde*] (*SF* 7:73). But only if one makes a proper use of one's freedom does one in fact lift oneself over the rest of nature.

The two-fold structure of Kant's conception of dignity can also be found in other writings, and it helps to solve some puzzling features of his remarks on dignity. In his writings Kant sometimes says that the capacity for freedom (or morality) has dignity, and sometimes that it is actually being morally good that has such dignity (cf. *TL* 6:420; *GMS* 4:435). The tension can be seen, for instance, in the passage quoted under heading 1). There Kant spoke in the same paragraph of the "*dignity* in the person who fulfills all his duties" and of "the dignity of humanity", which "consists just in this capacity to give universal law" (*GMS* 4:440). The first phrase refers to someone who is actually morally good, while the second refers to the *capacity* for being morally good. This is no problem if one keeps in mind that Kant has a two-fold conception of dignity. The capacity for morality is one's initial dignity, while actually being morally good is the fully realized form of one's dignity.

The same two-fold structure also helps to make sense of puzzling passages about being an end in itself and having autonomy. Those concepts are related to dignity in that Kant mainly uses them in relation to free-

---

170 *Reflection* 6856, 19:181; my translation; cf. *Päd* 9:488.

dom, they merely highlight different aspects of freedom. In virtue of freedom someone is an end in himself (as I have argued in Chapter 3), is autonomous and has dignity. 'End in itself' expresses that someone is not merely a means to someone else's will; autonomy more positively expresses that someone is self-governed, while in this context dignity expresses that freedom uplifts one over the rest of nature. But the same two-fold structure can be found for all three concepts. For instance Kant famously says that "every rational being *exists* as an end in itself" (*GMS* 4:428), but that "morality is the condition under which alone a rational being can be an end in itself" (*GMS* 4:435). Unless all rational beings are morally good there does seem to be a tension between these two statements. However, the tension disappears if one keeps the two-fold structure in mind. All rational beings have the *capacity* for freedom (i. e., they exist as ends in themselves), however, only if one makes (proper) use of one's freedom is one *actually* an end in oneself (i. e., is really free: 'end in itself' is foremost not a normative term, but merely describes freedom – as I have argued in Chapter 3 above). Similarly autonomy can sometimes refer to the capacity for self-governance (cf. *GMS* 4:446 f.), and sometimes to the actual giving of universal law (cf. *GMS* 4:435 f.).

3.) For Kant dignity is connected to a duty, and by itself it does not generate rights

The third feature Kant's conception of dignity has in common with the traditional paradigm has already been mentioned in other contexts. For Kant dignity is not a feature (e.g., a value) that by itself generates rights. Rather for Kant the rights one can claim follow from a duty of the agent:

> But why is the doctrine of morals usually called (especially by Cicero) a doctrine of *duties* and not also a doctrine of *rights*, even though rights have reference to duties? – The reason is that we know our own freedom (from which all moral laws, and so all rights as well as duties proceed) only through the *moral imperative*, which is a proposition commanding duty, from which the capacity for putting others under obligation, that is, the concept of right, can afterwards be explicated. (*TL* 6:239)

Thus in Kant's view, the concept of claim rights is preceded by the concept of duty. Someone can claim rights by reminding the agent of his or her duty to follow the Categorical Imperative. Accordingly, the '*innate right* of each' is a right to freedom that can coexist with the freedom of everyone else in accordance with a universal law (cf. *TP* 8:292 f.; cf. *RL* 6:230). One's freedom is only restricted by the Categorical Imperative (cf. Seel 2009). If another human being restricts one's freedom unlawfully, one can remind him of his duty to follow the imperative.

Dignity as the elevation of human beings over the rest of nature is grounded in freedom; freedom comes with the moral law. What is moral is described by that law which comprises one's duty. If one follows the law one realizes one's initial dignity in truly elevating oneself over the rest of nature. Dignity is therefore connected to duty and only indirectly to rights. Furthermore, one's duty is primarily a duty to oneself.

4.) Kant uses 'dignity' primarily in reference to duties towards oneself
Finally, Kant's usage of 'dignity' as it relates to all human beings also exhibits the fourth feature of the traditional paradigm – that it is used primarily in the context of duties towards self. Having freedom yields a duty (in the first instance to oneself) to make a proper use of one's freedom. Accordingly, Kant brings up dignity in connection with duties to oneself, as the duty is to realise and preserve one's initial dignity:

> duties towards himself. – These do not consist [...] in seeking to satisfy his cravings and inclinations [...]. But they consist in his being conscious that man possesses a certain dignity, which ennobles him above all other creatures, and that it is his duty so to act as not to violate in his own person this dignity of mankind.[171]

In Kant's view human beings are ennobled or elevated over the rest of nature in virtue of being free (i.e., not necessarily being determined by one's inclinations). This freedom is said to be connected to a duty to use one's freedom in a proper way, especially to realise and preserve one's initial dignity. Any demand as to what one should do is justified with reference to the Categorical Imperative (cf. Part I). What is important to note, however, is that for Kant too one's initial dignity yields a duty, and that this duty is primarily to oneself. As I have stressed before, for Kant, the primary duty is to follow the Categorical Imperative and in this way acquire a good will. Without this duty to oneself there would be no duty to others, as duties towards others are expressed by the Categorical Imperative as well (cf. again *TL* 6:417 f.):

> I can recognize that I am under obligation to others only insofar as I at the same time put myself under obligation, since the law by virtue of which I regard myself under obligation [the Categorical Imperative] proceeds in

---

171 *Päd.* 9:488, tra. by A. Churton in: Kant, *Kant on Education* (London: Kegan Paul, 1899).

every case from my own practical reason; and in being constrained by my own reason, I am also the one constraining myself.[172]

To realize one's initial dignity, to elevate oneself in following the moral law, is therefore in the first instance a duty towards oneself. I have already argued in the last chapter that this is even true for the following passage that seems to make the opposite claim: "The *respect* that I have for others or that another can require from me [...] is therefore recognition of a *dignity* (*dignitas*) in other human beings" (*TL* 6:462). The reference to dignity in this passage indicates *what* should be respected, the striving of the other to fully realize his initial dignity, rather than giving a justification of *why* the other should be respected. This comes out as Kant continues:

> But just as he cannot give himself away for any price (this would conflict with his duty of self-esteem), so neither can he act contrary to the equally necessary self-esteem of others, as human beings, that is, he is under obligation to acknowledge, in a practical way, the dignity of humanity in every other human being. (*TL* 6:462)

The individual has the duty to realize his initial dignity. If one should respect others, one should respect their striving for dignity. Dignity is primarily related to duties towards self.

Kant repeatedly uses 'dignity' in this context of duties towards self to express that a proper moral motive is respect for the higher aspect of one's person (freedom and rationality). Dignity expresses that this aspect is higher, ennobled or more important. Kant does not say that this aspect is more important because of a value property adhering to it, but because it is the seat of the moral law which alone expresses what duty is (cf. *RL* 6:225; *TL* 6:393). This usage of 'dignity' in the context of the proper moral motive already came out in the passage cited from the *Lectures on Pedagogy*. There Kant says that duties towards self "consist in his being conscious that man possesses a certain dignity, which ennobles him above all other creatures, and that it is his duty so to act as not to violate in his own person this dignity of mankind" (*Päd* 9:488). However, this is also a recurrent thought in other writings. For instance, Kant calls the morally commanded or "real self-esteem (pride in the dignity of humanity in one's own person)" (*TL* 6:459). And he says that "unless the dignity of virtue is exalted above everything else in one's actions, the concept of duty itself vanishes and dissolves [...], since a human being's consciousness of his own nobility then disappears" (*TL* 6:483). This is in

---

172 See again Schönecker 2010; Denis 2010b; Timmermann 2012.

line with Kant's claim that one's "insignificance as a *human animal* may not infringe upon his consciousness of his dignity as a *rational being*, and he should not disavow the moral self-esteem of such a being"; instead one should pursue one's end by "not disavowing his dignity, but always with consciousness of his sublime moral predisposition" (*TL* 6:435). Kant sums it up in the following passage:

> True humility follows unavoidably from our sincere and exact comparison of ourselves with the moral law [...]. But [...] from the (natural) human being's feeling himself compelled to revere the (moral) human being within his own person, at the same time there comes *exaltation* of the highest self-esteem, the feeling of his inner worth (*valor*), in terms of which he [...] possesses an inalienable dignity (*dignitas interna*), which instills in him respect for himself (*reverentia*). (*TL* 6:436)

The proper moral motive is respect for the moral law or the idea of a moral human being. Dignity expresses the idea that this aspect is higher or to be preferred (since the moral law says so, and strikes down any self-conceit opposing it; cf. *KpV* 5:73). Accordingly, Kant says that "the pure moral motive [...] teaches the human being to feel his own dignity [...] and the greatness of soul to which he sees that he is called" (*KpV* 5:152). Kant sometimes expresses the thought without using the term 'dignity', but using 'sublimity' instead:

> This is how the genuine moral incentive of pure practical reason is constituted; it is nothing other than the pure moral law itself insofar as it lets us discover the sublimity of our own supersensible existence and subjectively effects respect for their higher vocation in human beings (*KpV* 5:88).

Although Kant does not use the term 'dignity' in this passage, the thought is the same. The moral motivation can also be expressed as respect for the sublimity of the moral aspect within, i.e., the moral law. I shall argue in the next chapter that this is also the thought Kant wants to express in the *Groundwork* passage on dignity. There Kant says that a morally good being universalizes its maxim "from the idea of the *dignity* of a rational being, who obeys no law other than that which he himself at the same time gives" (*GMS* 4:434).

In sum: In accordance with the traditional paradigm of dignity, Kant uses 'dignity' predominantly in the context of duties towards oneself. Respect for the dignity of the moral law is the proper moral motive (cf. also *RGV* 6:183; *SF* 7:58). As respect is connected to the duty to oneself to follow the moral law, dignity appears foremost in connection with duties towards self.

Concluding Remarks

The aim of this chapter was to point out that dignity does not have to be understood as an inherent value property (or an ascription of value), and to introduce the idea of dignity as rank or elevated position. This older conception was very prominent in the history of philosophy, and it is not clear that the contemporary paradigm even existed before the 20th century.[173] In this chapter I have already given some evidence that Kant too used 'dignity' in a way that accords with the traditional paradigm. This explains why Kant uses the term merely sporadically, and not at all in places one would expect him to if he had the contemporary paradigm in mind. As such dignity is not a concept that carries any justificatory weight. Kant uses it sometimes to express his core ideas. But this should not be surprising. Kant often takes popular concepts of his time and subordinates them to his theory (e.g., the enthusiasts of his time or religious terms like holiness, cf. *KpV* 5:86 f., or Stoic conceptions like dignity).

But does Kant not also sometimes use 'dignity' as a name for a value? How else can one make sense of the famous passages in the *Groundwork* and *Doctrine of Virtue* where he seems to equate dignity with an unconditional value? This will be the topic of my next chapter.

---

173 The earliest passage I have found in which rights are based on dignity is in G.W.F. Schiller's *Don Carlos*, Act III/Scene 3. However, Schiller understands dignity as a nobility in nature, a conception akin to the traditional paradigm of dignity. I have not found a passage in which dignity is said to be an inherent metaphysical value property before the twentieth century – although I realize that Kant is currently often read this way.

Chapter 5: Kant's Conception of Human Dignity

Introduction

In the last chapter I contrasted the contemporary paradigm of dignity as an absolute inner value all human beings possess, a value that grounds the requirement to respect others, with a different conception; and I gave evidence that Kant knew and frequently employed that conception. The question for this chapter is whether Kant did not also adhere to the popular contemporary conception that is often ascribed to him. For how else should one read passages in which Kant uses phrases like "inner worth, that is, *dignity*" (*GMS* 4:435), "dignity, that is, an unconditional, incomparable worth" (*GMS* 4:436), "*dignity* (an absolute inner worth)" (*TL* 6:435), or "*dignity* [...] that is, of a worth that has no price" (*TL* 6:462)? Are these not clear definitions of 'dignity' as an absolute inner value? Even if Kant sometimes uses the traditional conception of dignity, does he not also use the contemporary one?

The first thing to note is that we have good reason to suspect that, in these passages, Kant does not adhere to the contemporary paradigm in its standard form. For we have seen that Kant does not have a conception of value that could *ground* moral requirements (see Chapter 1). More specifically, value is not the ground of the requirement to respect others (see Chapters 2 and 3). So it cannot be that Kant uses a value 'dignity' to ground the requirement to respect others. And, in fact he seems to explicitly reverse the relationship between dignity and respect. It is not that someone should be respected because he has dignity, but he has dignity because he should be respected:

> Humanity itself is a dignity; for a human being cannot be used merely as a means by any human being [...] but must always be used at the same time as an end. It is just in this that his dignity (personality) consists, by which he raises himself above all other beings in the world that are not human beings and yet can be used, and so over all *things*. (*TL* 6:462; similarly 6:434 f.)

A human being has dignity because he should be treated as an end in itself, not the other way around. So in passages where 'dignity' appears next to 'worth', I infer that Kant cannot adhere to the contemporary paradigm of dignity strictly speaking.

However, this leaves open the possibility that Kant sometimes conceives of dignity as an absolute inner value in the different sense specified in Chapter 1. It could be that instead of the prescription 'x should be valued unconditionally' Kant sometimes uses the phrases 'x has absolute inner value' or 'x has dignity'. This would not introduce a new justification for the requirement to respect others (different from the one sketched in Chapter 3 above), but it might explain the phrases where 'dignity' appears next to 'worth'. While I think that this is a possible reading, I do not think that it is exactly what Kant is saying in these passages.

In this chapter I shall argue that even in the passages where 'dignity' appears in conjunction with 'worth', Kant adheres to the traditional paradigm, and understands dignity as elevation or sublimity (*Erhabenheit*). In the last chapter I argued that Kant often conceives of dignity as sublimity or the elevation of something over something else.[174] In these cases 'dignity' refers to a relational property of being elevated. 'X has dignity' is then equivalent to 'X is elevated over Y' or 'X is higher than Y'. But this means that one has to specify what is elevated over something else, and in which respect it is higher. In the last chapter I mainly talked about instances of the aristocratic use of dignity, when, for instance, Kant talks about the "dignity of a monarch" (*SF* 7:19.26), or about the first stage of the traditional conception, when Kant talks about the "dignity of humanity"[175].

In the few passages where 'dignity' appears in conjunction with 'worth' it could be that Kant introduces a very different usage of dignity, but it is important to note that the passages fit perfectly well with the usage of 'dignity' as elevation, or the realized stage of the traditional conception. There are three passages in particular in which 'dignity' appears next to 'worth': one in the *Groundwork* (4:434–6), one in the *Doctrine of Virtue* in connection with a duty against servility (6:434–6), and one a few pages later in the section on respect towards others (6:462 f.). To give a brief preview of my argument: All three of these passages can be read as instances of the traditional paradigm of dignity. In the *Groundwork* passage Kant talks about the value of morality. His claim there is that morality does not merely have a price, but that it is *raised above* all price (cf.

174 Cf. *BDG* 2:117.35, *NG* 212.01, 215.20, *GSE* 241.18; *GMS* 4:425.28, 440.01; *KpV* 5:71.21; *TL* 6:435.20; *Log* 9:30.12.
175 For instance, in: *GMS* 4:439.04, 440.11; *KU* 5:273.13 f.; *RGV* 6:80.18, 183.24; *TL* 6:420.16, 429.16, 436.16, 449.28 f., 459.23, 462.30; *Päd* 9:488.36, 489.01.

GMS 4:435). In this context too 'dignity' means 'raised above'. It express-es the relation of being elevated. The phrase "inner worth, that is, *dignity*" (cf. *GMS* 4:435) can then be read as saying that the worth of morality is elevated over other forms of worth. 'Dignity' specifies 'inner' in saying that inner worth is elevated or more important than mere relative worth. Second, in the *Doctrine of Virtue* passage on servility 'dignity' also appears next to 'worth' in the context of the higher importance of morality. Kant's point is that the natural human being should revere the higher moral aspect within (cf. *TL* 6:436). Kant uses 'dignity' to ex-press that this moral aspect is "sublime" (*TL* 6:435), elevated or more im-portant than the natural aspects of human beings. Third, during his dis-cussion of respect owed to others in the *Doctrine of Virtue* (6:462), Kant says that what one should respect in others is their striving for morality, "that is, of a worth that has no price". Human beings have a "dignity; for a human being cannot be used merely as a means [...] by which he raises himself [...] over all *things*" (*TL* 6:462). 'Dignity' expresses that human beings are elevated over the rest of nature because they should be respect-ed directly (while the rest of nature is to be respected only indirectly). Kant uses 'worth' in this passage to specify what should be respected in others, their striving for morality which has an unconditional worth.

In all three passages where 'dignity' appears in conjunction with 'worth' the topic is the worth of morality. This worth is more important than and raised above all other worth. (I have argued in Chapter 1 that this is to be read as: 'Only morality should be pursued unconditionally.') Kant's usage of 'dignity' becomes consistent if in these passages too he uses it to express an elevation. The particular elevation he is talking about is that morality is more important than or raised above all price. I therefore think that one is too quick if one just takes 'dignity' to be a definition of 'absolute inner value'. However, I do not think that much is at stake if one wants to read 'dignity' in these passages as such a defi-nition of 'absolute value'. This is because Kant's notion of value is not a substantive conception that is offered as a justification of moral claims (see again Chapter 1). However, in the following I shall expand upon my argument that Kant in fact uses the more complicated but unifying conception according to which 'dignity' expresses an elevation.

In order to argue for these claims I shall first point out how seldom Kant uses 'dignity' in conjunction with 'worth' (Section 1). I shall then give a thorough reading of the famous *Groundwork* passage in which Kant talks about dignity (Section 2), before I do the same for the *Doctrine of Virtue* passages (Section 3). Finally I shall reflect upon the importance of dignity in Kant's thought, the value of dignity, so to speak (Section 4).

Section 1: The Appearance of 'Dignity' in Kant's Works

The aim of this Section is to give an overview of all the usages of 'dignity' in Kant's published works. What is striking is how seldom 'dignity' appears in conjunction with 'worth'. In contrast, Kant frequently uses 'dignity' in the aristocratic sense, to express that one member is elevated within a certain group (for instance, a teacher in the classroom or mathematics among disciplines). And Kant frequently uses 'dignity' in the traditional sense, to express that all human beings are elevated over the rest of nature in virtue of being free, and that they realize this initial dignity in being morally good.

In his published writings Kant uses the term 'dignity' 111 times.[176] In addition, there is one lecture[177] and two reflection notes[178] that are helpful in clarifying Kant's view of dignity. In his published works the use of 'dignity' is spread over 18 writings. The works in which the word is used most often are (ordered by the number of appearances): the *Doctrine of Virtue* (21 times), the *Groundwork of the Metaphysics of Morals* (17 times), *Religion within the Boundaries of Mere Reason* (eleven times), and the *Lectures on Pedagogy* (ten times).[179]

---

176 See *Kant-Konkordanz* 1995, 306–308. Passage 6:58.25 is mistakenly listed there and not counted here. In addition, I counted four occurrences where Kant talks about "Menschenwürde" (human dignity) in contrast to the more common "Würde der Menschheit" (dignity of humanity). The four passages are: *TL* 6:429.24, 436.29, 465.17, and *Anth* 7:295.19.

177 "Kants Naturrecht gelesen im Winterhalben Jahre 1784. Gottf. Feyerabend", *NF* 27:1319–1322.

178 *Refl* 6856 19:181; *Refl* 7305, 19:307.

179 The others are: "Observations on the Feeling of the Beautiful and Sublime" (ten times); *Critique of Pure Reason* (seven times); "The Conflict of the Faculties" (six times); *Critique of Practical Reason* (five times); *Doctrine of Right* (five times); *Anthropology from a Pragmatic Point of View* (five times); "Toward Perpetual Peace" (four times); *Critique of the Powers of Judgment* (three times); "The Only Possible Argument in Support of a Demonstration of the Existence of God" (twice); *Lectures on Logic* (twice); "Attempt to Introduce the Concept of Negative Magnitudes into Philosophy" (once); "An Answer to the Question: What is Enlightenment?" (once); "On the Miscarriage of All Philosophical Trials in Theodicy" (once); "Kraus's Review of Ulrich's *Eleutheriology*" (once).

In different contexts and throughout different writings Kant consistently elucidates dignity as sublimity (*Erhabenheit*) or the (the highest form of) elevation.[180] The elevation he has in mind is sometimes that indicated by the aristocratic conception of dignity, and sometimes that indicated by the traditional conception I distinguished in Chapter 4. He clearly uses the aristocratic conception when – for instance – he talks about "kingly dignity" (*Anth* 7:131.09), the "dignity of a monarch" (*SF* 7:19.26), the "dignity of a regent" and of "a minister" (*ZeF* 8:344.06–08). In these passages Kant uses 'dignity' in the aristocratic sense to indicate some aspect of rank, with which he sometimes equates it explicitly (so in *RL* 6:328.33; *TL* 468.09; and *Anth* 7:127.09). In this sense Kant also uses the plural 'dignities' (cf. *RL* 6:315; 328). For instance, he calls the three authorities in a state (the legislative, executive, and juridical powers) "*civic dignities*", and says that they "comprise the relation of a *superior* over all". The superiority is not a moral quality, but merely the "relation of a *commander* (*imperans*) to *those who obey*" (*RL* 6:315). It expresses that someone is elevated over the rest in terms of political power. In this exclusive sense, by which Kant points out the elevation of one member of a class, he also talks about the "dignity of philosophy" (*KrV* 3:81.22; 4:203.08; cf. 3:322.29) or the "dignity of a philosopher" (*Päd* 9:26.14), the "dignity of mathematics" (*KrV* 3:323.09), and the "dignity of a teacher" (*RGV* 6:162.19). As these usages all rank one member of a group over others, I have counted them as instances of the aristocratic conception of dignity (even if they do not refer to the rank of one human being in society, as the Roman conception did). All in all, he uses the aristocratic conception of dignity 39 times.[181]

In contrast to the exclusive and hierarchical aristocratic usage of dignity, Kant often talks about the dignity of *all* human beings, or – as he

---

180 Cf. *BDG* 2:117.35, *NG* 212.01, 215.20, *GSE* 241.18; *GMS* 4:425.28, 440.01; *KpV* 5:71.21; *TL* 6:435.20; *Log* 9:30.12. Sometimes Kant expresses this as something being below someone's dignity, e.g., in: *KrV* 3:419.20; *KpV* 5:327.14; *RGV* 6:113.26, *RL* 327.27; *Päd* 9:489.11. Cf. also *GMS* 4:438.13 and *TL* 6:420.16 f. where he elucidates dignity as a prerogative. For a specification of Kant's usage of 'sublimity' see esp. *KU* 5:248.05 and 250.05.

181 In addition to the 13 passages cited see: *BDG* 2:117.35, 123.06, *NG* 198.02, 212.01, 215.20; *KrV* 3:419.20, 549.32; 4:159.33; *KpV* 5:25.06, 71.21, *KU* 327.14, 336.10; *RGV* 6:113.26, 123.16, 165.25, *RL* 327.27, 329.33 & 36, 363.27, *TL* 467.26; *SF* 7:19.18, 34.10, 52.22, *Anth* 316.05; *ZeF* 8:365.14, 368.27.

often puts it – the "dignity of humanity [*Würde der Menschheit*]"[182]. Kant says that the dignity of humanity consists in freedom as the capacity to act independently of inclinations (cf. *RGV* 6:57.27, 183.24; *TL* 420.22; *SF* 7:73.03; 8:42.01; *Refl* 19:181; *NF* 27:1319–1322). Because freedom in this sense is also the capacity to act morally, Kant also says that the dignity of humanity consists in the capacity to act morally (cf. *GMS* 4:435.08, 440.11; *SF* 7:58.20). Kant specifies what he means by dignity in this context by saying that the capacity to act morally is a pre-rogative human beings have over the rest of nature (cf. *GMS* 4:438.13; *TL* 6:420.17, 434 f.; *Päd* 9:488.36). Interestingly, in these passages he does not refer to worth or value, but he does call human dignity "innate" (*TL* 6:420.22) and "inalienable [*unverlierbar*]" (*TL* 6:436.12). In accord-ance with Kant I will call this usage of dignity the "initial dignity [*ur-sprüngliche Würde*]" (*SF* 7:73.03), as it expresses the first stage of what I have called the traditional pattern of thought. All in all he uses dignity in this sense 41 times throughout his published writings.[183]

In addition, Kant often speaks of dignity in relation to morality and morally good behavior in a way that suggests the realized dignity in the traditional paradigm. In this sense Kant talks about the "dignity of virtue" (*GSE* 2:216.29; *TL* 6:483.03), the dignity of the concept of duty (cf. *RGV* 6:23.23 f.), the dignity of the moral law (cf. *KpV* 5:147.17 f.; *TL* 6:464.18), or the "sublimity and *dignity* in the person who fulfills all his duties" (*GMS* 4:440.01 f.). Kant uses 'dignity' in the realized sense es-pecially to express the claim that morality should be valued above all else. Accordingly, it is in passages where Kant talks about the realized sense that 'dignity' appears in conjunction with 'worth' (cf. esp. *GMS* 4:435.04 f.; *TL* 6:435.02 and below). Morality is said to have an elevated worth because of its independence from inclinations: "[T]he sublimity and inner dignity of the command in duty is all the more manifest the fewer are the subjective causes in favour of it" (*GMS* 4:425.27–29).

---

182 Literally in: *GMS* 4:439.04, 440.11; *KU* 5:273.14; *RGV* 6:80.18, 183.24, *TL* 420.16, 429.16, 436.16 & 29, 449.29, 459.23, 462.30; *Päd* 9:488.36, 489.01/07/11 & 34; but see also: *GSE* 2:212.11, 217.17, 219.11, 221.29; *GMS* 4:435.08, 438.13; *KpV* 5:88.07, 152.28; *RGV* 6:57.27, *TL* 420.22, 429.24, 435.02 & 19, 436.12, 462.13/21 & 24, 465.17; *SF* 7:58.20, 73.03; *WA* 8:42.01, *RezUlrich* 454.20; *Päd* 9:488.35, 489.08.

183 See previous footnote for references.

Counted together there are 31 passages that connect dignity to morality.[184]

I claim that – setting aside passages where Kant uses the aristocratic conception of dignity – his usage of 'dignity' always conforms to the traditional paradigm of dignity. The 41 passages in which Kant talks about the dignity of *all* human beings refer to the first stage of the traditional conception, i. e., a capacity that elevates human beings over the rest of nature. The 31 times when Kant refers to dignity in relation to morality, he emphasizes the duty to make a certain use of one's freedom, i. e., to realize one's dignity fully.

What is also noteworthy about Kant's usages of dignity is that, out of 111 occurrences, only eight relate dignity to worth or value (*Werth*).[185] As these passages are the source of the claim in the literature that Kant adheres to the contemporary paradigm of dignity,[186] I shall now have a closer look at them. In the following section (Section 2) I shall look at the passages in the *Groundwork* that are often read this way. In the subsequent section (Section 3) I shall look at the passages from the *Doctrine of Virtue*. I shall argue that even those passages are in fact in line with the traditional paradigm of dignity.

Section 2: Dignity in the *Groundwork*

Introduction

In the following I shall have a close look at those passages in the *Groundwork* that seem to link dignity and worth, because they are the ones most likely to be seen as a challenge to the interpretation of Kant I have advanced. I shall argue that, if one closely looks at the content and context of these passages, one can see that Kant even here adheres to the traditional pattern of thought.

All in all in the *Groundwork* Kant uses the term 'dignity' only 17 times. What is striking is that Kant does not use the term at all where

---

184 In addition to the seven cited cf. *GSE* 2:227.35, 241.18; *Aufsätze* 2:450.32; *GMS* 4:405.17, 411.02 & 13, 434.29/32 & 34, 435.04 & 25, 436.03 & 06, 442.29; *RGV* 6:23.19, 114.11, *TL* 467.25; *Anth* 7:295.19 & 22; 8:257.27; *Log* 9:30.12, *Päd* 9:490.01 & 31, 493.04.
185 Cf. *GMS* 4:435.04, 435.25, 436.03; *TL* 6:435.02, 436.10–12, 462.12 f.; *Anth* 7:295.19; cf. *KrV* 3:322.09.
186 For references see again the introduction to Part I.

one would most expect it if one reads Kant as adhering to the contemporary paradigm. He neither uses the term in connection with the Formula of Humanity and the respect one owes to others (cf. *GMS* 4:426–431), nor where he justifies his moral views in the Third Section of the *Groundwork*. This is striking; if Kant saw dignity as his "most fundamental value" (Wood 1998b, 189), and as a value that is the foundation even of the Categorical Imperative (cf. Guyer 2000, 150–7), one would expect a sustained treatment of the issue for instance in the Third Section of the *Groundwork* (cf. *GMS* 4:446–463), where Kant aims to justify the Categorical Imperative (cf. *GMS* 4:431.32–34 and 445.01 f.). However, Kant neither uses the term 'dignity' in the Third Section, nor does he present an argument for an absolute value of human beings there.[187]

Instead, eight occurrences of 'dignity' appear in a peripheral addition to the Formulas of Autonomy and Kingdom of Ends (cf. *GMS* 4:434.20–436.07). He then uses the term four times in a summary of his argument for these formulas (cf. *GMS* 4:438.08–440.13). In addition, there are five isolated occurrences scattered throughout the *Groundwork* that clearly do not deal with *human* dignity at all, but with the elevation of morality over other forms of behavior (cf. *GMS* 4:405.17, 411.02 & 13, 425.28, 442.29). As the three passages in which Kant relates dignity to worth appear in the addendum to the Formula of Autonomy, I shall here go through the one and a half pages of the addendum which contain eight occurrences of dignity. In analyzing the addendum I shall refer to the summary of the argument as well.

I shall argue, to anticipate, that the addendum answers a question about moral motivation in the widest sense. The passage is not about the justification of moral requirements. Rather the question is why one should abide by the Categorical Imperative in its Formula of Autonomy, a formula that emphasizes the exclusion of all interest from moral motivation (cf. *GMS* 4:431.25–432.04). Kant's answer is that one should abide by the Categorical Imperative because following the imperative, that is morality, has an elevated worth (i. e., morality alone should be pursued unconditionally). Rather than putting forward the contemporary paradigm of dignity, I argue, Kant repeats familiar claims of the *Ground-*

---

187 In the Third Section Kant uses the phrase 'inner worth' once (see 4:454.37), where it is clearly tied to morality and not said to be a value of all human beings; and he uses the phrase 'absolute worth' three times in connection with the Formula of Humanity (cf. *GMS* 4:428.04, 15 & 30), where, however, it receives only passing mention.

work. Only a morally good will can have an unconditional worth. While it is possible to read 'dignity' as a definition of 'unconditional worth' in a more modest sense (as a prescription of what one should value), this would be inconsistent with Kant's usages elsewhere and lose the special meaning 'dignity' adds in this passage: 'Dignity' expresses the sublimity of morality, in that this worth is *higher* than or to be preferred over other worth: Morality, and not the objects of one's inclinations, should be sought above all else.

The Context of the Passage

In more detail: The passage appears at the end of Kant's discussion of the Formula of Autonomy and the Formula of Kingdom of Ends. In his discussion Kant switches back and forth between both formulas. Kant introduces the Formula of Autonomy, "namely the idea of the will of every rational being as a *will giving universal law*" (*GMS* 4:432.03 f.),[188] in order to make explicit the categorical nature of the Categorical Imperative, or "to indicate in the imperative itself the renunciation of all interest, in volition from duty, by means of some determination the imperative contains" (*GMS* 4:431.35–37).[189] Kant continues by noting that the idea of the Formula of Autonomy, that every rational being should give universal law, leads to the idea of a kingdom of ends. A kingdom of ends is "a systematic union of various rational beings through common laws" (*GMS* 4:433.17 f.). Such a kingdom is only an ideal, but it would come actually into existence if everyone were to act on the Categorical Imperative (cf. *GMS* 4:438.29–32).[190]

---

188 At this point Kant does not state the Formula of Autonomy in an imperative form. He first does so on page 4:434.12–14.

189 The requirement to give universal law makes an imperative categorical, that is not dependent upon something else one wants (by inclination), in that a *universal* or supreme lawgiver cannot be governed by inclinations: "for, a will that is dependent in this way would itself need yet another law that would limit the interest of its self-love to the condition of a validity for universal law" (*GMS* 4:432.08–11). Behind Kant's argument is the view that all inclinations propel to self-love, cf. *KpV* 5:22–25.

190 In his first discussion of the kingdom of ends Kant likewise does not state the formula. Only in a repetition of his argument he states: "every rational being must act as if he were by his maxims at all times a lawgiving member of the universal kingdom of ends" (*GMS* 4:438.18–21).

He concludes: "Morality consists, then, in the reference of all action to the lawgiving by which alone a kingdom of ends is possible." (*GMS* 4:434.07 f.) Kant reformulates the requirement of the kingdom of ends as the requirement of the Formula of Autonomy, because the requirement to universalize must be able to arise from an agent's will without looking at the scope of concern of the requirement.[191] For the first time he spells out the Formula of Autonomy thus: "[A]ct only *so that the will could regard itself as at the same time giving universal law through its maxim*" (*GMS* 4:434.12–14). It is to this law that the passage about dignity refers.

The Passage

What is important to note in reading the passage that contains the eight references to dignity is that it is an addendum to the Formula of Autonomy, and that this formula excludes inclinations as one's proper moral motivation. The passage does not address the issue of the *justification* of moral requirements, as one would expect if dignity were a foundational value. The addendum is a very dense and complicated passage. This is because it tries to link four key concepts, each of which is expressed differently over the one and a half pages. The four concepts are: 'autonomy', 'morality', 'dignity', and 'worth'. Those concepts are linked in the claim that a morally good person is autonomous (or abides by the Formula of Autonomy) because morality has an elevated worth.

Given the complicated character of the passage, I shall first lay out why the passage should be read as an instance of the traditional paradigm if one follows it closely in its context. In order not to complicate matters further, I shall not emphasize at each junction why the passage is not an instance of the contemporary pattern of thought. However, after I have gone through the whole one-and-a-half pages I shall address in a separate discussion the objection that the appearance of 'worth' makes the *Groundwork* passage an example of the contemporary paradigm of dignity. In that discussion I shall again point out, first, that for Kant the good is dependent upon the right; second, that it is not humanity as such that has

---

191 Accordingly, Paton classifies the Formula of Kingdom of Ends as a sub-formula of the Formula of Autonomy, see his 1947, 129. The scope of concern emphasizes the receiving end of one's duty, not who has duties, cf. Gibbard 1999, 151.

an absolute inner worth, but morality; and, third, that Kant does not conceive of worth as a distinct metaphysical property. The passage begins:

> [Occurrence *1*:] The practical necessity of acting in accordance with this principle [...] does not rest at all on feelings, impulses, and inclinations [...]. Reason [...] does so not for the sake of any other practical motive or any future advantage but from the idea of the **dignity** of a rational being, who obeys no law other than that which he himself at the same time gives. (*GMS* 4:434.20–30[192])

The first occurrence links the concepts of 'autonomy', 'morality' and 'dignity'. A morally good being does not abide by the Formula of Autonomy out of any inclination or thought about his advantage, but from the idea of the dignity (or sublimity) of a morally good being, that is a being who abides by the Formula of Autonomy, or – as the last phrase puts it – "who obeys no law other than that which he himself at the same time gives". As the summary of the argument later in the *Groundwork* indicates, Kant has the dignity of *the agent's own* morally good will in mind.[193] Although it is a common theme throughout Kant's ethical writings that the idea of the dignity or sublimity of one's own morally good will is a proper moral motive,[194] one has to be careful to construe this thought in the proper way. To be morally good, a person could not be moved by any liking of himself as a morally good person or any thoughts about the advantages that it might yield in the eyes of others (cf., e.g., *GMS* 4:397.19–32). One could express this requirement more adequately by saying that a morally good person abides by the Formula of Autonomy because of the dignity of morality. It is the dignity of morality, then, that accounts for the practical necessity to abide by the Formula of Autonomy.

In the next two occurrences Kant elucidates dignity as elevation:

> [Occurrences *2* & *3*:] In the kingdom of ends everything has either a *price* or a **dignity**. What has a price can be replaced by something else as its *equivalent*; what on the other hand is raised above all price and therefore admits of no equivalent has a **dignity.** (*GMS* 4:434.31–34)

What these occurrences do is to elucidate dignity as sublimity or the highest form of elevation. In this passage Kant talks about the special case in which something is elevated over things to which a price can be

---

192 I have put *"dignity"* in bold in this and the following quotations.
193 See *GMS* 4:440.07–10 (my emphasis): *"Our own will* insofar as it would act only under the condition of a possible giving of universal law through its maxims – this will possible for us in idea – is the proper object of respect".
194 Cf., e.g., *TL* 6:483, 459; *KpV* 5:152; *RGV* 6:183; *SF* 7:58.

assigned, and which can be traded for other things of equal value. What is elevated above price and what has an *elevated* worth is morality, as the next occurrences make clear:

> [Occurrences **4** & **5**:] What is related to general human inclinations and needs has a *market price*; [...] but that which constitutes the condition under which alone something can be an end in itself has not merely a relative worth, that is, a price, but an inner worth, that is, **dignity.**

> Now morality is the condition under which alone a rational being can be an end in itself [...]. Hence morality, and humanity insofar as it is capable of morality, is that which alone has **dignity.** (*GMS* 4:434.35–435.09)

These occurrences link the concepts of 'morality', 'dignity' and 'worth'. It is morality that has an inner worth. Kant uses 'inner' to express how one has to judge something in isolation, i.e., independently of any relations that may hold (cf. *KrV* A324 f./B381 f.). Given his usage of worth as a prescription of what one should value (see Chapter 1 above), what he is saying is that one should value morality whether one has an inclination to do so or not. The prescription to pursue morality is not conditioned upon any relation that may hold, e.g., the utility of moral actions or whether one is inclined towards the action or not. It is in this respect that moral worth is elevated over relative or conditional worth. To say that something has relative or conditional worth is a different way of expressing that something should be valued because something else holds, e.g., because one is inclined towards it (cf. *GMS* 4:428).

When Kant uses 'dignity' in this context, it could merely be a definition of 'inner worth' (in the sense just specified). However, this usage would be contrary to the vast majority of passages in which Kant uses 'dignity' (see Section 1 above). And the specific meaning of this passage would be lost. Kant's question was why a morally good being abides by the Formula of Autonomy. What Kant is saying is that morality is more important than other value, i.e., morality is higher or elevated in value. 'Dignity' is exactly the term he uses throughout his writings in order to express that something is raised above all else (in a certain respect). Accordingly, the phrase "inner worth, that is, *dignity*" should not be read as a definition of 'dignity', but as a specification that 'inner' is more important than or elevated over 'relative'. The whole sentence can be paraphrased as follows: Morality has not just a subordinate relative value (a price), but an *elevated* inner worth (a dignity in worth). 'Dignity' is used to express the thought that moral worth is *higher than* other worth.[195] While morality has dignity in the sense that it should be sought above all else, humanity has dignity in the sense of being elevated over the rest of nature in being capable of morality (cf. *GMS* 4:438.12 f.). In the traditional paradigm these are two stages of elevation or dignity. The initial elevation of humanity is only realized if one makes a proper use of one's moral capacity. At this part of the *Groundwork* Kant is mainly concerned with realized dignity, a morally good will, as the next occurrence makes clear:

> [Occurrence *6:*] Skill and diligence in work have a market price; [...] fidelity in promises and benevolence from basic principles (not from instinct) have an inner worth. [...] Such actions [...] present the will that practices them as the object of an immediate respect [...]. This estimation therefore lets the worth of such a cast of mind be cognized as **dignity** and puts it infinitely above all price (*GMS* 4:435.09–28).

This occurrence confirms that Kant is talking about morality in this passage. It is morality that has a value that is raised beyond all price, and 'dignity' appears in the context of something's (morality's) being raised above all else (moral worth is raised above all price). Here he talks more specifically in terms of a morally good will or a moral cast of mind, thereby bringing the passage closer to the famous opening sentence of the First Section of the *Groundwork* – that only a good will could be called unconditionally good (cf. *GMS* 4:393.05–07). Kant says that it is a morally good cast of mind that has inner worth, and is therefore elevated over other talents and casts of mind which do not have this special worth (i. e., which should not be valued unconditionally). In accordance with the traditional paradigm, this is what the realized dignity of a morally good person consists in.

The next occurrences specify why morality is said to have an elevated worth, and in doing so they link autonomy back to the elevated worth of morality:

> [Occurrences *7* & *8:*] And what is it, then, that justifies a morally good disposition [*Gesinnung*], or virtue, in making such high claims? It is nothing less than the *share* it affords a rational being *in the giving of universal law* [...] For, nothing can have a worth other than that which the law determines

---

195 But if 'inner value' just means the prescription to value something unconditionally, is dignity not an inner value insofar as the term has the connotation of being worthy of esteem? Does Kant not mean the same thing in saying that something should be valued and that it is worthy to be valued? However, the requirement to value something unconditionally is not a necessary connotation of Kant's usage of 'dignity', e. g., when he speaks of the dignity of mathematics or a teacher.

for it. But the lawgiving itself, which determines all worth, must for that very reason have a **dignity**, that is, an unconditional, incomparable worth[196] [...] *Autonomy* is therefore the ground of the **dignity** of human nature and of every rational nature." (*GMS* 4:435.29–436.07)

These occurrences tie the claim that morality has an elevated worth back to the original question of why a morally good person abides by the Formula of Autonomy. They connect morality, dignity, and worth to autonomy, or – as Kant shortens it here – lawgiving. To act with autonomy is to regard the adoption of one's maxim as giving a law for all others (cf. *GMS* 4:432 f.). The lawgiving Kant is talking about in the above passage is therefore Kant's way of bringing the discussion back to autonomy. Kant begins the passage with the question of why a moral cast of mind has an absolute worth, or why it is elevated over other casts of mind (i.e., has a dignity). Kant's answer is that this cast of mind affords a share in universal lawgiving or autonomy. He further explains his answer that lawgiving has an elevated worth as follows: The moral law as a principle of right is prior to the good and determines it: The (moral) law determines all (moral) worth (cf. Chapter 1 above). If the law determines all (moral) worth, then doing what the law says means that one is morally good and has moral worth. Since doing what the law says amounts to lawgiving (as autonomy), it is the lawgiving that has an unconditional worth, or an elevated worth (i.e., a dignity in worth). Kant can therefore conclude that it is autonomy that is the ground of the (realized) dignity of human beings. Autonomy is the ground of the high claim a moral cast of mind can make (of being elevated or possessing dignity). This answers the question Kant had posed at the beginning of the passage (containing occurrences 7 and 8).

This explanation – "the lawgiving itself, which determines all worth, must for that very reason have [...] an unconditional, incomparable worth" – is not an argument for why the law is prior, or why morality has an elevated worth. Those arguments are given in the *Critique of Practical Reason* and the First Section of the *Groundwork*. Nor is this explanation an argument for the view that human beings possess a value in virtue of which they should be respected.[197] Such an argument would be a

---

196 Here too the phrase **"dignity**, that is, an unconditional, incomparable worth" does not have to be read as a definition of 'dignity'. It should be read as saying: 'morality has an elevated position (dignity), in that it should be valued above all else (it has an incomparable worth)'.

197 *Pace* Porcheddu 2012.

version of Korsgaard's initial Regress Argument (as discussed in Chapter 2, Section 1). I have argued that this argument would not work (cf. *ibid.*), but the question why other human beings should be respected is also not Kant's topic at this point. His topic is why a morally good being follows the Formula of Autonomy, or what is so special about such a cast of mind. The explanation unfolds the link between different concepts, and ties autonomy to Kant's views on moral motivation.

In sum: What makes the one-and-a-half pages on dignity in the *Groundwork* so complicated is that they tie together four concepts ('autonomy', 'morality', 'dignity', 'worth') that are each expressed differently. Unfolding this complicated structure yields a picture that fits perfectly well with the traditional paradigm of thought. Kant's claim in the whole addendum to the Formula of Autonomy is that morality is to be valued above all else. This answers the question of why a morally good person abides by the Formula of Autonomy. The person does so not from any advantage he might hope to achieve or from any inclinations, but from the idea of the elevated standing of moral worth (i. e., its dignity). These are familiar claims Kant makes throughout the *Groundwork*, and there is no need for him to argue for them at this point. Kant's key passage on dignity in the *Groundwork* can therefore very well be explained as adhering to the traditional paradigm of dignity.

Dignity as a Value

Now that I have laid out how the *Groundwork* passage suggests that Kant uses the traditional paradigm of dignity, it is important also to spell out directly my negative claim that he does not use the contemporary pattern of thought. This is because the appearance of phrases like: "inner worth, that is, *dignity*" (occurrence *4*), or: "worth [...] be cognized as **dignity**" (*6*), or: "**dignity**, that is, an unconditional, incomparable worth" (*7*) might be read as an instance of the contemporary paradigm. If one reads dignity as inner worth, and if humanity has dignity (*5*), then humanity has inner worth, and one might be led to think that one should respect humanity because it has an inner worth.

However, this is not what Kant actually says, and it is important to keep in mind three points I have stressed: First, for Kant the good is dependent upon the right; second, it is not humanity that has an inner worth, but morality; and third, Kant does not conceive of worth as a distinct metaphysical property.

On the first point, Kant makes clear also in the *Groundwork* that the good is dependent upon the right: "For, nothing can have a worth other than that which the law determines for it" (*GMS* 4:436.01 f.). There is therefore no independent worth that could ground the requirement to respect others, but for Kant the relationship is the other way around: One should respect others because it is commanded by the Categorical Imperative in the Formula of Humanity. It is in virtue of the moral law – and not because of an inner worth of human beings – that one should respect them (see Chapters 1 and 3 above).

This is further supported, second, by the fact that, in the *Groundwork* and elsewhere, Kant ties absolute inner worth (almost) exclusively to morality and not to human beings as such.[198] This comes out not just in that famous opening of the *Groundwork* in which Kant claims that only a good will can be called absolutely good (cf. *GMS* 4:393), but also in the passage on dignity itself. To recall: The passage starts out by asking about the practical necessity or duty of acting in accordance with a moral principle, the Formula of Autonomy (cf. *GMS* 4:434). While Kant says that morality and humanity have dignity (**5**), it is morality that is said to have an inner worth: "that which constitutes the condition under which alone something can be an end in itself has [...] an inner worth [...]. Now, morality is the condition" (*GMS* 4:435). He goes on to explain that only morality has an inner worth, that morality causes an immediate respect, and he asks: "And what is it, then, that justifies a morally good disposition, or virtue, in making such high claims?" (*ibid.*) His answer is that only in acting morally (by participating in lawgiving) does one act as one unconditionally should (in accordance with what the law determines). Likewise in the dignity passage Kant ties absolute inner value exclusively to morality (similarly Darwall 2008).

This is a clear expression of a recurrent thought in Kant's writings. Throughout his works Kant repeats the claim that the inner or absolute worth of human beings is one that the human being can only give himself in being morally good:

> [I]t is the value that he alone can give to himself, and which consists in what he does, in how and in accordance with which principles he acts, not as a link in nature but in the freedom of his faculty of desire; i.e., a good will

---

198 Cf. also Mulholland 1990, 104. Two rare exceptions, *GMS* 4:428.04 and *TL* 6:462.13, are discussed in Chapter 3 and Section 3 below respectively.

is that alone by means of which his existence can have an absolute value. (*KU* 5:443.07–13.)[199]

The absolute worth of human beings is secondary to and depends upon a morally good will. This does not mean that one can treat morally bad human beings in an inhumane way – to repeat, Kant claims that even a criminal deserves respect[200] – but it emphasizes again that Kant's ethics is not built upon an inner or unconditional worth of human beings as its foundation, and that for Kant rights are not grounded on a value human beings possess (cf. again *TL* 6:239.13–21): If one should respect all human beings, but if not all human beings have an absolute worth (of a morally good will), then absolute worth is not the ground of the requirement to respect others.

Kant therefore neither grounds the requirement to respect others on an absolute inner value all human beings possess, nor does he advance such a value. This is further supported, third, by Kant's conception of worth. Kant does not give a positive specification of worth as a distinct metaphysical property. In the *Groundwork* passage on dignity – as elsewhere[201] – Kant specifies inner worth merely negatively. Kant says that inner worth is "*raised above* all price", "admits of *no* equivalent" (occurrence *3*), "has *not* merely a relative worth" (*4*), but an "*un*conditional, *in*comparable worth" (*7*; all emphasis mine). Again – as I have argued in Chapter 1 – I agree with scholars who say that 'inner worth' is merely a different expression for what one *should* value independently of its usefulness,[202] or something that one *would* value if one were fully governed by reason.[203]

So there is no indication in the *Groundwork* passage that Kant breaks here from his claim that value is not the ground of moral requirements (cf. Chapter 1). To the contrary, he directly affirms that value is dependent upon the moral law (cf. *GMS* 4:436). However, this leaves open the possibility that in *Groundwork* 4:434–6 Kant conceives of dignity as a value in the more modest sense (as being a prescription of reason). In a way this is the natural reading, because of the way Kant sets it up.

---

199 See, e.g., *GMS* 4:439, 449 f., 454; *KpV* 5:110 f., 147 f.; *KU* 5:208 f. Matthew Caswell argues that Kant's conception of evil rules out an absolute value that humanity would have as such, cf. his 2006.
200 Cf. Kant: *TL* 6:463.12 f.; see Hill 1992, 53; Wood 1999, 132–139.
201 See Löhrer 1995, 36; cf. Santeler 1962, 61; cf. Schwartländer 1968, 183.
202 Cf. again Ross 1954, 50 f.; Hill 2003, 19; Engstrom 2009, 11–14.
203 Cf. once more Hill 1992, 48; Dean 2000, 34; cf. *GMS* 4:414, 449, 454.

He seems to set up a parallel between two types of value, price and dignity: morality "has not merely a relative worth, that is, a price, but an inner worth, that is, *dignity*" (*GMS* 4:435). So, again, I think this reading is possible, but at the same time it has little effect on my overall argument, because it does not introduce a new justification for the requirement to respect others.

Nonetheless, I do not think that this is all that Kant wants to say here, as I have argued above. This usage would be at odds with Kant's other usages of 'dignity' (and out of tune with how 'dignity' was used in his time). But more importantly, on this interpretation of dignity one would lose the further dimension and subtlety that accompanies the term 'dignity'. Kant does not merely use a different term for 'absolute value', but in speaking of dignity he wants to express the idea that morality is elevated and special. In this particular context Kant uses the term 'dignity' to express the thought that moral value is raised above all other value.

I therefore do not read Kant as putting forward the contemporary pattern of thought, nor as defining 'dignity' as 'value' even in the most suggestive passages of the *Groundwork*.

Section 3: Dignity in the *Doctrine of Virtue*

In this section I shall have a close look at Kant's usage of 'dignity' in the *Doctrine of Virtue*. Even if one grants that Kant does use the traditional rather than the contemporary paradigm of dignity in the *Groundwork*, one could still argue that he has changed his mind in the *Doctrine of Virtue* (cf. Darwall 2008, 175–177). Consider the following passages. Kant says that

> a human being regarded as a *person* [...] possesses a *dignity* (an absolute inner worth) by which he exacts *respect* for himself from all other rational beings in the world (*TL* 6:434 f.).

Later he says:

> The *respect* that I have for others or that another can require from me [...] is therefore recognition of a *dignity* (*dignitas*) in other human beings, that is, of a worth that has no price, no equivalent for which the object evaluated [...] could be exchanged. (*TL* 6:462)

Both passages might lead one to think that Kant adheres to the contemporary paradigm of dignity. His claim would then be that all human beings possess an absolute inner value called 'dignity', which is the reason why one should respect them. In this section I shall therefore have a close look at the passages.

In the following I shall first give an overview of Kant's usage of 'dignity' in the *Doctrine of Virtue*. I shall then closely examine the two passages where 'dignity' appears next to 'worth' to see whether Kant puts forth the contemporary paradigm of dignity. I shall then reflect upon the sense in which the *Doctrine of Virtue* is a break from Kant's earlier works in this respect.

Kant's Usage of 'Dignity' in the *Doctrine of Virtue*

In the *Doctrine of Virtue* Kant uses 'dignity' 21 times.[204] These are isolated and scattered occurrences that do not follow a systematic pattern. Kant uses the term six times in relation to a duty against servility or false humility (cf. *TL* 6:435 f.). Nine times 'dignity' appears in connection with duties of respect owed to others (cf. *TL* 449, 462, 464, 467 f.). Twice it appears in the introduction to duties towards self (cf. *TL* 6:420), and twice in Kant's treatment of the duty not to lie (cf. *TL* 6:429). It appears once in the discussion of duties of love towards others (cf. *TL* 6:459), and once more in the 'Doctrine of Method' (cf. *TL* 6:483). This scattered and sparse usage makes one wonder whether Kant considers 'dignity' to be a key concept for the *Doctrine of Virtue*.

More illuminating is in which sense Kant talks about dignity in this work. Out of the 21 usages, three are an instance of the aristocratic paradigm. Kant emphasizes that one element is raised above another, but he is not referring to a moral ranking, or to a higher place of all human beings in nature. Instead Kant talks about the respect that should be shown to differences in "rank and dignity [*Stand und Würde*]" (*TL* 6:468.9) that someone contingently occupies in society, and about mere customs that are falsely "raised to the dignity of a law" (*TL* 6:464.18 f.). In the third instance, Kant says that against mockery it is right "either to put up no defense [...] or to conduct it with dignity and seriousness" (*TL* 6:467.26 f.). In these instances Kant is not talking about morality (nor

---

204 See *TL* 6:420.16 & 22; 429.16 & 24; 435.2 & 15 & 19; 436.12 & 16 & 29; 449.28; 459.23; 462.12 & 21 & 24 & 30; 464.18; 467.25 & 26; 468.09; 483.03.

a foundational moral value), but about a higher rank one entity occupies over another (and the conduct befitting one's higher position).

Three times Kant talks about the dignity of morality, for instance when he talks about the "dignity of virtue" (*TL* 6:483.03), the dignity of reason's moral interest (cf. *TL* 6:467.25), and the dignity of one's morally practical reason (cf. *TL* 6:435.02). The other 15 usages, I contend, refer to the 'dignity of humanity' ('*Würde der Menschheit*' or akin to the modern German '*Menschenwürde*', cf. *TL* 6:429.24, 436.29). It will turn out that here too Kant uses 'humanity' in the sense of one's idea of a morally good being (humanity as ideal or *noumenon* as specified in Chapter 3 above). This is not the same as someone's actually being morally good, or the dignity of fully realized morality. Rather humanity in this sense is the same as the capacity for morality, which for Kant is the same as free will (see Chapter 3). The idea is that all human beings are raised above the rest of nature in virtue of being free, which is the same as being *under* the moral law.

For instance, Kant specifies the "*dignity* of humanity in his person" as the "*prerogative* of a moral being, that of acting in accordance with principles, that is, inner freedom" (*TL* 6:420.16). Kant uses 'dignity' to express the thought that human beings are raised above the rest of nature: "his dignity [...] by which he raises himself above all other beings in the world" (*TL* 6:462.24). It is freedom that gives human beings a prerogative or raises them over the rest of nature. Kant calls this "inner freedom, the innate dignity of a human being" (*TL* 6:420.22). All human beings have this form of dignity innately.

What is most important to note is that only in three instances out of 21 does 'dignity' appear in conjunction with 'worth' (cf. *TL* 6:435.02; 436.12; 462.12). I shall now have a close look at these passages, the duty against false humility (*TL* 6:434–6), and the introduction to the duties of respect owed to others (*TL* 6:462–4). To anticipate: It shall turn out that even in this context Kant talks about the dignity of humanity (as the capacity to be moral). Throughout the *Doctrine of Virtue* Kant's point is that one should not deprive oneself of the prerogative of being able to act freely (i.e., in accordance with morality). This is not a new justification or application of morality, but is just a different way of saying that one should act as the Categorical Imperative commands. In the context of the duty against false humility the idea is that one's "real self-esteem" is "pride in the dignity of humanity in one's person" (*TL* 6:459.23). One should not lower oneself in regard to others because one has the most important thing in oneself: the moral law and the ability to follow it. Therefore: "He can measure himself with every other being of this kind and value himself on a footing of equality with them." (*TL* 6:435) The worth or value Kant mentions in this context is the value of a good will that one should have before one's eyes. This is the same reason why Kant mentions dignity in conjunction with worth in the introduction to duties of respect: "as he cannot give himself away for any price (this would conflict with the duty of self-esteem), so neither can he act contrary to the equally necessary self-esteem of others" (*TL* 6:462). This means that when Kant says that respecting others is "recognition of a *dignity* (*dignitas*) in other human beings, that is, of a worth that has no price" (*TL* 6:462), he merely says *what* should be respected – their striving for moral worth; it is not the *justification* for why one should respect them.

After this general overview of Kant's usage of 'dignity' in the *Doctrine of Virtue*, I shall now have a close look at the passages in which 'dignity' appears in conjunction with 'worth'. I shall start with the passage on the duty against false humility (cf. *TL* 6:434–6).

Dignity and the Duty Against Servility

Kant discusses the duty against servility as one of the duties a human being has to himself merely as a moral being. By this he means that he regards a human being without taking his animality or bodily nature into consideration (cf. *TL* 6:420). The other two vices he discusses in that context are lying and avarice. Kant rules out these three vices because they directly violate the moral law in its form: "These adopt principles that are directly contrary to his character as a moral being (in terms of its very form)" (*TL* 6:420). For Kant a character is a law of causality (cf. *KrV* A539/B567). The causal law of a moral being is the moral law or Categorical Imperative (cf. again *GMS* 4:446 f.). This means that the three vices directly violate an existing moral command, to act on universalizable principles and thereby to be free: "they make it one's basic principle to have no basic principle and hence no character" (*TL* 6:420). This is why these vices are described as "depriving himself of the *prerogative* of a moral being, that of acting in accordance with principles, that is, inner freedom" (*TL* 6:420). Lying, avarice and servility are therefore directly opposed to one's freedom (understood as acting in accordance with the Categorical Imperative). They deny one the prerogative or dignity of being able to act in accordance with principle, and are "so making himself a plaything of the mere inclination and hence a thing" (*TL* 6:420). Kant uses 'dignity' to rephrase his central claim that one should act in accordance with the Categorical Imperative. If one does not so act, one deprives oneself of one's prerogative (freedom), and lowers oneself into a thing that is determined by external forces. Kant's usage of 'dignity' does not introduce a new justification for why it is wrong to engage in the three vices, but he uses 'dignity' and the language of lowering oneself to bring out one aspect of these vices.

This is confirmed if one looks more closely at the vice of servility or false humility (*TL* 6:434–6). I have already discussed this vice in connection with respect in Chapter 3 above. In this context I am interested in his usage of 'value' and 'dignity'. My claim is that in this passage Kant talks about moral value. His usage of 'value' does then not introduce a new conception of value and dignity, but repeats the familiar claim that morality is more important or is raised in value (i. e., has a dignity in value). Recall that the vice of servility is "belittling one's own moral worth merely as a means to acquiring the favour of another" (*TL* 6:435 f.). One should not belittle oneself, but revere the moral law within (cf. *TL* 6:436, 468). As a subject of the law the human being "can measure himself with every other being of this kind and value himself on a footing of equality with them" (*TL* 6:434.32 f., 435.3–5; cf. *Vigil* 27:609 f.). Again the idea is that in following the moral law one can acquire the unconditional worth of a morally good will (in the sense specified in Chapter 1). To gain the favour of another is in comparison only of conditional value, and one should therefore not belittle oneself. In the context of the duty against servility Kant does not introduce a new kind of value.

There is therefore no reason to assume that Kant in the following passage wants to introduce a new conception of value, one that could justify moral requirements, but would violate everything else he has argued for on this subject (cf. Chapter 1). The passage reads:

> a human being regarded as a *person* [...] possesses a *dignity* (an absolute inner worth) by which he exacts *respect* for himself from all other rational beings in the world (*TL* 6:434 f.).

There is no specification in this passage that suggests that value is something else than Kant had argued for elsewhere (cf. Chapter 1 above). In fact, it seems to me that the passage makes it even harder to attribute to Kant a view that all human beings as such have a value that grounds the requirement to respect them. For Kant says that "a human being (*homo phaenomenon, animal rationale*) is a being of slight importance", it merely has "an ordinary value". Although he "can set himself ends, even this gives him only an *extrinsic* value for his usefulness". This value is even "a lower value than the universal medium of exchange, money". Instead, his absolute worth comes from being "the subject of a morally practical reason" (*TL* 6:434). This is in line with my earlier interpretation of Kant's usage of 'value' and the requirement to respect others (cf. Chapters 1 and 3). As the subject of a morally practical reason, a human being is subject to the Categorical Imperative and can acquire a good will. This will is the only thing that is worth striving for unconditionally (i.e., it 'has' an absolute inner worth). When Kant says that a being exacts respect for himself, he is not talking about the commanded respect owed to others. Rather he is talking about the moral feeling of respect, which Kant had said is properly speaking respect for the moral law of which the other gives one an example (cf. *GMS* 4:401 note; *KpV* 5:81 note). In virtue of his morally practical reason a human being is under the Categorical Imperative, which commands unconditionally and exacts respect from others if followed. This is not a new justification for why one should respect others (cf. Chapter 3), but rather an explanation of why one should not be servile. One can achieve what is most important, a good will, and therefore should not think lower of oneself towards anyone.

Kant uses 'dignity' to express the *same* claims in terms of higher and lower. The duty of self-esteem is based on the thought that one can attain what is of prime importance: a good will as commanded by the moral law. This aspect of oneself is therefore higher in importance: It is sublime in its importance and can exalt oneself over the rest of nature. This is how Kant puts it in his discussion of the vice of false humility: "In the system of nature, a human being [...] is a being of slight importance [...]." However, "his insignificance as a *human animal* may not infringe upon the consciousness of his dignity as a *rational human being*". A human being therefore "should not disavow the moral self-esteem of such a being", and should maintain this esteem "with consciousness of his sublime moral predisposition". This means that "from our capacity for internal lawgiving and from the (natural) human being's feeling himself compelled to revere the (moral) human being within his own person, at the same time there comes *exaltation* of the highest self-esteem". The moral aspect of human beings is connected with a "feeling of his inner worth (*valor*), in terms of which he is above any price (*pretium*) and possesses an inalienable dignity" (*TL* 6:434–6).

Self-esteem is therefore pride in the dignity of one's moral calling.[205]
Kant uses 'dignity' to express the idea that something is "sublime", "exalted" or "above any price". In this context what is exalted is the *moral* vocation (in the sense that only morality should be pursued unconditionally), or the idea of oneself as morally good (cf. *TL* 4:436; *Vigil* 27:593; cf.
GMS 4:434; *Päd* 9:488 f.). In this context dignity is clearly connected to
morality. It is not itself a value, but is used to express a higher standing of
moral value over other forms of behavior.

The fact that Kant uses 'dignity' in conjunction with 'worth' in his
discussion of the vice of servility therefore does not mean that Kant adheres to the contemporary paradigm of dignity. Rather Kant talks about
the value of a morally practical reason, i.e., the familiar claim that morality is to be pursued above all else (i.e., has an absolute value). Kant uses
'dignity' to express the idea that moral value is higher or more important
than other forms of behavior. Granted, if one picks out one sentence and
reads it in isolation, one could get the impression that Kant puts forth a
new justification for why one should respect others (because they have a
value). However, on a close reading of the passage it is clear that he does
nothing of that sort. I shall now examine the second passage where Kant
uses 'dignity' in conjunction with 'worth'.

'Dignity' and the Requirement to Respect Others

Kant's introduction to the duties of respect owed to others contains the
other instance in which Kant uses 'dignity' in conjunction with 'worth'
in the *Doctrine of Virtue* (cf. *TL* 6:462). Here too, if one reads the passage
in isolation, one could get the impression that Kant uses the contemporary paradigm of dignity:

> The *respect* that I have for others or that another can require from me [...] is
> therefore recognition of a *dignity* (*dignitas*) in other human beings, that is, of
> a worth that has no price, no equivalent for which the object evaluated [...]
> could be exchanged. (*TL* 6:462)

In this passage Kant seems to say that one can make (moral) claims on
others because of an inner worth one possesses, and that this worth is
called 'dignity'. This would be an instance of the contemporary paradigm

---

205 Kant uses 'moral calling' here in the sense of personality, or the being under the
    moral law, cf. *Vigil* 27:627, *TL* 6:459; cf. *GMS* 4:434.

of dignity. One should respect others because one recognizes that they have a special kind of worth. On this reading, the good would be prior to the right, and rights prior to duties.

However, if one reads the passage in its context, it becomes clear that here too Kant ties the worth of human beings to morality, that worth is not the reason why one should respect others, and that the passage is merely about *what* one should respect in others (their striving for morality and an absolute worth) – it is not a justification for *why* one should respect them. As it turns out, the passage is not meant to offer a *justification* for why one should respect others, but merely explains *what* one should respect in them. In the following I shall present a careful reading of the passage in which the above quote appears.

The passage is the beginning of Kant's discussion of duties that are owed to *others* from respect due to them (*TL* 6:462–8). He discusses them in the second section of a chapter on duties towards other human beings, the first section of which dealt with duties of love.[206] Duties of respect emphasize a negative aspect of one's duty. They are limiting conditions, admonishing to keep oneself within certain limits with regard to others. Everyone owes these duties to everyone else without putting the other person under a further obligation (of gratitude etc.). They are analogous to duties of right as presented in Kant's *Doctrine of Right*, "not to encroach upon what belongs to anyone" (*TL* 6:449.33; cf. 6:448–450).

The section on duties toward others from respect is divided into eight sub-sections (§§37–44). The first five are general remarks, containing definitions (§37), the justification for why one should respect others (§38), clarifications of what should be respected (§39), a contrast to the feeling of respect (§40), and a clarification of the nature of the vices of disrespect (§41). Kant then elucidates the three vices of disrespect: arrogance (§42), defamation (§43), and ridicule (§44), which I have already discussed in detail in Chapter 3 above.

The paragraph in which the above quote appears, §37, contains definitions regarding the respect due to others. In the introduction to duties towards others in general (§25) Kant had characterized duties of respect as "not exalting oneself above others" (*TL* 6:449.32; cf. Chapter 3). In respecting others one does not "detract anything from the worth that the other, as a human being, is authorized to put upon himself" (*TL* 6:450.12 f.). Accordingly, in §37 Kant defines modesty as the "willing re-

---

206 For the relation between the two sections see Baron 2002, 393–400; Esser 2004, 370–4; and Gregor 1963, 182–8.

striction of one's self-love in view of the self-love of others" (*TL* 6:462.5–7). If one does not restrict one's self-love, but exalts it over the self-love of others, the attitude would be "*self-conceit (arrogantia)* [*Eigendünkel*]" (*TL* 6:462.10). The most extreme vice of disrespect is to deny the other any worth: "Judging something to be worthless is contempt." (*TL* 6:462.15 f.)

Respect for others is therefore "recognition of a *dignity (dignitas)* in other human beings" (*TL* 6:462.12 f.). In respecting others one does not place oneself above them, but recognizes a certain rank or standing (i. e., dignity). One leaves intact the worth that the other is justified placing upon himself. This worth is not the *justification* for why one should respect others – 'worth' here merely refers to self-esteem – but it explains *what* should be respected in others. One should acknowledge the self-respect the other is justified in placing on himself. But why does Kant say that recognition of a dignity in others is recognition "of a worth that has no price, no equivalent for which the object evaluated (*aestimii*) could be exchanged" (*TL* 6:462.13–5)? He explains this in §38.

§38 contains the justification for the requirement to respect others. It is a dense passage that relies on Kant's fuller treatment elsewhere. It begins: "Every human being has a legitimate claim to respect from his fellow human beings and is *in turn* bound to respect every other." (*TL* 6:462.18–20) At first this just reads as the thesis to be proven. However, it already contains a reference to the justification. One can make a claim for respect on others, but it could only be binding if one "*in turn*" grants it to others. This does not mean that one only needs to respect people who reciprocate.[207] For Kant, even a criminal deserves respect, as I have emphasized (cf. *TL* 6:463). Rather it is a statement about the nature and origin of moral obligation. The moral bindingness of a maxim comes about because the maxim is qualified to be a universal law.[208] However, Kant also spells out the justification as he proceeds.

He continues: "Humanity itself is a dignity" (*TL* 6:462.21). I have argued in Chapter 4 that this should be read as saying: 'Humanity is elevated over the rest of nature.' Why is it elevated? "[F]or a human being cannot be used merely as a means [...] but must always be used at the same time as an end." (*TL* 6:462.21–3) Human beings have a dignity

---

207 I thank Samuel Kahn for pressing me on this.
208 Cf. *TL* 6:393.19–22: "we [...] make ourselves an end for others; and the only way this maxim can be binding is through its qualification as a universal law". Cf. *TL* 6:451; and *Vigil* 27:580.

because ("for") the moral law, as articulated in the Formula of Humanity, demands respect for human beings. Dignity is not the ground of that requirement (similarly 6:434.32–435.2). In this context Kant uses 'dignity' to express the idea that human beings are special in nature because they are protected by the requirement to respect others, as expressed in the Formula of Humanity: "It is just in this that his dignity (personality[209]) consists, by which he raises himself above all other beings in the world that are not human beings and yet can be used, and so over all *things*[210]." (*TL* 6:462.24–6) The Formula of Humanity is the justification for why one should respect others, confirming what Kant had said earlier (cf. §25), that the requirement to respect others is already contained in the requirement not to degrade others to mere means (cf. *TL* 6:450).

The rest of §38 specifies *what* should be respected in others. Kant continues:

> But just as he cannot give himself away for any price (this would conflict with his duty of self-esteem), so neither can he act contrary to the equally necessary self-esteem of others, as human beings, that is, he is under obligation to acknowledge, in a practical way, the dignity of humanity in every other human being. (*TL* 6:462.26–31)

What one should respect in others is their self-esteem. As one is under a duty to esteem oneself, so everyone else is under this duty also. This self-esteem is said to be necessary and linked to dignity.

Kant had explained the sense in which self-esteem is necessary and linked to dignity in the discussion of the duty against servility. To repeat: Everyone is under the moral law. One esteems it, and it makes one realize the sublimity or dignity of one's moral calling. So this also explains why Kant had said in §37 that respecting others means respecting their dignity and a worth that has no price (their moral calling): As one is oneself under the duty of moral self-esteem to realize one's initial dignity and form a morally good will, so everyone else is under the same duty. If one should respect others – as is commanded by the Formula of Humanity – then one should respect them in their striving to realize their dignity and form a morally good will.

On a close reading of the passage there is therefore no reason to assume that Kant wanted to introduce a new justification based on a value.

---

209 Kant's use of "personality" here indicates that it is being under the moral law, freedom, that elevates one over the rest of nature and that is to be respected. This will come out as §38 continues.

210 On Kant's views about duties towards animals, cf. Chapter 3 above.

Dignity is explicitly said to *follow* from the demand of the Formula of Humanity, it is not the ground of it. And nothing Kant says about value indicates that he means value in a very different sense from the one specified in other works (cf. Chapter 1 above). Another reason that the value Kant talks about here is not the *reason* for why one should respect others is that even someone who does not in fact possess a morally good will and its absolute value, still should be respected. This comes out in §39.

In §39 Kant makes clear that the duty to respect the moral striving of others does not mean that one should only respect morally worthy people: "To be *contemptuous* of others (*contemnere*), that is, to deny them the respect owed to human beings in general, is in every case contrary to duty; for they are human beings." (*TL* 6:463.2–4) One does not owe respect only to human beings who are morally good, and does not just owe it because they might be good after all (even though they do not show any sign of it). If one should respect all others, but not all have moral worth, then moral worth is not the justification for respecting others. The Formula of Humanity commands that one respect all human beings as such: Even a vicious man deserves respect "as a human being, even though by his deeds he makes himself unworthy of it" (*TL* 4:643.13–5). Kant does not say that a vicious human being really is good deep down, or that his striving gives him worth, or that the capacity for morality has worth. Even if one could judge that a vicious being has no moral worth, one still should not treat him as if he were a thing or with complete contempt (cf. also Denis 2010a). He remains a human being and is to be respected. Neither moral vice nor faulty reasoning justifies contempt: "for on this supposition he could never be improved, and this is not consistent with the idea of a *human being*, who as such (as a moral being) can never lose entirely his predisposition for the good." (*TL* 6:463.36–464.3) One should respect all human beings as such. What one should respect in them is their moral capacity (freedom and the Categorical Imperative), but the degree to which the other is moral – and his corresponding moral worth – do not justify a lack of respect. Kant grants that one often cannot help but *feel* contempt (e. g., for a villain), however, the respect owed to others is not a feeling, but the *maxim* of limiting one's self-esteem by the equal high rank or dignity of others (cf. *TL* 6:449.23–30). Even if one cannot help but feel contempt for a villain in the first sense of respect, "the outward manifestation of this is, nevertheless, an offense" (*TL* 6:463.4–6).

To sum up: The question in this chapter so far has been whether Kant – in passages where he uses 'dignity' in conjunction with 'worth' – does not adhere to the contemporary paradigm of dignity. I have argued that this is not the case even in the most suggestive passages. The *Doctrine of Virtue* does not give such a justification. It does not break with what Kant had said before. He merely uses 'dignity' and the Formula of Humanity to bring the same claims closer to intuition. But if this is all there is to Kant's notion of 'dignity', is it relevant for moral philosophy? What is to be said about a claim that Kant is the founder of the contemporary paradigm of dignity that is so prominent in UN documents and the constitution of many states? And if this claim is not correct, what are the implications?

Section 4: The Relevance of Kant's Conception of Dignity

In this last section I want to reflect upon the significance of Kant's conception of dignity (as I interpret it) for moral and political philosophy more generally. The aim is not to give a systematic defense of Kant's views – this would be a whole project of its own. Rather I want to raise three points in order to show that Kant's views – even if they are different from the contemporary conception of dignity – are not therefore far-fetched, but do have an initial plausibility.

The question of the significance of Kant's conception of dignity arises because today there are high hopes placed on the conception of human dignity. Dignity is an important part of the justification of human rights in United Nations documents, and it is the cornerstone of the constitution for many states (see again Chapter 4). For a justification of this idea people mostly turn to Kant.[211] In contrast, I have argued that dignity is a secondary concept in Kant's moral philosophy. He uses the term to express the idea that morality is more important than other forms of behavior. But by itself it does not ground any moral requirement. This interpretation makes Kant's texts coherent, and it explains why Kant uses 'dignity' so sparsely and not at all in passages where one would expect it, were Kant to adhere to the contemporary pattern of thought. But if dignity is a secondary concept for Kant, does my interpretation not undermine the high expectations that are often placed on human dignity in moral phi-

---

211 Cf. again Gewirth 1982, 28; Seifert 1997, 98; Wood 2008, 94; and Dürig's object formula in German constitutional law; cf. Wetz 1998, ch. 3.

losophy? Does it weaken the case that can be made for human rights and the requirement to respect others? What is the significance of Kant's conception of dignity for moral and political philosophy?

There are two considerations upfront that might mitigate the discrepancy between Kant's views on dignity and the contemporary conception of dignity. First, even if dignity is a secondary concept for Kant, this does not mean that one need not respect others. Kant and the contemporary paradigm converge on the view that one should respect all human beings. They merely offer a different justification for this requirement. Second, the implication of my interpretation of Kant is not that the contemporary conception of dignity is unfounded, or that there is no value all human beings possess as such. The result is merely that Kant does not provide such a conception. If one could justify the contemporary paradigm in some other way, this would seem like a highly desirable result. It would add an additional justification and defense of human rights. Kant argues that value cannot be the foundation of morality, on the basis of his epistemology from the *Critique of Pure Reason*. This does not mean that there is not such a foundation, but it shows how deep such a conception has to go: One would have to provide a different epistemology that refutes Kant's views from the first *Critique*. My interpretation then merely poses a dilemma: If one wants to uphold the contemporary conception of dignity, one cannot simply refer to Kant for a justification of this view; and if one wants to follow Kant, one would have to endorse a different conception of dignity. But what if one does follow Kant? Is his notion of dignity of any relevance for moral and political philosophy?

Dignity is less central for Kant's ethics than it is for the contemporary conception of dignity. However, this does not make either dignity or Kant's ethics irrelevant. By itself dignity does not play a foundational role for Kant. It indicates that morality is more important than actions based on inclinations, but dignity is not the reason why morality is more important. But the fact that dignity is a secondary concept for Kant does not by itself make Kant's moral philosophy inferior to the contemporary conception of dignity. In the following I shall point out three reasons why Kant's ethics might be better equipped to meet the demands placed on a moral theory. My aim is not to defend Kant systematically, nor to argue that the contemporary conception of dignity is false. I just want to give some indication that Kant's ethics is not far-fetched. I shall argue that: 1) unless there is a justification for the contemporary conception of dignity that is convincing to all, Kant's ethics seems to start from a more realistic starting point; 2) Kant's Categorical Imperative is an important normative condition for the coordination of a plurality of agents; and that 3) there is some indication that the imperative really is embedded in common moral cognition.

1.) The Starting Point of Kant's Ethics

The first step in defense of Kant's views is to shift the burden of proof. The contemporary conception of dignity, if defended convincingly, would be a solid foundation of morality. But what is the proof that there is such a prior and independent value? For Kant it is nothing that we already have or that one can perceive: "the existence of man is not by itself a *factum* that produces any obligation" (*Vigil* 27:545). Kant does not think that there is any moral fact one can start with, like a value of human beings:

> Here, then, we see philosophy put in fact in a precarious position, which is to be firm even though there is nothing in heaven or on earth from which it depends or on which it is based. (*GMS* 4:425)

This means that for Kant the burden of proof is on a defender of a prior value of human beings. For Kant the initial situation of human beings is that there is a plurality of finite agents that cannot avoid each other (cf. *RL* 6:311–3; *ZeF* 8:366). In this initial situation human beings have different needs and opinions.[212] The Categorical Imperative applies to this situation.

2.) The Categorical Imperative as a Condition for Coordination

The second point in support of Kant's view is that in such a situation as described under 1) the Categorical Imperative is a condition for coordinating a plurality of finite yet connected agents. In this situation relativism – the view that different people can hold on to fundamentally different moral truths (or that there is not any truth to be had) – is too early or too late (cf. Williams 1985, ch. 9). It is too early for a group with moral laws in common that does not know about other groups with different morals. However, once one knows about other groups with different rules, relativism is too late, as people with differing views have to find a way of living together. The new laws (political and moral) that have

---

212 Cf. O'Neill 1989, ch. 1; and her 1996, 50–65. This does not mean that human beings are wholly unsocial. Rather they possess an 'unsocial sociability', according to Kant (cf. *IaG* 8:20–2).

to be established cannot be justified with reference to subjective reasons, i. e., reasons that hold for some but not for others. Kant calls this a "private use of reason" (*WDO* 8:38)[213]. If one merely speaks for a particular group, tradition or a particular interest based on one's own desires, the reason is only valid for the group which shares this outlook. This agreement seems fine as long as the group is isolated and relativism is too early. However, once there are conflicting groups, the shared outlook of one group is per se no reason for another group. If, for instance, one proposes a law because one's preacher told one to, the law is only valid if all accept the authority of the preacher. Even if different people desire the same thing, this is not a good basis for moral (and political) laws. For instance, if everyone desires their happiness, this might be the cause for more strife rather than harmony, e. g., if two men desire the same woman. But even if the desires of different people harmonize, this harmony is merely contingent, as the desires can change. If a dispute were to arise, there would be no law as arbiter (cf. *RL* 6:312; *KpV* 5:28 f.).

So if there is to be a law to coordinate a plurality of finite agents, and if all particular desires are excluded, then only the form of the law remains (cf. *KpV* 5:28 f.; *GMS* 4:420 f., 400–2). This form is the Categorical Imperative, to ask oneself whether one's reasons or the rule that follows from it can be willed as a universal law. The imperative is a condition for what can count as a reason for a plurality of finite agents.[214] In the first instance it spells out what can be a moral reason, or what accounts for obligation: "The categorical imperative, which as such only affirms what obligation is, is: act upon a maxim that can also hold as a universal law" (*RL* 6:225; cf. *Vigil* 27:578; and Baum 2012). The imperative expresses what moral obligation is, its nature or essence so to speak. Neither the mere existence of others, nor the fact that they make claims on one another (e. g., to be helped) by itself generates an obligation for Kant. It is the imperative that makes it an obligation rather than a mere wish. It is

> our need to be loved (helped in the case of need) [...], we therefore make ourselves an end for others; and the only way this maxim can be binding is through its qualification as a universal law (*TL* 6:393).

---

213 Cf. O'Neill 1989, ch. 2; and her 1996, 61 f.
214 Cf. O'Neill 1989, ch. 1; her 1996, 51; and Hill 1992, 111 f.

By itself the Categorical Imperative is not so much a guide for a decision procedure for deriving concrete duties, but a condition for what can count as a moral reason.

The traditional charge that the imperative is empty (cf. again Hegel 1820, §135) is true to an extent, but this is a strength rather than a weakness. Why would one expect a person in 18th century Prussia to come up with one sentence that will decide once and for all every moral issue (including the ones about technologies that have not yet been invented)? Instead Kant gives us a framework within which the details are to be worked out by each group. A few requirements are directly entailed by the imperative. In addition to the requirement not to make exceptions for oneself (the Formula of Law of Nature), the imperative requires that one not exalt oneself above other rational beings (the Formula of Humanity), and not act on selfish motives (the Formula of Autonomy). In adding a few general facts about human beings (that we are not autarkic, that we can be injured and deceived), further moral rules can be derived.[215] But what one can say a priori is limited and leaves a lot of room for empirical differences.

Even in the *Doctrine of Virtue* in which Kant gives the fullest account of more concrete duties, he can only give a few general rules that leave room for casuistical questions and empirical differences. The question remains: "How should people be treated in accordance with their differences in rank, age, sex, health, prosperity or poverty and so forth?" (*TL* 6:469) The answers "cannot be set forth in detail and classified in the *metaphysical* first principles of a doctrine of virtue, since this has to do only with its pure rational principles" (*TL* 6:468). So even the principles set forth in the *Doctrine of Virtue* need "a transition having its own special rules" (*TL* 6:469) to apply the general rules to experience. It is to be expected that there will be different levels of rules, answering to a greater specificity in empirical knowledge (cf. Hill 1992, ch. 3; Oberer 2006, 264). For instance, there will be very general rules valid for all human beings as such (if there are any rational beings other than humans), rules for finite human beings, rules for finite human beings in specific situations (e. g., certain geographical conditions), and so forth. This includes concrete wishes of individual people or groups. The imperative allows each party its freedom, unless it interferes with the freedom of others (cf. *RL* 6:230). If a practice does interfere, a new rule has to be found that can be willed as a universal law. So besides a priori knowledge and em-

---

215 Cf. O'Neill 1989, ch. 5; her 1996, ch. 6; and Oberer 2006, 264.

pirical knowledge about all human beings, there is further room for individual wishes. The Categorical Imperative does not demand uniform behavior. Mostly it does not prescribe the solution (e. g., whether to drive on the left or right side of the road), but it merely demands that the agreed-upon law can be universal (in the domain under consideration). If one proposes a rule as a law, it fails to be universal if one party wants to make exceptions (cf. *GMS* 4:424), or if the law cannot be adopted by others (cf. Engstrom 2009, 167–183; and Reath 2012b). So the derivation of concrete duties is not as simple as it is often made to seem.[216] But this room for circumstances and judgment is a strength, not a weakness. It leaves room for individual differences and freedoms.

In sum: The Categorical Imperative is a condition for a plurality of finite rational agents to coordinate and move toward a resolution of strife. But even if this is granted as an interpretation of Kant – much more would have to be said to justify it systematically – the question arises whether what I have said so far establishes that the imperative is *categorical*. Kant uses 'categorical' in the sense that the Categorical Imperative is valid *regardless of what one wants*. In contrast an imperative is only hypothetical if its validity is conditioned upon something else one wants (cf. *GMS* 4:414, 441), or something someone else wants. A hypothetical imperative is not, however, objectively and universally valid, as it is only valid if the condition is met. But as I have presented it, it seems that the imperative is only valid *if* one wants to avoid strife, or isolation and dispersion. Does this mean that the imperative is only hypothetical and not categorical?

Kant seems to think that living in isolation is not an option. In his essay 'Idea of a Universal History from a Cosmopolitan Point of View' (1784) he argues that humans could not live next to each other in isolation, as they would kill each other, nor would isolation allow one to flourish and bring out one's talents. Rather one would be "stunted, bent and twisted" (*IaG* 8:22). Kant describes the impulse to join society as "sheer necessity" (*IaG* 8:22). However, what if someone does not mind this state of isolation with all its dangers and harsh consequences? In this very extreme case, where someone does not mind forfeiting reason and living by instinct, it seems that the Categorical Imperative – as here construed by the previous argument alone – is not valid for such a being.

---

216 For the complexities of the derivations cf. Timmons/Smit 2012; Timmons 2012; and Hanna (unpublished).

This is not an option for Kant. According to the reading I have been putting forward in this book, the Categorical Imperative is not an optional principle that applies only if one wants to cooperate. For Kant, all human beings are under the imperative in virtue of freedom, and even the "most hardened scoundrel" (*GMS* 4:454) wishes to follow it. But is this correct? What might be said in favour of Kant's claim that everyone is under the moral law? This leads to the third step in defense of Kant.

3) The Categorical Imperative as an Existing Command

The third step that is needed for a defense of Kant's views is some indication that there really is such an imperative. This mirrors Kant's questions in the *Groundwork*. He first established the conditional that if there is morality, then it must be expressed in categorical imperatives. He then asks the question whether there really is such an imperative (cf. *GMS* 4:425 f., 445). Kant of course thought that every human being is under the Categorical Imperative, and – even without knowing the exact formulation of it – always "uses the norm for its appraisals" (*GMS* 4:403 f., cf. 402–6; *KpV* 5:8 note). But is this really the case? Is the exact requirement – that one's maxim can be willed as a universal law – really something that is guiding everyone? I shall argue that this requirement is not as far-fetched as it might seem in the abstract.

Support for Kant's views – I think – comes from an unlikely source: empirical philosophy. Kant of course is adamant that morality cannot be *derived* from empirical observations (cf. *GMS* 4:389, 407–412, 425, 430 f.). However, if Kant is right that morality is a priori, then it should also be found in all human beings. Experience should be able to *confirm* morality. This is because being a priori (for Kant) is the same as being necessary and universal (cf. *KrV* B4). So, if the Categorical Imperative has an a priori source, then one should be able to find traces of it in all human beings. And this is where empirical philosophy can support Kant.

What traces should one expect to find? I want to pick out three that seem to be essentially connected with the Categorical Imperative. I shall argue that a) the Categorical Imperative is basically a requirement of fairness, that b) the requirement is connected with an ability to detect cheaters or people who break the rules, and that c) an important point of Kant's imperative is captured in the distinction between moral laws (which are valid categorically) and conventions (which are merely hypothetically valid). Finally, d) I shall argue that all three elements are supported by empirical philosophy as being deeply engrained in human beings.

a) Fairness: Kant describes the essence of the Categorical Imperative as ruling out that someone makes an exception for himself to a rule that is willed as a general law:

> If we now attend to ourselves in any transgression of duty, we find that we do not really will that our maxim should become a universal law, since that is impossible for us, but that the opposite of our maxim should instead remain a universal law, only we take the liberty of making an *exception* to it for ourselves (or just for this once) to the advantage of our inclination. (*GMS* 4:424.15–20)

The requirement not to make exceptions is not a far-fetched or abstract requirement. It describes what is moral about Kant's imperative, and it seems to resonate with our sense of fairness. The requirement does not demand uniform behavior, and it does not demand rule-worship. It merely demands that one does not make an exception for oneself to an agreed-upon rule without a good reason, or simply because one is oneself. If something is to be divided, e.g., a cake at a children's birthday party, there is a presumption that each gets the same amount. However, there might be good reasons to give some more than others. It seems fine if the child whose birthday it is gets a bigger piece, or the child who has baked the cake, or the one that is hungriest, the one that has bought the ingredients etc. The point is just that it would be unfair to demand an exception without good reason simply because one is oneself. Empirical philosophy tells us that the sense of fairness is more or less a human universal.[217] An equal-division norm was found even in three-year olds (cf. Nichols 2009, 8).

b) Cheater Detection: Kant's Categorical Imperative can be described as a requirement for fairness, and against free riders or cheaters. If the imperative is thought to be deeply engrained in human beings, then it might be thought that human beings are adept at detecting cheaters. Again empirical philosophy supports the view that cheater detection is deeply engrained, and even children as early as four years old can detect transgressions to rules.[218]

---

217 Cf. Darwall 2006, 175, 173; Prinz 2008, 264–7; and Nichols 2009.
218 Cf. Nichols 2005, 6; Prinz 2008, 249–252.

c) The Moral/Conventional Distinction: An essential part of Kant's moral philosophy is the view that moral rules are categorically valid, while prudential rules and conventions which are based on particular desires are only hypothetically valid. Kant thinks that even an eight-year old could distinguish between what is unconditionally wrong (e. g., not returning a deposit or giving false testimony) and rules that are dependent upon desires (cf. *TP* 8:286; *KpV* 5:155). And again empirical philosophy supports the view that the moral/conventional distinction is deeply engrained in human beings. Studies support the idea that from a young age children draw the moral/conventional distinction. Like Kant, they see moral rules as being generalizably valid, e. g., as valid in different countries, and like Kant they explain the validity of these rules in terms of fairness and harm to victims (cf. Nichols 2005, 6).

d) Empirical Philosophy: There are strands within empirical philosophy that support basic elements of Kant's position. There is support for the claim that judgments of fairness are more or less a human universal, that the capacity to detect cheaters is deeply embedded, and that a distinction between categorical and hypothetical rules is drawn from very early age. However, this is not meant to be a proof of Kant's position. Empirical philosophy is a method, not a unified position that speaks in one voice without dissent. Furthermore, the emphasis is on empirical observation, not on a priori insights (as it is for Kant), and some proponents emphasize the role of emotions in contrast to laws of reason. One could even say that sometimes empirical philosophy shows too much. When, for instance, a mechanism for cheater-detection is also found in bats and chimpanzees,[219] it does not seem to be something that is unique to rational beings, in which Kant seems to be most interested.

However, the findings of empirical philosophy raised so far are also not at odds with Kant's views. Kant is interested in showing that the Categorical Imperative is necessary and universal. The findings of empirical philosophy allow for the possibility that the recognition of non-hypothetical imperatives and the capacity for cheater-detection are innate.[220] The question of innateness is not completely identical to Kant's questions whether morality is a priori (i. e., necessary and universal), but if the capacity for categorical imperatives is innate, it points to the conclusion that it is also

---

219 Cf. Prinz 2008, 264–7, 249–252.
220 Cf. Nichols 2005, 4, 7; Prinz 2008, 264–7.

universal and deeply embedded in human beings. But even if this is correct, a problem remains. It is not only categorical imperatives and judgments of fairness that are universal, but also immoral desires like hatred, revenge and crushing punishment. It is not enough to show that something is universal, one also has to justify that it is a morally right element. Even if empirical philosophy does in fact support some of Kant's basic ideas, it does not make obsolete a normative justification of Kant's views (like the one I have sketched under heading 2 above).

Concluding Remarks

In this Chapter I have argued that Kant adheres to a traditional conception of dignity. According to his view, all human beings are elevated over the rest of nature in virtue of freedom. Being free, human beings are subject to the Categorical Imperative that demands that one fulfill one's initial dignity (in making a proper use of one's freedom), and that one respect others.

While this means that 'dignity' is not itself a concept that carries any justificatory weight, this result should not be surprising. It not only makes sense of Kant's sporadic use of 'dignity' throughout his writings, it also accords with the overall framework of Kant's ethics. He always refers to the Categorical Imperative as the supreme principle of morality; and when he tries to justify the imperative, he does *not* rely on a conception of worth or dignity – as the prevailing reading would have led one to expect. My reading therefore helps to bring out the coherence of Kant's moral writings.

In addition, I have tried to show that Kant's views have some initial plausibility. My aim in the last section has not been to defend Kant systematically. Nothing I have said would be strong enough to accomplish this. My aim has merely been to show that Kant's ideas are not far-fetched. There is some support for his ideas from empirical philosophy; his Categorical Imperative does spell out a condition for what can be a moral reason; and Kant seems to work from a more realistic starting-point than the contemporary paradigm of dignity employs.

What then is the relevance of Kant's conception of dignity – as I interpret it – for moral philosophy? Kant's views do not fulfill all the hopes that are placed on it by proponents of the contemporary paradigm of dignity. Kant does not propose a value on which moral philosophy can be based. Instead, Kant reminds us that we do not directly perceive a value that would induce respect. Rather respect for others is a task that is required of us. Kant's conception of dignity is important because it emphasizes our sense that this task is nobler and more sublime than the selfish pursuit of our own desires.

Conclusion

The place of human dignity in Kant's framework, on my reading, is more modest than it is often taken to be; but it is not insignificant. Human dignity does not ground moral imperatives, but human beings have dignity because they are free and so bound by moral imperatives.

Kant bases his moral philosophy on an a priori law of reason. He argues that if one grounds morality in anything else, such as a property of objects or human beings, the unconditional character of morality will be destroyed and heteronomy results:

> If the will seeks the law that is to determine it *anywhere else* than in the fitness of its maxims for its own giving of universal law – consequently if, in going beyond itself, it seeks this law in a property of any of its objects – *heteronomy* always results. (*GMS* 4:441; cf. *KpV* 5:39 f.)

The temptation in interpreting Kant's passages on dignity and the requirement to respect others is to introduce through the back door a property of objects as the basis for moral requirements, such as a value all human beings possess, or their having a normative property of being an end in themselves. In assuming such a prior value of human beings, one would go beyond the will and its internal a priori principle. This is a step that Kant rules out. Heteronomy would result and no unconditional moral requirement would be possible (cf. Chapter 1).

Prominent arguments in the Kant literature that claim that the value of human beings can be known as an internal property of the will have failed to ground the requirement to respect others (cf. Chapter 2). Instead, Kant justifies this requirement with reference to the a priori moral law (cf. Chapter 3). For Kant 'dignity' is then not the name for a value that grounds respect. Rather he adheres to a different, basically Stoic conception of dignity (Chapter 4), even in famous passages in which 'dignity' appears in conjunction with 'worth' (Chapter 5). For Kant 'dignity' expresses the idea that something is raised above something else, for instance that human beings are special in nature because they should be treated as equal, while non-rational things need not be (cf. *TL* 6:462), or that morality is elevated over other forms of behavior because only being moral is commanded unconditionally (cf. *GMS* 4:434–6).

So I am led to the conclusion that the key to understanding Kant's views on moral philosophy is to understand how morality can be an a priori law of reason, not based on any value. In my book I have only sketched Kant's answer: For Kant the moral law is the causal law of freedom. Every causality needs a law, Kant argues, and if freedom is a causality of human beings to determine themselves independently of nature, this capacity too operates under a causal law: the moral law or Categorical Imperative. The moral law is an operating principle of reason so to speak. When reason deliberates about what one should do, it is guided by the law – akin to the non-contradiction-principle in theoretical reasoning. I have documented Kant's answer, but a full defense or even explanation of this goes beyond the scope of the present work. One has to explain why freedom as a descriptive metaphysical property (the ability to determine oneself independently of nature) should yield a *moral* law. In addition, one has to make plausible the idea that moral obligation can only be expressed in a categorical imperative. These questions were not the subject of this book. My arguments here rather lead up to a dilemma: If one wants a justification for human dignity as a value at the foundation of the requirement to respect others, one cannot simply rely on Kant. But if one finds Kant's views of the matter appealing, one finds support in his texts for a different justification of the requirement to respect others.

In the Kant literature there is a growing reaction against the view that Kant bases morality on a value. My book is part of this trend: It explains how one can read Kant's views on dignity, respect, and humanity as an end in itself without reference to a value as the foundation. My interpretation agrees with the contemporary paradigm that one should respect all human beings, I merely offer a different justification for this view. On the one hand, my argument supports the anti-value reading of Kant, but on the other hand it does not require one to rely on the formal Categorical Imperative in order to derive concrete duties. Instead, on my reading of Kant, one can conduct moral deliberation in terms of the deep-seated question of respect for persons.

References

Alföldy, Géza (1986), *Die römische Gesellschaft*. Stuttgart: Franz Steiner.

Allison, Henry (2011), *Kant's* Groundwork for the Metaphysics of Morals. Oxford: Oxford University Press.

—: (2012) "The Singleness of the Categorical Imperative." In Bacin (2012b).

Ameriks, Karl (2003), *Interpreting Kant's Critiques*. Oxford: Clarendon Press.

Appiah, Anthony (2003), "Grounding Human Rights." In *Human Rights as Politics and Idolatry*, ed. A. Gutman. Princeton: Princeton University Press, pp. 101–116.

Bacin, Stefano (2012a), "Perfect Duties to Oneself as a Moral Being." In Trampota (2012).

—: et al. (2012b) (eds.), *Kant and Philosophy in a Cosmopolitan Sense*. Berlin/New York: Walter de Gruyter.

Baiasu, Sorin, and Timmons, Mark (2012) (eds.), *Kant on Practical Justification*. Oxford: Oxford University Press.

Baker, Herschel (1947), *The Dignity of Man. Studies in the Persistence of an Idea*. Cambridge/MA: Harvard University Press.

Baron, Marcia (1995), *Kantian Ethics Almost without Apology*. Ithaca: Cornell University Press.

—: (2002), "Love and Respect in the *Doctrine of Virtue*." In Timmons (2002), pp. 391–407.

Baum, Manfred (2012), "Prior Concepts of the Metaphysics of Morals." In Trampota (2012).

Baxley, Anne Margaret (2009), "Allen Wood. *Kantian Morality*." *Journal of the History of Philosophy* 47, pp. 627–9.

Betzler, Monika (2008) (ed.), *Kant's Ethics of Virtue*. Berlin/New York: Walter de Gruyter.

Bruch, Richard (1981), "Die Würde des Menschen in der partistischen und scholastischen Tradition." In *Wissen – Glaube – Politik*, ed. W. Gruber et al. Graz: Styria, pp. 139–154.

Carnois, Bernard (1987), *The Coherence of Kant's Doctrine of Freedom*. Chicago: University of Chicago Press.

Catechism of the Catholic Church (1999). London: Geoffrey Chapman.

Cancik, Hubert (2002), "'Dignity of Man' and 'Persona' in Stoic Anthropology: Some Remarks on Cicero, *De Officiis* I, 105–107." In Kretzmer/Klein (2002), pp. 19–40.

Caswell, Matthew (2006), "The Value of Humanity and Kant's Conception of Evil." *Journal of the History of Philosophy* 44, pp. 635–662

Christiano, Thomas (2008), "Two Conceptions of the Dignity of Persons." *Annual Review of Law and Ethics* 16, pp. 101–126.

Cicero, M.T. (1913), *De Officiis*, tra. W. Miller. Cambridge/MA: Harvard University Press.

Clewis, Robert R. (2009), *The Kantian Sublime and the Revelations of Freedom*. Cambridge: Cambridge University Press.

Cohon, R. (2000), "The Roots of Reasons." *The Philosophical Review* 109, pp. 63 – 85.

Copp, David (1999), "Korsgaard on Normativity, Identity, and the Ground of Obligation." In *Rationality, Realism, Revision*, ed. J. Nida-Rümelin. Berlin/ New York: Walter de Gruyter.

Craven, Matthew C.R. (1995), *The International Covenant on Economic, Social, and Cultural Rights*. Oxford: Clarendon Press.

Cummiskey, David (1996), *Kantian Consequentialism*. Oxford: Oxford University Press.

Darwall, Stephen (2006), *The Second-Person Standpoint*. Cambridge/MA: Harvard University Press.

—: (2008), "Kant on Respect, Dignity, and the Duty of Respect." In: Betzler (2008), pp. 175 – 199.

—: (2009), "Why Kant Needs the Second-Person Standpoint." In Hill (2009), pp. 138 – 158.

Dean, Richard (2000), "Cummiskey's Kantian Consequentialism." *Utilitas* 12, pp. 25 – 40.

—: (2006), *The Value of Humanity in Kant's Moral Theory*. Oxford: Clarendon Press.

Denis, Lara (2000), "Kant's Cold Sage and the Sublimity of Apathy." *Kantian Review* 4, pp. 48 – 73.

—: (2010a), "Humanity, Obligation, and the Good Will: An Argument against Dean's Interpretation of Humanity." *Kantian Review* 15, pp. 118 – 141.

—: (2010b), "Freedom, Primacy, and Perfect Duties to Oneself." In *Kant's Metaphysics of Morals: A Critical Guide*, ed. Lara Denis. Cambridge: Cambridge University Press.

Dicke, Klaus (2002), "The Founding Function of Human Dignity in the Universal Declaration of Human Rights." In Kretzmer/Klein (2002), pp. 111 – 120.

Donagan, Alan (1977), *The Theory of Morality*. Chicago: The University of Chicago Press.

Downie, R.S., and Telfer, E. (1970), *Respect for Persons*. New York: Schocken.

Drexler, Hans (1944), "Dignitas." In *Das Staatsdenken der Römer*, ed. R. Klein. Darmstadt: Wissenschaftlicher Buchgesellschaft, 1966, pp. 231 – 254.

Duden. Etymologie. Herkunftswörterbuch der deutschen Sprache (1997), ed. G. Drosdowski. Mannheim: Dudenverlag.

Dürig, W. (1957), "Dignitas." In *Reallexikon für Antike und Christentum* Vol. III, ed. by T. Klauser. Stuttgart: Hiersemann, pp. 1024 – 1035.

Duncan, A.R.C. (1957), *Practical Reason and Morality*. London: Thomas Nelson and Sons LTD.

Dyck, Andrew (1996), *A Commentary on Cicero, De Officiis*. Ann Arbor: The University of Michigan Press.

Ebbinghaus, Julius (1959), "Die Formeln des Kategorischen Imperativs und die Ableitung inhaltlich bestimmter Pflichten." In *Gesammelte Schriften* Vol. 2, ed. Georg Geismann et al. Bonn: Bouvier, 1988.

Encyclopedia of Human Rights (1996), ed. E. Lawson. Washington D.C.: Taylor & Francis.

Engstrom, Stephen, and Whiting, Jennifer (1996) (eds.), *Aristotle, Kant, and the Stoics*. Cambridge: Cambridge University Press.

—: (2009), *The Form of Practical Knowledge. A Study of the Categorical Imperative*. Cambridge/MA: Harvard University Press.

Esser, Andrea (2004), *Eine Ethik für Endliche. Kants Tugendlehre in der Gegenwart*. Stuttgart-Bad Cannstatt: Frommann-Holzboog.

FitzPatrick, William (2005), "The Practical Turn in Ethical Theory: Korsgaard's Constructivism, Realism, and the Nature of Normativity." *Ethics* 115, pp. 651–691.

—: and Watkins, Eric (2002), see Watkins.

Flikschuh, Katrin (2000), *Kant and Modern Political Philosophy*. Cambridge: Cambridge University Press.

—: (2010), "Kant's Kingdom of Ends: Metaphysical, Not Political." In Timmermann (2010), pp. 119–139.

Foreman, Elizabeth (2010), "Jens Timmermann (ed.): Kant's *Groundwork of the Metaphysics of Morals: A Critical Guide*." *Notre Dame Philosophical Reviews* 2010.08.23 (http://ndpr.nd.edu/review.cfm?id=20990)

Formosa, Paul (2012), "Is Kant a Moral Constructivist or a Moral Realist?" In Bacin (2012b).

Forschner, Maximilian (1998), "Marktpreis und Würde; oder vom Adel der menschlichen Natur." In *Die Würde des Menschen. Fünf Vorträge*, ed. H. Kössler. Erlangen: Universitätsbund Erlangen-Nürnberg e.V., pp. 33–59.

Frohwein, Jochen A. (2002), "Human Dignity in International Law." In Kretzmer/Klein (2002), pp. 121–135.

Gadamer, Hans-Georg (1988), "Die Menschenwürde auf ihrem Weg von der Antike bis heute." *Humanistische Bildung* 12, pp. 95–106.

Gaut, B. (1997), "The Structure of Practical Reason." In *Ethics and Practical Reason*, ed. Cullity/Gaut. Oxford: Oxford University Press.

Geuss, Raymond (1996), "Morality and Identity." In Korsgaard (1996b), pp. 189–199.

Gewirth, Alan (1978), *Reason and Morality*. Chicago: Chicago University Press.

—: (1982), *Human Rights*. Chicago: Chicago University Press.

Gibbard, A. (1999), "Morality as Consistency in Living: Korsgaard's Kantian Lectures." *Ethics* 110, pp. 140–164.

Glasgow, Joshua (2007), "Kant's Conception of Humanity." *Journal of the History of Philosophy* 45, pp. 291–308.

Glendon, Mary Ann (1999), "Foundations of Human Rights: The Unfinished Business." *The American Journal of Jurisprudence* 44, pp. 1–14.

—: (2001), *A World Made New*. New York: Random House.

Gregor, Mary (1963), *Laws of Freedom*. Oxford: Basil Blackwell.

Griffin, James (2001), "Discrepancies between the Best Philosophical Account of Human Rights and the International Law of Human Rights." *Proceedings of the Aristotelian Society* 101, pp. 1–28.

Guyer, Paul (1992) (ed.), *The Cambridge Companion to Kant.* Cambridge: Cambridge University Press.

—: (1998a), "The Value of Reason and the Value of Freedom." *Ethics* 109, pp. 22–35.

—: (1998b) (ed.), *Kant's* Groundwork of the Metaphysics of Morals. Lanham: Rowman & Littlefield.

—: (2000), *Kant on Freedom, Law, and Happiness.* Cambridge: Cambridge University Press.

—: (2006a), *Kant.* London: Routledge.

—: (2006b) (ed.), *The Cambridge Companion to Kant and Modern Philosophy.* Cambridge: Cambridge University Press.

—: (2007), *Kant's* Groundwork for the Metaphysics of Morals. *A Reader's Guide.* London/New York: Continuum.

Haezrahi, Pepita (1962), "The Concept of Man as End-in-Himself." *Kant-Studien* 53, pp. 209–224.

Hanna, Robert (unpublished), "Living with Contradictions: The Logic of Kantian Moral Principles in Nonideal World."

Hegel, Georg Wilhelm Friedrich (1820), *Elements of the Philosophy of Right*, tra. by H.B. Nisbet. Cambridge: Cambridge University Press, 1991.

Henkin, Louis (1981), *The International Bill of Rights.* New York: Columbia University Press.

Herman, Barbara (1993), *The Practice of Moral Judgment.* Cambridge/MA: Harvard University Press.

—: (2010), "The Difference that Ends Make." In *Perfecting Virtue: Kantian Ethics and Virtue Ethics*, ed. Julian Wuerth et al. Cambridge: Cambridge University Press.

Hill, Thomas (1992), *Dignity and Practical Reason in Kant's Moral Philosophy.* Ithaca: Cornell University Press.

—: (2000), *Respect, Pluralism, and Justice.* Oxford: Oxford University Press.

—: (2002), *Human Welfare and Moral Worth.* Oxford: Oxford University Press.

—: (2003), "Treating Criminals as Ends in Themselves." *Annual Review of Law and Ethics* 11, pp. 17–36.

—: (2009) (ed.), *The Blackwell Guide to Kant's Ethics.* Oxford: Wiley-Blackwell.

Hills, Alison (2005), "Rational Nature as the Source of Value." *Kantian Review* 10, pp. 60–81.

Höffe, Otfried (ed.) (1989), *Grundlegung zur Metaphysik der Sitten. Ein kooperativer Kommentar.* Frankfurt: Klostermann.

—: (1992), *Ethik und Politik.* Stuttgart: Suhrkamp.

—: (2002) (ed.), *Kritik der praktischen Vernunft.* Berlin: Akademie Verlag.

—: (2008), "Urteilskraft und Sittlichkeit. Ein moralischer Rückblick auf die dritte Kritik." In *Kritik der Urteilskraft*, ed. O. Höffe. Berlin: Akademie Verlag, pp. 351–366.

Horn, Christian, and Schönecker, Dieter (2006) (eds.), *Kant's* Groundwork of the Metaphysics of Morals: *New Interpretations*. Berlin/New York: Walter de Gruyter.

Horstmann, R.P. (1980), "Menschenwürde." In *Historisches Wörterbuch der Philosophie* Vol. 5, ed. J. Ritter and K. Gründer. Basel/Stuttgart: Schwabe & Co., pp. 1124–27.

Hruschka, Joachim (2006), "Kant and Human Dignity." In *Kant and Law*, ed. S. Byrd/J. Hruschka. London: Ashgate, pp. 69–84.

Hügli, A. (2004), "Wert I." In *Historisches Wörterbuch der Philosophie*, vol. 12, ed. J. Ritter et al. Basel: Schwabe, pp. 556–558.

Hutchings, Patrick (1972), *Kant on Absolute Value*. Detroit: Wayne State University Press.

Ibsen, Knut (1990), *Völkerrecht. Ein Studienbuch.* München: C. H. Beck'sche Verlagsbuchhandlung.

Jones, H.E. (1971), *Kant's Principle of Personality.* Madison: University of Wisconsin Press.

Johnson, Robert (2007), "Value and Autonomy in Kantian Ethics." In *Oxford Studies in Metaethics* Vol. 2, ed. Russ Shafer-Landau. Oxford: Oxford University Press, pp. 133–148.

—: (2010), "The Moral Law as Causal Law." In Timmermann (2010), pp. 82–101.

Kain, Patrick (2010), "Allen W. Wood, *Kantian Ethics.*" *Philosophical Review* 119, pp. 104–108.

Kant, Immanuel (1996), *Practical Philosophy*, trans. M. Gregor. Cambridge: Cambridge University Press.

Kant-Konkordanz Vol. 9 (1995), ed. Wilhelm Lütterfelds et al. Hildesheim: Olms.

Kerstein, Samuel J. (2002), *Kant's Search for the Supreme Principle of Morality.* Cambridge: Cambridge University Press.

—: (2006), "Deriving the Formula of Humanity." In Horn/Schönecker (2006), pp. 200–221.

Klemme, Heiner (2010), "Immanuel Kant." In *Handbuch Menschenrechte*, ed. Georg Lohmann et al. Metzler: Stuttgart.

Korsgaard, Christine (1996a), *Creating the Kingdom of Ends.* Cambridge: Cambridge University Press.

—: (1996b), *The Sources of Normativity.* Cambridge: Cambridge University Press.

—: (1998), "Motivation, Metaphysics, and the Value of the Self: A Reply to Ginsborg, Guyer, and Schneewind." In *Ethics* 109, pp. 49–66.

Kretzmer, D., and Klein E. (2002) (eds.), *The Concept of Human Dignity in Human Rights Discourse.* The Hague/London/New York: Kluwer Law International.

Kristeller, Paul O. (1964), *Eight Philosophers of the Italian Renaissance.* Stanford: Stanford University Press.

Langton, Rae (2007), "Objective and Unconditioned Value." *Philosophical Review* 116, pp. 157–185.

Leist, Anton (1996), "Persons as 'Self-Originating Sources of Value.'" In Bayertz (1996), pp. 177–199.

Leo the Great (1996), *Sermons*, tra. by J.P. Freeland and A.J. Conway. Washington D.C.: The Catholic University of America Press.

Lichtblau, Klaus (2004), "Wert/Preis." In *Historisches Wörterbuch der Philosophie*, vol. 12, ed. J. Ritter et al. Basel: Schwabe, pp. 586–591.

Lo, P.C. (1987), *Treating Persons as Ends*. Lanham: University Press of America.

Löhrer, Guido (1995), *Menschliche Würde*. Alber: Freiburg.

Lovejoy, Arthur (1961), *The Great Chain of Being, a Study of the History of an Idea*. New York: Harper & Row.

MacIntyre, Alasdair (1981), *After Virtue*. South Bend: University of Notre Dame Press.

Mackie, John (1977), *Ethics*. New York: Penguin Books.

Martin, Adrienne (2006), "How to Argue for the Value of Humanity." *Pacific Philosophical Quarterly* 87, pp. 96–125.

McDowell, John (1985), "Value and Secondary Qualities." In *Morality and Objectivity*, ed. Ted Honderich. London: Routledge & Kegan Paul.

Mendonça, W.P. (1993), "Die Person als Zweck an sich." *Kant-Studien* 84, pp.167–184.

Meyer, Michael (1989), "Dignity, Rights, and Self-Control." In *Ethics* 99, pp. 520–534.

Mohr, Georg (2007), "Ein ‚Wert, der keinen Preis hat‘ – Philosophiegeschichtliche Grundlagen der Menschenwürde bei Kant und Fichte." In *Menschenwürde*, ed. H.J. Sandkühler. Frankfurt a.M.: Lang, pp. 13–39.

Moore, G.E. (1903), *Principia Ethica*, ed. T. Baldwin. Cambridge: Cambridge University Press: Cambridge, 1993.

Mulholland, Leslie (1990), *Kant's System of Rights*. New York: Columbia University Press.

Murchland, Bernard (1966), *Two Views of Man*. New York: Frederick Ungar.

Nichols, Shaun (2005), "Innateness and Moral Psychology." In *The Innate Mind*, ed. P. Carruthers et al. Oxford: Oxford University Press.

—: (2009), "Emotions, norms, and the genealogy of fairness." *PPE* 9, pp. 1–22.

Noggle, Robert (1999), "Kantian Respect and Particular Persons." *Canadian Journal of Philosophy* 29, pp. 449–478.

Nussbaum, Martha (1997), "Kant and Stoic Cosmopolitanism." *Journal of Political Philosophy* 5, pp. 1–25.

Oberer, Hariolf (2006), "Sittlichkeit, Ethik und Recht bei Kant." *Annual Review of Law and Ethics* 14, pp. 259–267.

O'Neill, Onora (1989), *Constructions of Reason*. Cambridge: Cambridge University Press.

—: (1991), "Kantian Ethics." In *A Companion to Ethics*, ed. P. Singer. Oxford: Blackwell.

—: (1996), *Towards Justice and Virtue*. Cambridge: Cambridge University Press.

—: (1998), "Kant on Duties Regarding Nonrational Nature." *Aristotelian Society. Supplement* 72, pp. 211–228.

Oxford Latin Dictionary (1996), ed. by P.G.W. Glare. Oxford: Oxford University Press.

Parfit, Derek (2011), *On What Matters*. Oxford: Oxford University Press.

Paton, Herbert James (1947), *The Categorical Imperative. A Study in Kant's Moral Philosophy*. London: Hutchinson.

Pfordten, D. von der (2009), "On the Dignity of Man." *Philosophy* 84, pp. 371–391.

Pico della Mirandola (1486), *On the Dignity of Man*, tra. by C.G. Wallis. Indianapolis: The Bobbs-Merrill Company,1998.

Pieper, Annemarie (2002), "Zweites Hauptstück (57–71)." In Höffe (2002), pp. 115–133.

Plotinus, *The Enneads*, tra. by S. MacKenna. London: Faber and Faber, 1969.

Pöschl, Viktor (1969), "Der Begriff der Würde im antiken Rom und später." *Sitzungsberichte der Heidelberger Akademie der Wissenschaften. Philosophisch-historische Klasse* 3. Heidelberg: Carl Winter, pp. 7–67.

Porcheddu, Rocco (2012), "Der Zweck an sich selbst und die Deduktion des Kategorischen Imperativs." In Bacin (2012b).

Prauss, Gerold (1983), *Kant über Freiheit als Autonomie*. Frankfurt: Klostermann.

Prinz, Jesse (2008), *The Emotional Construction of Morals*. Oxford: Oxford University Press.

Rauscher, Frederick (2002), "Kant's Moral Anti-Realism." *Journal of the History of Philosophy* 40, pp. 477–499.

Rawls, John (1971), *A Theory of Justice*. Cambridge/MA: Harvard University Press.

Reath, Andrews (2003), "Value and Law in Kant's Moral Theory." *Ethics* 114, pp. 127–155.

—: (2006): *Agency & Autonomy in Kant's Moral Theory*. Oxford: Oxford University Press.

—: (2012a): "Formal Approaches to Kant's Formula of Humanity." In Baiasu/Timmons (2012).

—: (2012b): "The Ground of Practical Laws." In Bacin (2012b).

Regan, D. (2002), "The Value of Rational Nature." In *Ethics* 112, pp. 267–291.

Reich, Klaus (1939), "Kant and Greek Ethics II." *Mind* 48, pp. 446–463.

Ricken, Friedo (1989), "Homo Noumenon und Homo Phaenomenon." In O. Höffe (1989), pp. 234–252.

—: (1998a), *Allgemeine Ethik*. Stuttgart: Kohlhammer.

—: (1998b), "Aristotelische Interpretationen zum Traktat *De passionibus animae* (Summa theologiae I II 22–48) des Thomas von Aquin." In *Die Einheit der Person*, ed. M. Thurner. Stuttgart: Kohlhammer.

Ross, David (1954), *Kant's Ethical Theory*. Oxford: Clarendon Press.

Santeler, Josef (1962), *Die Grundlegung der Menschenwürde bei I. Kant*. Innsbruck: Innsbruck University Press.

Scanlon, Thomas (1998), *What We Owe to Each Other*. Cambridge/MA: Harvard University Press.

Scheler, Max (1913/16), *Der Formalismus in der Ethik und die materiale Wertethik*. Bern: Francke, 1980.

Schneewind, Jerome B. (1992), "Autonomy, Obligation, and Virtue: An Overview of Kant's Moral Philosophy." In Guyer (1992).

—: (1996), "Kant and Stoic Ethics." In Engstrom/Whiting (1996), pp. 285–301.

—: (1997), "Introduction." In *Immanuel Kant. Lectures on Ethics*, ed. Peter Heath and Jerome B. Schneewind. Cambridge: Cambridge University Press.

—: (1998), *The Invention of Autonomy. A History of Modern Moral Philosophy*. Cambridge: Cambridge University Press.

Schönecker, Dieter (1999), *Kant: Grundlegung III. Die Deduktion des kategorischen Imperativs*. Freiburg: Alber.

—: and Wood, Allan (2003), *Immanuel Kant „Grundlegung zur Metaphysik der Sitten": ein einführender Kommentar*. Paderborn: Schöningh.

—: (2010), "Kant über die Möglichkeit von Pflichten gegen sich selbst (*Tugendlehre* §§ 1–3)." In *Kant als Bezugspunkt philosophischen Denkens*, ed. H. Busche/A. Schmitt. Würzburg: Königshausen & Neumann, pp. 235–260.

Schwartländer, Johannes (1968), *Der Mensch ist Person*. Stuttgart: Kohlhammer.

Sedgwick, Sally (2008), *Kant's Groundwork of the Metaphysics of Morals*. Cambridge: Cambridge University Press.

Seel, Gerhard (2009), "How Does Kant Justify the Universal Objective Validity of the Law of Right?" *International Journal of Philosophical Studies* 17, pp. 71–94.

Seifert, Josef (1997), *The Value of Life*. Amsterdam: Rodopi.

Shafer-Landau, Russ (2003), *Moral Realism*. Oxford: Clarendon Press.

Shell, Susan (2003), "Kant on Human Dignity." In *In Defense of Human Dignity*, ed. R. Kraynak/G. Tinder. South Bend: University of Notre Dame Press.

Silber, John (1959/60), "The Copernican Revolution in Ethics. The Good Re-examined." *Kant-Studien* 51, pp. 85–101.

Smit, Houston, and Timmons, Mark (2012), "Kant's Grounding Project in *The Doctrine of Virtue*." In Baiasu/Timmons (2012).

Smith, Michael (1999), "Search for the Source." *The Philosophical Quarterly* 49, pp. 384–394.

Stern, Robert (2012), "On Hegel's Critique of Kant's Ethics. Beyond the 'Empty Formalism' Objection." In *Hegel's Philosophy of Right*, ed. Thom Brooks. Oxford: Wiley-Blackwell.

Stratton-Lake, Philip (2002) (ed.), *Ethical Intuitionism: Re-Evaluations*. Oxford: Clarendon Press.

Sullivan, Roger (1989), *Immanuel Kant's Moral Theory*. Cambridge: Cambridge University Press.

Sussman, David (2003), "The Authority of Humanity." In *Ethics* 113, pp. 350–366.

Timmermann, Jens (2000), "Kant's Puzzling Ethics of Maxims." *Harvard Review of Philosophy* 8, pp. 39–52.

—: (2003), *Sittengesetz und Freiheit*. Berlin/New York: Walter de Gruyter.

—: (2006), "Value Without Regress: Kant's 'Formula of Humanity' Revisited." *European Journal of Philosophy* 14, pp. 69–83.

—: (2007), *Kant's Groundwork of the Metaphysics of Morals. A Commentary*. Cambridge: Cambridge University Press.

—: (2010) (ed.), *Kant's Groundwork: A Critical Guide*. Cambridge: Cambridge University Press.

—: (2012), "On duties to the self as such." In Trampota (2012).

Timmons, Mark (2002) (ed.), *Kant's Metaphysics of Morals. Interpretative Essays.* Oxford: Oxford University Press.

—: and Smit, Houston (2012), see Smit.

—: (2012), "Kant on Duties to Oneself qua Animal Being." In Trampota (2012).

Trampota, Andreas (2003), *Autonome Vernunft oder moralische Sehkraft?* Stuttgart: Kohlhammer.

—: et al. (2012) (eds.), *Kant's* Tugendlehre. *A Comprehensive Commentary.* Berlin/ New York: Walter de Gruyter.

Tuck, Richard (1979), *Natural Rights Theories. Their Origin and Development.* Cambridge: Cambridge University Press.

Uleman, Jennifer (2010), *An Introduction to Kant's Moral Philosophy.* Cambridge: Cambridge University Press.

Vogt, Katja (unpublished), "Do Human Beings Have Non-Relative Value?"

Waldron, Jeremy (2007), "Dignity and Rank." *European Journal of Sociology* 48, pp. 201–237.

Wasianski, E.A.Ch. (1804), "Immanuel Kant in seinen letzten Lebensjahren." In *Immanuel Kant. Sein Leben in Darstellungen von Zeitgenossen*, ed. Felix Gross. Darmstadt: Wissenschaftliche Buchgesellschaft, pp. 189–271.

Watkins, Eric, and FitzPatrick, William (2002), "O'Neill and Korsgaard on the Construction of Normativity." *Journal of Value Inquiry* 36, pp. 349–367.

Wegehaupt, Helmut (1932), *Die Bedeutung und Anwendung von dignitas in den Schriften der republikanischen Zeit.* Ohlau i. Schl.: Eschenhagen.

Wetz, Franz Josef (1998), *Die Würde der Menschen ist antastbar.* Stuttgart: Klett-Cotta.

Whitman, J. (2003), "From Fascist 'Honour' to European 'Dignity.'" In *The Darker Legacy of European Law*, ed. C. Joerges/N. Ghaleigh. Cambridge: Hart, pp. 243–266.

Williams Bernard (1985), *Ethics and the Limits of Philosophy.* Cambridge/MA: Harvard University Press.

Wolff, Robert Paul (1973), *The Autonomy of Reason.* New York: Harper & Row.

Wood, Allen (1996), "General Introduction." In *Immanuel Kant. Practical Philosophy*, ed. Mary Gregor. Cambridge: Cambridge University Press, pp. xiii-xxxiii.

—: (1998a), "Humanity as an End in Itself." In Guyer (1998b), pp. 165–187.

—: (1998b), "Kant on Duties Regarding Nonrational Nature I." In *Aristotelian Society Supplement* 72, pp. 189–210.

—: (1999), *Kant's Ethical Thought.* Cambridge: Cambridge University Press.

—: (2006), "The supreme principle of morality." In Guyer (2006b), pp. 342–380.

—: (2008), *Kantian Ethics.* Cambridge: Cambridge University Press.

Wright, Georg Henrik von (1963), *The Varieties of Goodness.* London: Routledge & Kegan Paul.

Author Index

Subject Index

www.ingramcontent.com/pod-product-compliance
Lightning Source LLC
Chambersburg PA
CBHW070030100426
42740CB00013B/2644